# EDITOR'S FOREWORD

To make a psycho-analytic relationship with patients, suffering from the severe psychotic disorders was long regarded as impossible because of the profound withdrawal in these patients of interest in the outer world. Using the pioneering investigations of Melanie Klein as a basis for understanding the origin and growth of the capacity to relate to others, some of her students have been able to maintain intensive psycho-analytic treatment over long periods with a wide range of illnesses. Too few cases have been treated for the therapeutic effects to be judged, but there can be no question of the great value of such work as a contribution to our understanding of the nature and origin of the psychoses and possibly of early development of the personality in general.

As with all psycho-analytic work, investigation proceeds with methods which are themselves closely related to theory. For scientific purposes it would be simpler if theory and practice could be separated; but as Dr Rosenfeld amply demonstrates, it is only through the use of one theoretical approach that the transference relationship with these different patients has been understood and allowed to develop. His work has the status of the pioneering venture and as such will be of great interest to all those eager to advance our resources in treating and possibly preventing these tragic illnesses.

J. D. S.

# CONTENTS

# ACKNOWLEDGEMENTS

I WANT first to acknowledge my deep gratitude to the late Mrs Melanie Klein, whose work and personal help has made it possible for me to undertake the analysis of psychotic patients. My thanks are also due to the patients with whom I have been working and who have thus contributed to my understanding of psychosis. I should also like to thank my colleagues, in particular Miss Betty Joseph, for helpful suggestions and criticisms. To my wife I owe a special debt of gratitude – her support and encouragement has enabled me to see this book through.

# INTRODUCTION

THIS book brings together a number of papers written since 1946 from the viewpoint of the psycho-analyst dealing with the psychopathology and treatment of various psychotic and borderline conditions.

I had been interested in treating schizophrenics before I trained as a psycho-analyst and was impressed by the fact that it was possible to make contact with them. I concluded that these patients are able to form some kind of relationship to the therapist, a conclusion which Sullivan, and after him Fromm-Reichmann, had also reached about the same time. After I qualified as a psycho-analyst one of my early patients suffered from a schizophrenic state with depersonalization, and my experience with her encouraged me to continue using the psycho-analytic method with a number of acute and chronic schizophrenic patients. Later I also treated psycho-analytically other psychotic conditions such as severe hypochondriasis, drug addiction, severe depression, and manic depressive states. My aim was not only to achieve therapeutic results but to find out more about the psychopathology of schizophrenia and the other psychoses.

In his contributions to the psychopathology of paranoia and dementia praecox, Freud stressed the fixation of these patients at a very early phase of development. As early as 1911 he wrote that paranoid patients were fixated at, and had regressed to, the phase of narcissism, while schizophrenic patients had regressed 'not merely to narcissism, but to complete abandonment of object-love and a return to infantile auto-erotism'. Apart from his contributions to the psychopathology of paranoia and schizophrenia, Freud discussed hypochondriasis, depression and drug addiction but he felt always doubtful whether psychotic conditions could be treated psycho-analytically. In 1904 he had said: 'Psychoses, states of confusion, and deeply-rooted depression are not suitable for psycho-analysis; at least not for the method as it has been practised up to the present.' Subsequently he explained in more detail the difficulties he came up against in treating psychotic patients, saying 'experience shows that persons suffering from the narcissistic neuroses have no capacity for transference, or only insufficient remnants of it. They turn from the physician not in hostility but in indifference. Therefore they are not to be influenced by him. What he says leaves them cold, makes no impression on them and therefore the process of cure which can be carried through with others cannot be effected by them.' This point of view he repeated at the end of his life, in the posthumously published *Outline of Psycho-Analysis*: 'Thus we learn that we must renounce the idea of trying our plan of cure of psychotics, renounce it for ever perhaps or only for the moment until we have discovered some other plan better suited for the purpose.' From these quotations one gathers that Freud's investigation of psychotic conditions came to a halt through the difficulties he encountered in the transference of narcissistic patients. Any research into narcissistic states had therefore to be first and foremost directed to investigating whether psychotics formed any transference; if that question could be answered in the affirmative the second step lay in clarifying the difficulties which prevented the recognition and the understanding of the psychotic transference manifestations.

The work of Melanie Klein had gradually developed an analytic technique which made it possible to investigate very early infantile states in the transference analysis and I was stimulated and encouraged in my investigations by these possibilities. Klein had suggested from her experience that the infant from the beginning of life forms part-object and later whole-object relations to the breast and mother. The infant experiences love, hate, and anxiety in relation to these objects, and at the same time develops a variety of defences to deal with the resulting conflicts. In my work with psychotics I have used the psycho-analytic technique as described by Melanie Klein and the theory on which it is based; in the following papers this technique is explained in more detail. Here I want only to point out that I have found that if we avoid producing any positive transference by reassurance or expressions of love, and simply interpret any positive and negative transference manifestations of the psychotic patient, a transference psychosis develops. In all the cases I have treated I have attempted to study this transference psychosis and maintain the psycho-analytic situation. The treatment of acute psychotic patients resembles the analysis of children more than that of adults as they depend on the care of others for being brought for treatment; they generally do not use the couch, and they often have difficulties in expressing themselves in words, so that the analyst has to include in the material on which he can work communication through action or gesture. The psychotic patient in many different ways exerts conscious and unconscious pressure on the analyst to give up the analytic approach. In the chapter on 'Acting Out' I have attempted to throw some light on this problem. I found it essential to resist the pressure, while attempting to understand in detail the meaning and reasons for it. Even if I came up against apparently insuperable difficulties in the transference situation I decided to adhere to my analytic technique, following the principle that if I could not make contact with the patient through my interpretations it was not the technique that was wrong but my understanding of what was going on in the transference situation.

The contributions in this book are primarily based on the investigation of the transference of psychotic patients, in other words on the understanding of the transference psychosis. Occasionally I have mentioned that a particular treatment was a therapeutic success. I feel, however, that it is too early to attempt an appraisal of the value of the psycho-analytic treatment of schizophrenics and other psychotic patients. We have to remember that treatment is often interrupted, not so much because the patient is not responding to the analysis, but because those responsible for the treatment, the parents or other relatives, decide to stop it for a variety of reasons. The reasons are apparently practical ones; sometimes, however, they are more related to the emotional problems of the parents – problems which tend to be exacerbated by the intense acting out which I have learnt to expect in the treatment of the psychotic. There is reason to hope that as our understanding of the depth of the conflict of the schizophrenic progresses this type of acting out will diminish in intensity or duration.

Following my paper on the 'Considerations regarding the Psycho-Analytic Approach to Acute and Chronic Schizophrenia' (chap. 6), Ernest Jones said that he was glad that I had stressed the research and exploratory functions of my work and not the curative aspects, as only time could tell whether psychotic patients who are successfully analysed remain clinically well. Nevertheless, we should remember that any analysis of psychotic states, whether carried out for long or short periods and whether therapeutically successful or not, will enrich our understanding and will facilitate the treatment of other psychotic patients.

H. R.

# 1

# ANALYSIS OF A SCHIZOPHRENIC
# STATE WITH DEPERSONALIZATION[1]
## (1947)

THE patient I shall now discuss was sent to me for a variety of physical complaints of a functional origin. In the course of treatment it became apparent that I was dealing with a psychosis of the schizophrenic type. In this paper I shall concentrate only on certain aspects of the case; namely, the schizoid symptomatology and some of the schizoid mechanisms encountered. An additional aim will be to throw some light on depersonalization, and I will try to show the connexion between processes of ego disintegration and depersonalization.

### Short History of the Case

My patient, Mildred, is a young woman who was twenty-nine when the treatment started in March 1944. She is of average height and build, with straight fair hair. Her face is not exactly plain, but it usually appeared so because of its lack of expression. During the latter part of the treatment her expression became more alive and she sometimes smiled. She had her first breakdown in health when she was seventeen. Her second breakdown occurred at the age of twenty-five, in the early part of the war, while she was serving in the Auxiliary Territorial Service. She developed one physical illness after another, e.g. influenza and sore throats, until she had to be invalided from the Service. After some time she recovered and made another attempt to defeat the recurring illnesses by joining the Land Army, but again the physical disturbances prevented her from continuing. When I saw her in March 1944 for consultation she had been suffering from a so-called influenza for about four or five months. She agreed to analysis; but we soon realized that she had no desire to

[1] Based on a paper read at a meeting of the British Psycho-Analytical Society, March 5, 1947. First published in the *Int. J. Psycho-Anal.*, **28**.

come for treatment, and this was in the main due to a deep-seated hopelessness about any recovery.

## Family and Early History

There were no known schizoid disorders in the family, but one uncle is an alcoholic, and her father has suffered from a neurosis all his life. The patient described him as avoiding company and depending a great deal on his wife. She thought him old-fashioned, extremely dominating and very 'nervy'. She had always disliked him, but had, for the most part, ignored him. During the treatment her relationship with him improved considerably. She had always been very much attached to her mother, and had turned to her frequently in her childhood troubles. As a child she wrote poems and fairy stories and always found her mother a ready audience, and an adult who would treat her as an equal. She had one brother, Jack, nineteen months younger, and a sister, Ruth, six years younger.

Jack seems to have been a very attractive and intelligent boy, adored by everybody. Mildred, however, was ambivalent, but on the whole very fond of him and depended on him a great deal. She had quite consciously tried to adopt his personality and his interests, but had failed. When Jack was killed in a flying accident round about Christmas, 1940, she did not feel anything about it at the time; but during treatment she began to realize what a shock his death had been to her, and how responsible she felt for it. Her sister was very neurotic, suffering as a child from many anxieties, and as long as Ruth was small, Mildred felt quite motherly towards her, which enabled her to accept without much jealousy the greater attention which was shown to the anxious little sister. In contrast to Mildred, Ruth improved when she got older, and during the War did very well in the Women's Auxiliary Air Force. Socially, too, she became more self-confident; but both these circumstances roused considerable jealousy in my patient.

About Mildred's early development nothing abnormal was reported to me. I gathered that she cried but little as an infant and apparently showed no reaction on being weaned. We must remember, however, that schizoid reactions in small children are generally overlooked and we often get a history of a particularly good baby, as in this case. She started to talk and walk normally.

In addition to her mother, who breast-fed her, she had a nurse who was very devoted to her. As she was born in 1915, she did not see much of her father, who served all through the 1914–18 war; but whenever he was on leave he took a great deal of interest in his little daughter. When she was nineteen months old, Jack was born, and for three weeks her mother was away in a nursing home. This was the first time Mildred was separated from her mother for any length of time, and it was not until the tenth day that Mildred was allowed to visit her and the baby. Her mother told her later on that from the time she first saw Jack she became completely silent and withdrawn; and this reaction had disturbed the mother very much, since up to that time the child had talked normally. Four weeks after Jack's birth Mildred's nurse left to get married, and the new nurse had mainly to look after Jack. During the following years there were frequent changes of nurses. Mildred disliked them all, complaining to me that they treated her cruelly and often hit her, which might have been true, because she must have been an extremely difficult child to handle. She was frequently told she was no good, while Jack was held up to her as an example of goodness.

I had the impression that there was not only an impairment in her development after Jack's birth, but a definite regression to an earlier level of development. Not only did she give up speaking for a considerable time, but her ability to walk suffered as well, so that Jack developed far in advance of her. When Mildred was six a governess arrived, who seems to have been very prim and proper, but was liked by both children for her other good qualities. At eight years of age, Mildred fell ill with mastoiditis and had to have two operations, which greatly increased her paranoid reactions. She remembers feeling that for no apparent reason the doctors descended on her to frighten and hurt her, and afterwards she never quite overcame her fear of doctors. It took her many months to recover from these operations, and when she was better again she had to face another hard blow. Jack had been sent to school and they were no longer educated together.

She was educated at home by the governess, and for a long time she found it impossible to learn. Only when she was about twelve years of age did her intellectual capacity develop once more, and then she went to boarding-school, where she got on well, sometimes reaching the top of the class. On leaving school, she had a breakdown, which consisted in one physical illness after another, and culminated in a period of uncontrollable crying. The analysis revealed that envy of her best school friend, who got on better than she did, started this breakdown more than a year before leaving school. After school, until shortly before the war, she lived at home and was allowed to do exactly what she wanted. On the whole she felt fairly well, read a great deal; but took no interest in the running of the house. She had frequent periods of withdrawal from both friends and parents, and at these times she felt physically unwell, spending most of the time in bed. In addition, her mental state was always worse at the time of her periods when she suffered great discomfort and pain. As was mentioned earlier, she afterwards served in the A.T.S. and in the Women's Land Army.

### Condition when First Seen and during Early Stage of Treatment

When I saw her first, she was living in a large flat in London with her parents, and for some considerable time she continued to be withdrawn from the family life, leaving all the work of the flat to her mother and an elderly maid. Though consciously very fond of her mother, during analysis we realized that she tried to keep her mother completely under her control, ignoring her desire to be assisted, even when she was not feeling well. On the other hand, she wanted her mother to look after her, and give her her meals in bed, if she herself felt unwell. She expected her mother to take an interest in whatever she was doing, but she could stand no criticism from her nor even a suggestion or question referring to anything she might be doing. For example, she did not allow her mother to ask her whether she intended to stay in bed for the day or not, and when she was engaged in some occupation, such as reading, even a comment would be resented. If her mother did make one, Mildred immediately lost any desire to continue what she was doing, and would withdraw into herself. I later found out that there was a gradual improvement in this attitude after about a year's analysis.

Shortly after starting treatment she took up work again, doing some hours at an aircraft factory, and later on she succeeded in getting afternoon work at a well-known bookshop. Her physical health improved gradually and she attended analysis quite regularly, even while she had her periods, though at times she was very late. There were great difficulties with free association, and these increased rather than decreased. She generally made a long pause at the beginning of the hour, and at times she was silent for the whole session or only said a few words at the end. Sometimes the lack of material made it necessary to interpret on the basis of only one sentence. In addition, previous interviews or observations on her general behaviour had to be used for interpretations which were frequently of only a tentative character, and this created difficulties in assessing her reactions in the working-through period. Only on very rare occasions did she succeed in talking fairly fluently for most of the session, and then she spoke predominantly of actual events in the past or present.

Another technical difficulty was a particularly strong resistance to interpretations connecting together material of several interviews, because she could very seldom consciously remember what had been discussed at previous sessions.[1] This made it difficult to obtain the conscious and intellectual cooperation which is so helpful in those schizoid disorders when the intellect is little affected.

## The Depersonalization

Her conscious behaviour in analysis was marked by a rigid detachment and denial of all feelings, an attitude which at rare intervals was interrupted by paranoid suspicions or by despair about her lack of progress. Already at an early stage of the analysis she described symptoms and sensations of a distinctly schizoid type and feelings of depersonalization. She felt dim and sleepy, half unconscious and could hardly keep awake. At times when describing her experience she would say that there was something like a blanket separating her from the world, that she felt dead, or not here, or cut off from herself. At other times she called these feelings 'deadlock feelings', and explained that they had increased a few months before the treatment had started. She had felt giddy and faint at the time too.[2] She was frequently

[1] This attitude reminds one of Bergler and Eidelberg's (1935) depersonalized patient who could not remember any previous interpretations and at times gave the impression of being demented.

[2] It is interesting to note that both Mayer-Gross (1935) and Shorvon (1946) in their papers on depersonalization point out that the beginning of the depersonalization syndrome is often marked by feelings of faintness and giddiness.

B

afraid of not being able to speak at all and of getting into a completely unconscious state. I realized that she was aware of the danger of insanity, because she said if she tried to join up with herself she might force her mind completely out of joint.

I have the impression that although this state occurred frequently as a defence against impulses of all levels it was also, indeed perhaps mainly, a defence against feelings of guilt, depression and persecution. From time to time there seemed a small improvement in her condition, but the slightest difficulty, particularly any positive transference interpretation, produced long silences, and when she was able to speak again she related that she had experienced some of the schizoid symptoms I enumerated just now. As usual there was an amnesia of everything we had discussed previously. Her inability to deal particularly with positive transference interpretations had its basis in her marked ambivalence, which I shall discuss more fully later on.[1] Whenever the opportunity arose I interpreted her love and hate impulses towards the analyst, but I had to dose these interpretations very carefully because of the seriousness of the schizoid reactions which followed. The positive transference towards the analyst as a parent, sister or brother figure was always displaced on to other people; but her object-relations at this stage were very insecure, and on analysis it turned out that more often than not the other people represented a part of herself.

To give a short example of this process: Denis, the husband of her best friend, had a nervous breakdown while he was separated from his wife, who was expecting her second child. He tried his best to seduce my patient. At first she had great difficulty in controlling him. The wish to take him away from his wife soon came up as a conscious impulse, but it did not seem that she had any difficulty in coping with this wish directly. Her whole anxiety turned on whether she could control *his* wishes and arguments. She repeated some of his arguments to me, and it was clear that Denis stood for her own greedy sexual wishes which she had difficulty in dealing with and which she therefore projected on to him. Denis seemed a particularly suitable person for projection, because the precipitating factor of his neurosis corresponded to my patient's early situation, when the birth of her brother pre-

---

[1] It is of interest to note that one of Reik's (1927) patients became depersonalized whenever Reik tried to make conscious her positive feelings to her husband, to whom her relationship was consciously a bad one.

cipitated her first breakdown. The analysis of this mechanism helped Mildred to cope with Denis without having to avoid meeting him. Apart from the projection of impulses which were felt by the patient to be bad, there was also a continuous projection of good impulses into other people, particularly women friends, who not only represented good mother-figures, but the good part of herself. She felt excessively dependent on these friends and could hardly function without them. Her great dependency on Jack, which led to her inability to learn without him, was probably of the same nature.

## Details of the Analysis

Coming now to the details of the actual analysis, I shall bring forward the instances mainly in chronological order, but it will be understood that I have to select points from a vast collection of material, and I am trying to choose only that which is most relevant to the main theme of my paper. In the winter of 1944-5 the patient developed influenza for the first time since she started treatment. She was afraid that the illness would drag on for months, but it cleared up in the normal time. When she returned to analysis, she told me she had found out quite a lot about the meaning of her influenza, namely, that she liked her 'flu' and enjoyed staying in bed and withdrawing from the world. She spontaneously described fantasies of living warmly and comfortably inside another person whom she thought must be her mother, and remembered that she always told her mother that she had not wanted to be born. She herself related her overwhelming desire to go to sleep, or to become unconscious, to this particular state, and she admitted that she sometimes simply could not bear to remain awake and had to disappear into unconsciousness.[1]

This part of the analysis had a distinctly good effect on her physical symptoms; her difficulties then concentrated mostly on getting up in the morning to come to analysis at 10.30 a.m. For weeks she appeared up to *forty minutes* late. At first she seemed quite unworried about her inability to cooperate. Only gradually was I able to show her the anxiety which was hidden underneath her lack of feeling, and she then started to complain in these

[1] Other analysts, for example Nunberg (1924) and Reik (1927), have described fantasies of living inside the mother's womb in depersonalized patients.

words: 'There is nothing to *make me* get up and come for treatment.' I was at first not sure what she meant by this oft-repeated complaint. Then one day she came almost in tears. She had asked her mother to give her breakfast in bed; she hoped that with her breakfast inside her she would be able to get up. But when she got it, it did not work, and she said: 'It is no good to make it up in all sorts of ways.' I analysed this incident and similar ones in terms of internal and external object-relationships, and felt that her difficulties were mainly due to a failure in introjecting and maintaining a good inner object as represented by the breakfast. Her complaint that there was nothing to make her get up would therefore mean there was no good inner object inside her to help her to get up; the breakfast was supposed to fill this gap but had failed.

Shortly after this she told me of another spontaneous fantasy, which she had had since childhood and which she related now to her difficulties in cooperating. She felt there was a devil who attacked what she called the good people and was keeping them tied up in dungeons. They could not move and had gags in their mouths. No sooner did they manage to get a little freer than the devil appeared, attacked the victims violently and tied them up even more tightly than before. The victims were not killed, yet it was uncertain whether they were still alive. There was no point in fighting this devil because he was stronger than everybody. The only possible method of defence against him was *to ignore him*. This fantasy threw a light on the very strong negative therapeutic reaction of the patient which followed any improvement or freeing of her personality; it foreshadowed the depth of the paranoid situation which was to be expected in the analytic transference, when the analyst would turn into the devil father. For a while there was an improvement in her ability to come in time for treatment, and the positive transference then appeared, displaced, as always, on to a young relative whom she scarcely knew. After she heard that he was engaged, she felt very disappointed and became afraid of not being able to control her tears during the analytic session. She explained that if she started to cry she might not be able to stop again and would feel very ill. For a week she would not disclose the reason for her sadness. The hour after admitting what had happened, she felt dead and had lost her feelings so completely that she could not believe that she had ever had any feelings of love before. When I interpreted to her the strength of her love and hate, her fear of not being able to control them, and that she was defending herself against depression, she was at first incredulous and felt I was only reassuring her that she had feelings. By the end of the hour she realized that she was warding off feelings of pain and said: 'It is like squeezing one's finger in a door and saying one didn't feel anything.' In this situation the depersonalization was very marked. It followed a disappointment and appeared to be a mechanism of defence against depression. But this view appeared later on to be incomplete.[1]

During the next interview the depersonalization increased and was accompanied by feelings of persecution and *sensations of being split in two*. She talked about her fear of doctors and later on my talking was felt as an attack, making her feel I was pushing her into a hole, putting a lid over her and leaving her there. As a result of this assault she felt dead and although there was another part of her which was alive, the live part and the dead part did not know anything of each other. The connexion of this material with the devil fantasy where the objects were put into dungeons was obvious, and it seemed that the persecuting devil attacked not only her objects but her very self. After the attack her ego was completely divided. I did not interpret this to my patient in detail at the time, as she was quite incapable of following any elaborate interpretation of mechanisms until the later part of treatment. I confined myself here to demonstrating to her her ambivalent impulses, which made her feel split in two. In the following weeks, I expected the depression relating to the disappointment she had experienced over the marriage of her friend to come more to the surface. But instead she began to slip from a state of depersonalization gradually into a schizophrenic state, which was marked by the development of a strongly paranoid relationship to the analyst.

At the beginning of this schizoid period she was not entirely devoid of positive feelings, but these she split off and transferred on to a girl friend, with whom she went out frequently and who arranged parties for her. She told me nothing about this at the time. To make the division complete, nothing good was allowed to mix with anything bad and, as I was kept and thought of as almost entirely bad, she acted accordingly. She began to stay

[1] Particularly Reik (1927) and Feigenbaum (1937) have emphasized depersonalization as a mechanism of defence.

away from treatment, sometimes for two or three days on end, and when she did come she was often thirty to forty-five minutes late. At times she appeared confused and disconnected, and her forgetfulness concerning matters in the analysis was most marked. Occasionally she could admit her feelings of persecution and explained that she didn't tell me anything which mattered to her because either I would make it bad or take it away from her, or would cause her feelings about it to disappear. She was trying to sort things out in her mind. I was muddling it all up. Whenever and whatever I interpreted she firmly believed and felt that I was telling her to stop thinking about what she had in her mind and trying to make her think of something else. Her greatest suspicion was that I was making her think entirely in my way, so that she no longer knew what she had thought of before, and that thus she would lose her own self.

Acute fears appeared that when she met people she might one day find herself talking in a strange voice or accent. This voice would have talked, I am certain, with the analyst's voice and accent, but the patient could not admit this connexion consciously. About this time she frequently criticized her father for his selfishness and greed in his relationship to her mother and she herself could hardly bear speaking to him. Other material, for example, fears of hairy animals which attacked her, suggested the fear of an aggressive penis. Generally speaking, her persecutory fears were related to a bad father or penis and the sadistic impulses were mostly of an oral and anal nature. But the central anxiety was a fantasy of the persecuting analyst forcing himself into her to control her and rob her, not only of her inner possessions, for instance, her babies and her feelings, but her *very self*. It was not clear whether in this particular anxiety situation, I always stood for the bad father, or another figure. At this point of the analysis the girl friend she depended on was called up for war service, and her difficulties in coming for treatment and in speaking grew still worse. I realized that frequently she was not sufficiently aware of herself to come or talk or perform any action at all. At times she was more integrated, consequently more aware of herself. She was then able to complain that she felt so split up, and at times could not connect up enough to think or even talk. To get up or go to bed took her sometimes two hours because of the difficulty of consecutive action. Her sense of time was very confused. She could not judge time and often left home only shortly before or even after she was due to be at my house.

At the height of this transference-psychosis there was an alternative state to this split-up condition. She gave one the impression of being withdrawn into an omnipotent world of her own, where she was quite oblivious of external reality, where time and the passing of time did not matter, where she felt comfortable and not at all anxious about her serious mental condition. But sometimes she gave herself away and showed she was in fact controlling a severe threat coming from external reality. So she stated that she had a great deal to think about by herself, but she could not bring herself to tell it to me, because it would give me a handle with which to approach her and make her talk. This omnipotent withdrawal seemed very similar to the one she described in connexion with influenza, when she admitted to fantasies of living inside mother. But the force behind these fantasies seemed now increased. Indeed one sometimes had the feeling, when she showed no response, that she lived far away in another world.

I must admit that the alternation of states of narcissistic withdrawal and ego-disintegration seemed to me for some time a problem which I was unable to solve. In spite of the difficulties, I adhered all the time to the analytic technique in the hope that gradually a clearer pattern would show itself in the analytic situation. My understanding of the psychopathology of the schizoid mechanisms of my patient was very fragmentary at this point of the analysis, and her difficulties in cooperation did not make the task any easier. I was struck by the various phenomena I have been describing, but thought mainly of them as a defence against depression and persecution. Only gradually did I begin to realize the *specific* nature of the primitive schizoid processes which seemed to affect the very core of the ego. Fortunately the analysis somehow or other continued in spite of her short and rare appearances for the sessions. I am sure she must have unconsciously taken in some of my interpretations, but outwardly it appeared as if I were talking to a blank wall. Only quite gradually did she begin to show some response and understanding. She explained one day that she had realized that she could not stand coming for a treatment which made her aware of herself and the hopeless condition she felt herself to be in. Her fear of analysis failing was approached by her in a roundabout way.

She expressed fears of losing her job at the bookshop where she had been working for just a year. She explained to me that in her life everything started to go wrong after one year and that after eight or nine months more she always had to give in. As at that time she had been under treatment for exactly nineteen months I could demonstrate to her convincingly that her greatest deeply denied fear at the present moment was that I would not continue with her analysis. You will remember that she was nineteen months old when her brother Jack was born and we realized in analysis that his birth meant to her that everything had come to an end and that her parents, particularly her mother, had given her up. The realization of the repetition of the early childhood situation struck her forcibly. This produced a flicker of hope and a slightly more positive attitude to the treatment.

During the following weeks the pattern of the transference showed that after any particularly successful interview, when I was able to demonstrate to her some important connexions, she stayed away or did not talk at the following session. I was struck by the similarity of her present reaction to what had actually happened at Jack's birth when she had become completely silent. I now understood that in the transference I was the mother, and any particularly productive hour represented for her my giving birth to a baby to which she reacted with complete silence and withdrawal. Consciously she still denied any hostility to the analyst, but in my interpretations I reminded her of the sadistic envious attacks of the devil who, in her fantasy, always attacked the good objects; and I tried to show her that she was now behaving like the sadistic devil and that attacks against me as the envied and admired mother were hidden behind her silence.

These interpretations were, as always, at first ignored, but in the very lengthy working-through period she admitted that she had always been afraid of letting her women friends down. She gave me an important example of this. In the Land Army her friend Mary and she had arranged to form a partnership in looking after the cows. She herself had undertaken the milking, but Mary was to be in charge of the scheme. She remembered that she had felt that in one way or another she would let Mary down. Actually they never worked together because she broke down, and now she could offer the explanation herself. She thought it was the fear of hurting Mary which made her ill. The analysis of this incident with Mary, which went on for months, revealed that she was mainly afraid that she would not get up in the morning to milk the cows. She had dreams of forgetting about the cows for days, which meant that all the good and nourishing milk was wasted, and pain was inflicted on the animals. I suggested that Mary stood for the mother and the cows for the breasts. In addition, this situation showed a distinct similarity to the transference situation, when she stayed away and refused to take in the nourishing analysis. From this I concluded that I not only represented the pregnant mother, and the mother who gave birth to Jack, but a part object, namely, the breast which she attacked in a particularly aggressive and tantalizing way by refusing to take any milk. I had the impression that these attacks on the breasts sprung not only from the jealousy of Jack, who was breast-fed by her mother, or from a deeply-repressed fantasy of having stolen Jack from the mother, but it seemed that early sadistic impulses against the breasts had been revived.[1] The incident with Mary was not, of course, the only example of her difficulties with women. She admitted now that she often withdrew from her girl friends in the same way as she reacted to me in analysis. Formerly she had depicted herself as being in harmonious and idealized relationship with them.

In sorting out information I had obtained up to that time, I concluded that even as an infant Mildred's sadistic impulses must have been very powerful. She must have been still struggling with them without any great success when the mother became pregnant again. A positive bond with her father had developed early, but the birth of Jack had caused an acute disappointment, and had acted, in addition to the loss of her first nurse, as a severe trauma to the already weak ego, threatening the whole organization of it. In consequence, the situation of Jack's birth and the

---

[1] In analysing other schizoid patients, I have frequently observed a revival of similar sadistic attacks on the breast in the transference situation, which first showed themselves in the patient's inability to talk and to co-operate. The sadism, which gradually came to the surface, was of a particularly *tantalizing* quality: the patient appeared continuously to try to rouse interest and enthusiasm in the analyst, only to frustrate him and discourage him as soon as he showed any response by an interpretation. In spite of the history of an early weaning trauma in most of these cases, the patient had actually never refused the breast or other food as a baby. On the contrary, some of the patients were described as model babies. I want to suggest here an explanation of this fact. The sadistic attacks and the refusal of the breast exist in the fantasies only of these babies, while fear of starvation on the one hand, and persecuting anxieties on the other, compel the child to submit to taking food. In the analytic situation, a great number of these deeply-repressed fantasies are acted out before becoming conscious, and constitute our most valuable information about the impulses at work in earliest infancy.

separation from the mother were denied. The mother was idealized and at the same time omnipotently controlled. Part of her sadism was projected on to her father, in the typical way, who was thus turned into a violent devil persecutor, but regression to the early relationship to the breast, which caused a mobilization of the schizoid processes, absorbed the rest of her aggression. This method of absorbing aggression I shall show in some detail later on.[1]

Progress was now noticeable in that she came regularly and usually in time, but in spite of the intellectual understanding of the aggressive impulses inside her, she still could not experience them as conscious feelings. However, we observed that, whenever she had occasion to feel envy or frustration, some of the symptoms of depersonalization or ego-disintegration which I have described before appeared. It seemed that the destructive impulses, instead of being registered by her ego as aggression and being directed outwards against an external object, turned against her own libidinal impulses, causing a lack of desire and feeling, as well as against her ego, producing varying degrees of splitting and thus disturbances in the function of her ego. During the height of the paranoid schizoid state for periods lasting some days, her ego more or less ceased to function in relation to the analyst. She had, therefore, been unable to come to the sessions, and when she did come she was unable to feel, think or talk. The improvement in her condition showed itself in that now, even when she was in a bad phase, the destructive impulses left part of her ego intact, which meant that self-observation, talking and simple action were possible. In consequence, the schizoid processes of internal splitting and excessive projection of impulses and parts of her ego could be observed in greater detail. One had to be continuously on the look-out for those parts of herself which she projected into other people, mainly her friends, her sister or the analyst, and also for internal splits, which showed themselves in a monotonous form of speaking, complete inability to speak, drowsiness or other difficulties like disturbances of thinking and acting.

[1] The regression of my patient reminds me of Melanie Klein's (1946) suggestion that a regression from a later level to the paranoid position occurs frequently in cases where strong paranoid fears had impeded the normal working-through of the depressive position. Federn (1928), on the other hand, suggests that depersonalization is *directly* based on a shock in early childhood through which the ego becomes permanently weakened.

There was a great resistance to any attempt to integrate the projected and split-off parts, even after the intellectual recognition of such a process. A great deal of hate was hidden behind this resistance. This hostility only gradually came more to the surface and was part of the destructive forces inside her which divided practically anything and everything. By this I mean that this division was not only observed between good and bad impulses and objects, or between what occurred inside her and in outer reality, but it seemed as if all thought-processes, actions and impulses were split into innumerable parts, isolated from one another and kept in a state of division. The patient spontaneously referred to this condition as 'I am split up again'. The persistent interpretation of all the splits and divisions, wherever they were noticed, seemed to bring great relief to the patient; it stimulated integration and increased her hope of ultimate recovery. The splitting of thoughts and actions showed itself particularly in relation to the analytic situation; for example, her frequent lateness for analysis arose from her dividing up her coming to analysis into many isolated part-actions. Getting up, dressing, having breakfast, the bus-ride to the analysis and the analytical session itself were all acts which did not seem to her to have anything to do with one another; if she were early in getting up, it did not necessarily mean to say she would come in time. She might quite easily take an hour for dressing without any anxiety about the time getting late. Then she might hurry over breakfast, only to wait a long time before deciding to leave for her appointment. Sometimes she arrived quite in time, but would not start to talk, and it seemed that the action of arriving for analysis had finished and there was now a gap. The action of talking to me had become split off, and there was no desire to talk. As I pointed out before, owing to this division into part-actions, very little conscious anxiety was felt by her about her failure to come for treatment, and no adjustment in time or learning from experience could be achieved until she could think of all the part-actions together as a single whole. Similar difficulties showed themselves in her everyday life. She frequently took a great deal of trouble to fix an appointment with her hairdresser, who lived half an hour away from her, only to muddle up the appointment by leaving home at the time she was due there. She had not forgotten that the journey took thirty minutes, but this fact and the action of travelling had become completely dissociated from one

another. Frequently her emotional appreciation suffered through
the splitting process, even later on in the analysis when she had
greatly improved. It happened that her fiancé had to go to
Bombay where riots had broken out and shooting attacks on
British soldiers were reported. For days she was quite uncon-
cerned about him, because the fact of his being in Bombay remained disconnected from the dangerous situation which existed
there. When this split righted itself through the analysis, she felt
a great shock of anxiety and her normal concern for her fiancé
could come to the surface.

I have now chosen some material, from a time when she herself
had become aware of her impulses, in order to demonstrate the
turning inward of the aggression.

Throughout the treatment she had had a great desire to ask
questions, but only a few of her questions were actually asked,
because she knew I would only interpret them and this she could
not stand. Improvement was also shown in her increased
ability to ask questions, which were in themselves an important
source of information concerning her wishes and anxieties, and
which also threw light on her reactions to frustration. As soon as
I started to interpret a question, she complained of feelings of
deadness or could not remember what she had asked. This happened frequently, until one day she realized and admitted that
she was demanding an *immediate* answer from me. She said she
felt cross and tense. But what was the point of wanting to ask
questions if one did not get an answer? After that she fell into a
long silence. When I interpreted that she had got rid of her feelings, she replied that she was pleased not to feel any tension; but
soon after she showed her understanding of the danger of this
mechanism by saying: 'If one wanted to get rid of one's curiosity
one would just die, because one has no desire to live. It is not that
one wants to die; one just dies.' *Instead of attacking and destroying
the analyst, the destructive impulses had turned against her desire to live,
her libido, which left her half-dead, as it were, and so in a state of
depersonalization.*[1] The intensity of the ambivalence on this and
other similar occasions suggested that the impulses were of a pre-

---

[1] The importance of the ambivalent conflict in depersonalization was particularly
realized by Reik (1927), who points out that the lack of feeling is connected with
death-wishes directed against the ego. He quotes the words of one of his patients:
'Instead of knowing you want to kill somebody else, you wipe yourself out.' Melanie
Klein (1946) has recently described the turning of the destructive impulses against
the ego as a schizoid mechanism.

genital nature and her curiosity seemed to be primarily an oral impulse, while the aggressive impulses were linked with anal fantasies and symptoms. For instance, her desire to find out through looking or reading led frequently to indigestion; and once when I had interpreted her crossness as an attack on the analyst with faeces, she failed to appear for the next session. She explained later that she had become so constipated that, instead of coming to analysis, she had gone home to give herself an enema. Similar facts were over and over again demonstrated to the patient and gradually genital impulses appeared for the first time more clearly in the transference. For example, when she left the bookshop for her analytic interview she began to suspect the girls of thinking she went out to enjoy herself. After my interpretation that she felt she was coming to enjoy the analysis she fell asleep, but had a dream which she related to me on waking. The dream was that she held the lid of a teapot in her hand and felt it was getting larger through her touch—the lid had here a distinctly phallic significance.

In other ways too she began to show her feelings more openly. A boy friend wrote her a farewell letter on leaving her, which upset her very much, and for the first time she could quite openly allow herself to cry during the analytic session. But she could not bear to hear me speak because, as she said, it hurt her, jarred on her, felt like an attack splitting her up into a thousand pieces, as if one were to take a hammer and hit a drop of quick-silver. I suggested that her hate of the boy friend who deserted her was here turning against her feelings and herself. In an attempt to save herself, however, the destructive impulses were projected on to the analyst instead of herself, and so the feelings of persecution from without returned. As was almost to be expected after this interview, she stayed away for a few days to work through her hate by herself; but when she returned she told me that she had just made the discovery that she felt ashamed of never having been able to feel or to show affection. This realization was still completely split off from the analytical experience, and there was then a struggle for a week or so to make her aware of the split, so that she was able to become conscious of the positive transference. When she was at last able to express gratitude, it was for the fact that it was now possible for her to feel for the first time a whole and a live person.

It was shortly after this time that she came to know a young

man with whom she fell deeply in love. At the same time her
jealousy of other women could become fully conscious. This was
realized particularly in connexion with a girl friend who had
introduced this young man to her. The relationship between her
and the young man developed satisfactorily on both sides, and
after several weeks they got engaged. He had to go abroad for
two months and they arranged to get married after his return to
England. She reacted to his going away with an acute attack of
depersonalization. This situation coincided with my summer
vacation and there were no signs of a spontaneous recovery when
I saw her after the holiday. She had again lost all desire to talk
or to come for treatment, at the same time all her feelings for her
fiancé had disappeared. She had been crying for days before they
had to separate, because she had been afraid that something
might happen to him on his plane journey as a repetition of
what had happened to her brother Jack. But when he actually
had to go she had not felt anything, and now she wondered
whether she loved him at all, because she could only feel a
thrill about the prospect of getting married, but *he* did not
seem to exist. She was worried about this state and keen to
cooperate.

Apart from the lack of feeling, another symptom reappeared
which she had mentioned only once before at the height of the
psychotic state. She felt that she was swelling up like a balloon
twelve times her own size. At the same time she felt she was only
a tiny self inside this balloon. My patient described this state as
most unpleasant and the only clue she gave me was that *expect-
ancy* had something to do with it. If she expected something from
another person or from herself or someone wanted something
from her, this symptom greatly increased. This description reminded me of the time of her acute paranoid fears concerning the
analyst, when she had been afraid that whenever he spoke to her
or expected her to speak he would force himself into her. Her
active impulses of wanting to force herself into people to dominate, use and empty them, which corresponded to her passive
paranoid fears, had been particularly strongly repressed, denied,
and split off. I had the distinct impression that one of the reasons
why the aggressive impulses had so forcibly turned against her
libido, was a fusion of the libidinal impulses with her primitive,
greedy, dominating self, against which she felt a violent hatred.
Before, it had always been difficult to make her aware of wishes,

because any desire was unconsciously related to this greedy part of herself which had to be suppressed.

At this stage of the analysis it was sometimes possible for her to admit her wishes, and she now realized that she did not want her fiancé to go abroad. The frustration connected with his going had stirred up her greedy aggressive wishes. They had taken the form of fantasies in which she forced her way into him to compel him to do what she wanted and at the same time she felt she was emptying him of all that was good in him.[1] The result of this greedy aggressive attack was that she felt herself to be inside him. The sensation of the big balloon was connected with the fact that the object she had forced herself into was dead, emptied through her oral demands and full of air through her anal controlling attacks. She felt dead through the projective identification with the object. On the other hand, the loss of the feelings lost through this process seemed to correspond with that part of herself and her libido which through the projection had become split off from herself. This at once became related to the transference. I pointed out to her the anxiety about being separated from me during the holidays and her anxiety about the analysis coming to an end after her marriage. But when I interpreted that these fears had increased her desire and greed for treatment and that she had fantasies too of forcing herself into me to get from me all she wanted, she went into a long silence and I then wondered whether she could cope with what I had pointed out. At last she could speak again and said that she had felt immediately that my interpretations were right, but, with that realization, she had become so tired that she had lost consciousness for a few minutes; nevertheless had managed to get out of the state again by herself. We understood that this reaction was a confirmation of my interpretation and that this state of unconsciousness and complete loss of herself was connected with a fear of going completely into me and losing herself there. It struck me then that her present fear of losing her feelings and the depersonalization were only quantitatively different from the complete loss of herself in the schizoid state of disintegration. If in her greedy desires she felt

---

[1] Similar reactions in depersonalized patients have been described by Winnicot, (1945). Federn (1928) discusses depersonalization as a direct actual disturbance of the narcissistic libido and suggests that in depersonalization regression to ego-boundaries of earlier times takes place, which gives rise to disturbances in ego-feeling. Melanie Klein (1946) has shown the connexion of schizoid ego-splitting with projective identification.

that she completely entered into another object, she either went to sleep or felt severely split up. If smaller parts underwent the same process she still retained the awareness of herself and was only aware of loss of feelings.

I found a similar situation applying to the splitting processes inside the ego, which I have already described. Here, too, it appears to depend on the quantity and strength of the destructive forces turning against the self, whether depersonalization or a varying degree of ego-disintegration takes place. In the last few months of analysis other interesting material appeared. She admitted, after long resistance, that she had been completely frigid in her attempted sexual relations with her fiancé. The frigidity was distinctly related to her feelings of depersonalization. We found that she had masturbation fantasies of being raped, which were closely related to her fears of the penis and other objects being forced into her. Interpretations which established the connexion between her primitive oral fantasies and her depersonalization with later genital fantasies, themselves following the earlier pattern, brought great relief to my patient; this decreased her fear of her genital impulses and allowed them to come more to the surface, making a gradual simultaneous improvement of her depersonalization, her frigidity and her object-relationships become evident. Another fact became noticeable at the end of treatment. With the greater integration of her ego, the process of introjection came more into the open. Previously introjection had been largely overshadowed by projection mechanisms; or, to put it in another way, the process of introjection had become inhibited through the paranoid anxiety of objects being forced into her. It was particularly the decrease of these specific paranoid fears, through the understanding of the primitive impulses and processes described, which enabled the introjection mechanisms to function again.[1] When she got married and went with her husband to live abroad, the analysis had to be interrupted. I saw her a few times after her honeymoon. She was happy and confident, and her sexual relationship to her husband was developing satisfactorily.

From many points of view the analysis is still very incomplete and there is a danger of relapse. On the other hand, the marriage

---

[1] Melanie Klein (1946) has made similar observations, she points out: 'As a result of the mind or body being felt to be controlled by other people in a hostile way, there may be a severe disturbance in introjecting good objects.'

has a reasonable chance of success and since the patient will return with her husband in two or three years, I did not put any pressure on her to continue analysis at that time.

## Summary

I will briefly summarize my conclusions from the analysis of this case.

Schizoid processes, including depersonalization, can be used by the ego as a defence-mechanism at comparatively late stages of development. They are, however, processes which affect the very structure of the ego, causing varying degrees of splitting and projection of the ego. These processes are related to the working within the ego of destructive impulses, which are felt to be alien (split off) and therefore persecutors. Oral and anal sadistic impulses, directed against the inside of the mother's body, also increase the persecutory anxiety. These factors suggest an origin of these schizoid mechanisms on a paranoid level, which weakens the subsequent development of the ego. The weakened ego of my patient felt the birth of the brother and the circumstances related to it as a shock, and a considerable regression took place through which the schizoid processes became reinforced.

Depersonalization is still considered by psychiatrists and psycho-analysts alike as a very obscure subject. It is often found in the beginning or end of a neurosis or psychosis; it accompanies some organic diseases of the brain, schizophrenic conditions, depressions, obsessional neurosis, hysterical conditions, and has been described as a separate disease entity.

I have tried to show in this paper that there is a definite relationship between the schizoid process and depersonalization. The schizoid splitting mechanisms described were manifested both in the schizoid ego-disintegration and in the depersonalization of my patient. I suggest, therefore, that there is a quantitative difference only between the two clinical states. Among analysts, H. Deutsch (1942) has drawn attention to certain emotional states similar to depersonalization, and their relationship to schizophrenia, and lately Melanie Klein (1946) has suggested that in depersonalization regression to the paranoid schizoid position takes place.

# 2

# REMARKS ON THE RELATION OF MALE HOMOSEXUALITY TO PARANOIA, PARANOID ANXIETY AND NARCISSISM[1]

## (1949)

### Psycho-analytical Theories of Paranoia

THE problems I wish to discuss concern the interrelations between homosexuality and paranoia, paranoid anxiety and narcissism. As early as 1908, Freud discussed with some prominent analysts of that time, particularly Ferenczi and Jung, the intimate relationship which he felt invariably existed between paranoia and latent homosexuality; and since then many papers on paranoia have appeared in the analytic literature. Most of the earlier[2] and some of the later[3] authors think that the projection of latent homosexuality is the most important factor in this disease. Ferenczi (1911a) went so far as to suggest that paranoia may be simply a distorted form of homosexuality.[4] Freud (1911) stated his views on paranoia in his Schreber case.[5] There he put forward his famous formula for paranoia,[6] of how the consciously unbearable homosexual feelings are changed into hostile ones for defensive purposes, and then projected. At the same time he

---

[1] Enlarged from a short communication read as part of a symposium on Male Homosexuality in the British Psycho-Analytical Society, November 1948. First published in the *Int. J. Psycho-Anal.*, **30**.

[2] Freud (1911), Ferenczi (1911a, 1914), Grebelskaja (1912), Hassals (1913), Kempf (1921), Morichau-Beauchant (1912), Payne (1914–15), Shockley (1914), Wulff (1911).

[3] Later: Brunswick (1928), Gardner (1931), London (1931), Knight (1939), Reich (1936), Ackermann (1938).

[4] In the same paper, Ferenczi says: 'The paranoid defence mechanism is not directed against all kinds of libido cathexes but only against the homosexual cathexes.'

[5] In his earliest paper on paranoia (1896) Freud does not recognize homosexuality as a factor in the disease, but he there describes for the first time projection as a typical mechanism of defence in paranoia. In 1905 he stresses that the frequent change of tender impulses into hostile ones was on the whole characteristic for paranoia.

[6] I (a man) love him (a man). This is contradicted by: 'I do not love him—I hate him.' I hate him becomes transformed by projection into: He hates (persecutes) me, which will justify me in hating him.

demonstrated that the projective mechanism could be used for other purposes: 'In the beginning of the disease (dementia paranoides), all object cathexis is withdrawn from the objects of the environment and regression to narcissism takes place. In the process of recovery, the libido is brought back to the people it had abandoned. In paranoia, this process is carried out by the method of projection.'

Freud explains that for regression to take place, there must be a fixation of the libido, and he assumes that the fixation of paranoia is at the stage of narcissism.

The early fixation of the paranoiac has been stressed by many authors, as for example by Abraham (1924)[1] and later on by Bychowski (1930)[2] and Holstijn (1933)[3]; but it was mainly Melanie Klein[4] who insisted on the primary importance of this early fixation. Since 1919 she has gradually developed her views concerning the early stages of infantile development. She believes that the first three, four or five months of the child's life are dominated by paranoid anxieties, and she therefore calls this phase of maximal sadism the 'paranoid position'. It is to the paranoid position that the paranoiac regresses. It is also Klein (1932) who demonstrated that homosexuality frequently develops as a defence against paranoid anxieties, which may explain the frequency of the combination of paranoia and homosexuality.

I found only three authors beside Klein, namely Maeder (1910), Pfeiffer (1920) and Róheim (1922), who assume a primary paranoid attitude of some kind in the child. Maeder described a primitive paranoid tendency related to animism, which is not only characteristic of paranoia but can be observed in

[1] Abraham, stimulated by the work of Staerke and Ophhuijsen, described the fixation of the paranoiac at the earlier anal sadistic stage. Bibring's (1928, 1929) work is closely related to Abraham's views.

[2] Bychowski (1930) stressed the primary importance of the oral fixation of the paranoiac.

[3] Holstijn (1933) demonstrated the oral element in the delusions of the paraphrenic in a great number of patients.

[4] In her earlier papers, particularly 1930 and 1932, Melanie Klein still differentiates in her theoretical discussions between the fixation points of schizophrenia (oral sadistic level) and paranoia (early anal stage) following Abraham's terminology. In her case material she always connected early oral sadistic impulses with paranoid anxieties. In 1935, 1946, she describes the early oral sadistic level as the fixation point for both schizophrenia and paranoia (paranoid schizoid position). I want to remind readers that Freud differentiates (1911) between the schizophrenic's fixation on the autoerotic level and the paranoiac's fixation on the narcissistic level, both levels dominated by the oral libido. Freud, however, never made quite clear how long the autoerotic phase or narcissistic phase lasts. At one point he mentions that narcissism and autoerotism frequently overlap.

children. 'This probable biological tendency is revived in paranoia', though he finds it 'difficult to say whether this type of persecution exists alone'. It is, in his opinion, often combined with
the projection of latent homosexual tendencies.

Róheim (1922), when reviewing Freud's *Group Psychology and
the Analysis of the Ego*, refers to an unpublished paper of Pfeiffer
(1920), where the latter states that the phylogenetic root of paranoia goes back to the brother-horde. Róheim thinks that Freud
proves the correctness of Pfeiffer's theory, and he suggests that
Freud's formula should be followed up further: . . . 'I love him'
would really mean: 'I love the father,' but this would be a reaction formation against the original state of: 'I hate the father.'
Accordingly, 'homosexuality in the structure of the paranoia
would be only a secondary factor'.

Freud himself, in 1922 and 1923, gives hints of the importance of the ambivalent conflict in paranoia and emphasizes that
homosexuality may cover up the fear of the father (without
referring to the fear of the father as particularly paranoid in
nature).

My own experiences with paranoid patients closely coincide
with Klein's view of the fixation point of the paranoiac at the
early oral level (paranoid position) and of the secondary and
defensive nature of the paranoiac's homosexuality. It is to this
defensive function of the homosexuality that I wish particularly
to draw attention in this paper. In addition I shall bring forward
some clinical material to show that the fixation on this early level
of development may contribute considerably to the development
of later homosexuality.[1]

I have found that whereas the latent homosexuality in paranoia
has been accorded considerable attention by psycho-analytical
writers, the problem of manifest homosexuality and paranoia[2]
has been discussed by only a few authors.

---

[1] Compare Klein (1932), Bergler and Eidelberg (1933), Holstijn (1933),
G. Bibring (1940) and Bergler (1944).

[2] There are several authors, particularly Shockley (1914), who find that manifest
homosexuals frequently develop slight paranoid ideas when they do not engage
in any homosexual practices, but these authors attribute the paranoia simply to a
direct conversion of homosexual libido (perhaps in the sense of Ferenczi (1911a).
Shockley sums up his views: 'In paranoid dementia praecox, the homosexuality is
always connected with unconscious homosexual impulses breaking through into
conscious mentality and receiving distortion through the censor. The homosexual
inclinations may be open and well understood by the ego, in which case an attempt
at suppression, if unsuccessful, leads to a genesis of persecutory ideas which may be
either unsystematized or fairly well systematized, thus giving the individual a

*Manifest Homosexuality and Paranoia*

CASE A

I am treating at present a manifest homosexual patient who suffers from a certain type of paranoia which is referred to by some psychiatrists as paraphrenia.[1]

The patient is an artist whose homosexuality became manifest sixteen years ago, when the patient was twenty-five. Even when his homosexuality was still latent he occasionally felt persecuted and thought that people were referring to him as a homosexual. It is an interesting point that he decided to put his homosexual fantasies, which had existed for a long time, into practice after it became clear to him that homosexuals were in reality persecuted by English law—a fact which he had somehow or other managed to deny to himself until that time. For a period he had promiscuous relationships with men and was completely obsessed by the homosexual problem, but apparently did not feel persecuted.

It was probably about twelve months later that he became anxious, and suspected that he was followed by plain-clothes policemen who were trying to accost him and arrest him after he had responded to their homosexual advances. These paranoid suspicions never left him, but their intensity varied.

In most of his homosexual relationships he played the active role, but he was passive with an older friend who looked after him financially and with whom he has lived since he was twenty-six. Even after that time promiscuous homosexual relationships went on, but the intensity of his homosexual impulses varied.

Five years later, in 1939, he had an intense homosexual love

---

resulting compensatory reaction manifesting itself anywhere in the gradation from a paranoid character to an actual paranoid state.'

Hassals (1915) talks of two patients who both later on developed persecutory ideas and are described as outwardly homosexual and as having consciously homosexual inclinations respectively.

Schmideberg (1931) discusses two patients in her paper who both showed manifest homosexual behaviour and paranoid psychotic trends.

Bollmeier (1938) described a patient who frequently showed overt homosexual behaviour. He developed in consequence of a rebuff in his work the paranoid idea of being followed by thirty detectives. The analyst comes to the conclusion that the paranoid mechanism is a projection of the patient's repressed hostility.

Knight (1939) describes the successful short treatment of a patient, whom he diagnosed as a paranoid schizophrenic, who developed paranoid suspicions about his newly-wedded wife several months after his having been seduced by a homosexual. The paranoia developed *after* the homosexual relationship, which was sexually satisfactory, had finished.

[1] Paraphrenia is a non-deteriorating paranoid schizophrenia with auditory hallucinations.

affair; this was interrupted by the war, which came to him as a great shock, and since he held pacifist views he became a conscientious objector. During the war his paranoia grew worse. He was convinced that everybody in the village where he lived was against him and spread rumours about his homosexual activities.[1] Throughout the war he worked on the land and liked it. Towards the end of the war he became very depressed and made an attempt at suicide. On the advice of his doctor and a friend, he decided to have psycho-analytical treatment. He started analysis with a psycho-analyst, and very soon felt better.

After three months he stopped treatment in an elated state in which his homosexuality became violently active. The breaking off of the analysis coincided with the return of his homosexual lover of 1939, but after being disappointed with him he became more and more promiscuous with other men. He started to use lipstick, painted his cheeks, and used face-powder. He wanted to draw everybody's attention to himself, and quite deliberately got pleasure from the fact that people were talking about the way he was prostituting himself. Gradually he started to hear voices, which were generally abusive and sneering in character. The voices mostly called out words like: 'he is "kept" . . . a prostitute . . . cottage, . . . Oh, queen . . .' and other slang words used for homosexuals. The voices got worse and worse, and he started to shout at people whom he suspected of persecuting him.

He was sent to a mental hospital where a leucotomy was performed after only two months' stay. For a little while following the leucotomy the voices stopped, but he felt dull and depressed and without any energy. Then the voices re-started, and he suddenly decided that he must again have psycho-analytic treatment, which he had not consciously thought of since he had stopped. As his former analyst could not take him on, he was sent to me. The patient has now been under treatment for only one year, but has greatly improved. For example, his ability to paint, which he had almost completely lost, has returned.

The factor to which I want to draw attention in this case history is the manifestation of the homosexuality after the patient became aware that it was liable to prosecution and punishment by the law. Generally speaking, the patient is very sensitive to

---

[1] There was in reality some feeling against him in the village because of his conscientious objection. His homosexual activities stopped almost completely during the war, but continued in masturbatory fantasies, or were transformed into some fetishistic activity.

any external criticism and aggression, which enormously increases his fear of both internal and external persecution. The homosexuality was used to check and deny the persecutory anxiety, until the time when even the men he had intercourse with became persecutors (plain-clothes policemen).

Another interesting feature is that the homosexual activities only stopped when the paranoia became very much worse, such as during the war and before he was sent to hospital. I have the impression that if the paranoid anxieties are too severe, the homosexual defence breaks down. Subsequently the paranoia will show itself undisguised and unmitigated, which clinically manifests itself as a paranoid psychosis.

I have collected some analytical material to show a mechanism which the patient repeated again and again in the transference situation. It is taken from a period of the analysis when he worked through the reasons for breaking off his previous analysis, and when he was afraid of repeating the same process with me. It might therefore tell us something about the state of homosexual elation and the consequent deterioration of the patient's simple paranoia into a paraphrenia. There is a childhood memory which he mentions frequently. He remembers how he struggled as a small child against an impulse to smear himself all over with faeces. When he was four, he took a lot of soot from the chimney and blackened his face with it. His present impulses to powder and paint his face and lips are connected by the patient himself with this childhood memory.

In addition there is a memory of excitedly riding on his father's knee combined with a fantasy of defaecating in his own knickers on these occasions, without his father knowing this. Before this memory appeared he frequently felt very anxious and depressed about certain thoughts and feelings which he had in his mind. It was sufficient for him to tell me what he had in his mind to feel relieved and elated. It seemed that he relieved himself of his depression by the process of expelling it into me (projection) as if he had defaecated into me. He himself related this transference experience to anal processes. Detailed analysis revealed that internal depressive and persecutory thoughts and situations were connected with these anal fantasies, which in turn were related to objects and part objects which he had previously incorporated in an oral or anal way. We realized also that, apart from the obvious anal projection mechanism, in addition he had sexual fantasies of forcing his penis into me during these periods of elation. After each such occasion where he seemed to expel some material in the way I described, he first felt elated, but afterwards the persecution by his voices increased, a fact which could be related to the transference situation. It was found that he was terrified after he had expelled his thought material and that therefore he detached himself completely from any interpretation which I tried to make, as if he feared that something awful was then being forced back into him by me.

Two dreams will further demonstrate the points which I have tried to make clear.

The patient looks at a well-known, successful painter from behind; this painter is very depressed and looks smaller than in real life. My patient looks down on him in the dream. In the second dream, a man drives a herd of dirty pigs right through the patient's kitchen. The man is in a flippant mood and suggestively touches his penis and pulls up the tail of a pig as if it were a penis. The patient took both for homosexual gestures.

In the first dream, the patient is envious of the successful rival. He castrates and humiliates him and makes him depressed through homosexual intercourse; but in addition, through this homosexual intercourse the patient rids himself of his own depression. It is the other man now who is depressed. The second dream demonstrates the persecution. Since the man is not in reality a homosexual, the patient has put his own dirty homosexuality into this man. In the dream, this man drives the dirty homosexual penises (pigs) in a flippant way *back* into my patient.

In the whole of the material presented, the anal element is doubtless in the foreground, but in fact the patient never played the passive homosexual role during the elated state. In actual reality genitality (the penis) masked the anal attack which he makes on his rivals. We can therefore say that the active homosexual role is used as a defence against anal sadistic tendencies. However, the genitality fails in its defensive function. The penis becomes indistinguishable from faeces (dirty pigs) so that it is the inner mess after all which was thrown out into other men. On the other hand faeces, as we know from the work of Stärke (1919),[1]

---

[1] Stärke stressed the identification of the loved object with the skybalum (faeces), which acts as a persecutor through the patient's ambivalent attitude towards the internal and external love object: Ophhuijsen independently from Stärke found that the persecutor may be the personification of the skybalum.

Abraham (1924) took up Stärke and Ophhuijsen's observations, acknowledged

Ophhuijsen (1929), Abraham (1924) and particularly Klein (1932, 1935, 1946), may become identified with an internal object. In my patient's case the greedily or aggressively incorporated penis (father), or at other times the breast, causes an unbearable internal depressive or persecutory anxiety situation. It is the projection outside of this internal anxiety situation, identified with faeces, which produces the elation, a mechanism which is well known. But in our case it is the penis, functioning in a manifest homosexual way, which one might say carried out the projection mechanism.

The other point which seems significant is the failure of this defence. This manic mechanism leads to retaliatory measures from the men of the outer world. Clinically, the patient began to hear voices.

To summarize my conclusions: the manifest homosexuality in my patient's state of elation before the paraphrenia developed was, partially at least, in the service of a defensive projection mechanism which had distinctly manic features. The depression and persecution which were homosexually forced out into the outer world returned into the patient in the form of persecutory voices.

---

their full importance and developed them further. He says, after speaking about Stärke and Freud's Schreber case: 'We may now add that in this process of reconstruction (of the lost object cathexis) the paranoiac incorporates a part of his object. In doing this he undergoes much the same fate as the melancholiac who has introjected the whole of his object by a process of incorporation. Nor can he either escape his ambivalence in this way. Like the melancholiac, therefore, he tries to get rid of that part of his object which he has taken into himself. And on the psychosexual development level on which he is, this can only be an anal process for him. To a paranoiac, therefore, the loved object is equivalent to faeces which he cannot get rid of. The introjected part of his love object will not leave him, just as in the case of the melancholiac the object which has been introjected *in toto* continues to exercise its despotic power from within.'

So far it seems clear that Abraham has oral incorporation in mind, but he mentions later on that 'this partial introjection need not be effected in an oral way but can be thought of as an anal process'.

Abraham thinks that it is not to narcissism or the stage of total incorporation that the paranoiac regresses but to the earlier anal stage with partial love incorporation.

Melanie Klein (1935) described in detail the internal depressive and persecutory anxieties.

It is most frequently the bad object which becomes identified with faeces. The bad object represents the bad sadistic impulses, the bad part of the patient's personality and last, but not least, an internal sadistic or destroyed object (part object or whole object), which may become a persecutor.

In addition, E. Bibring, Bender, Alexander and Menninger, Young and others have stressed the anal factor in paranoia.

*Paranoid Anxiety and Manifest Homosexuality (Neurosis)*

CASE B

In the next case I wish to show that severe paranoid anxieties are frequently hidden underneath a manifest homosexuality. This is a fact which has been stressed and discussed, particularly by Melanie Klein (1932). Nunberg (1936) mentions that apart from the great importance of ambivalence in homosexuality, there is the frequency with which paranoid anxieties occur in manifest homosexuals. Benedek (1934)[1] describes a manifest homosexual who suffered at times severe anxieties which she described as paranoid.

Patient B is a manifest homosexual, thirty-eight years of age. He has a great number of conversion hysteric symptoms, and tends to have manic depressive moods, but generally speaking his disturbances are rather more of a neurotic than psychotic nature.

He had an acute attack of severe paranoid anxiety, lasting for nearly twelve hours soon after starting treatment. He used to come to the analysis by car at a time when there was no basic petrol ration. On leaving my house one day he noticed that a car was passing by and a man sitting beside the driver seemed to hide his face behind a newspaper. My patient later on overtook the car and for some time saw the car behind him in the mirror. He got into a panic and was suddenly convinced that he was being followed by a police-car. He thought that I had telephoned the police and informed them about his illegal use of his petrol allowance. The analysis of this incident was very revealing and I will relate the dream he brought me the day after the anxiety state. In the dream the patient came to see me for his analytic session. In this I was telling a friend of his that he (the patient) was no good, and I asked my patient to bring up material by being sick, which he failed to do. I then put a syringe into his mouth to help him. Later on the patient took the syringe out of my hand and put it into his mouth himself. He did not succeed in bringing up any material. I was so enraged with him, that I charged him a high fee and finished treatment with him.

[1] It is the persecuting mother figure which plays an important part in B's case. In the symposium and the subsequent discussion in the British Psycho-Analytical Society, Dr Usher, Dr Thorner and Dr Heimann drew attention to the persecuting and devouring mother, while Anna Freud discussed the biting and castrating mother figure in male homosexuals. I observed the presence of a persecutory mother figure in all the cases I am referring to in this paper. I have, however, selected mainly material connected with the persecuting father (penis) figure.

I cannot go into detail of the analysis of this dream, which stresses first the internal anxiety about something bad he had obviously swallowed, and secondly showed the syringe as an ambivalent penis, which could aggressively put still more material into him or helpfully remove his inner badness. The act of taking the syringe out of my hand, as later material showed, represents the repetition of the bad act, namely, the swallowing of the analyst's penis, to which the dream analyst reacts with final persecutory hostility and castration of the patient.

In short, the analysis of the paranoid incident revealed that hostile and greedy oral impulses directed against the analyst's penis, fear of a stolen and therefore bad internalized penis and fear of the analyst as an external retaliating figure, were mainly responsible for this paranoid anxiety state.

To summarize, one part of the patient's homosexuality was determined by his attempts to appease external persecutory figures by passive anal intercourse and by the need to test and to reassure himself by fellatio about the destructiveness of his oral impulses. However, I found another mechanism in the patient's homosexuality which he demonstrated with great clarity. I noticed that the patient's homosexuality always became specially compulsive when he was depressed. For some time any manifestation of the homosexuality in the outside world was controlled in the transference situation, where the depression disappeared as if by magic after a successful interpretation. After I drew the patient's attention to the fact of his apparently magical incorporating of something from me which, I interpreted, represented to him my penis, the patient became very severely depressed and wanted to break off the analysis. At the same time he again made homosexual advances to men in outside life.

The manifest homosexuality was here used as a defence against depression. In working through the depression we had noticed several periods where the patient had become completely heterosexual, but he found it very difficult to bear the slightest frustration imposed on him by any woman. He admitted a desire to become dependent on a woman, whom he wanted to be wealthy so that he would not have to work. Any such attempt to love a woman was followed by intense hate and depression and turning away from women in hopelessness, after which the homosexual interest reappeared.

At first it seemed as if the patient had simply transferred his love from the breast (he had been breast-fed for eighteen months) to the penis, but closer analysis revealed that in the depression he felt that he had incorporated and destroyed the loved breast and mother. He felt unable to restore this mother, which on the genital level meant to him an inability to use his penis satisfactorily with women. In such an anxiety-situation one day he suddenly felt that I was surely much better at looking after women than he was; perhaps if he told me all his difficulties I could sort them out for him and give him back his interest in women and his sexual potency. This was followed by a homosexual fantasy about me. This transference fantasy, I think, demonstrates the following mechanism:

The destroyed or injured mother (breast) and the whole heterosexuality, including the patient's own penis, were projected into other men (here into the analyst) for safety and reparation.[1]

The passive homosexual intercourse served the purpose of recapturing the lost interest in women and the lost penis and potency from the men he chose for his homosexual intercourse. The projection of the bad self or the bad penis played an equally important part in the patient's homosexuality. He described how frequently in the past he found that he had a homosexual impulse to approach men who had nothing in their personality, physically or mentally, that he desired, but represented everything he hated in himself, particularly his own small, and, as he felt, bad penis. He often dreamt of such men and we always found that when he had succeeded in seeing these men naked in his dreams, their penis looked as small and unattractive as he felt his own penis to be.

### Latent Homosexuality and Paranoia

CASE C

My third case is a paranoid character type with strong latent homosexual features. The patient was treated by me eight years ago for difficulties and anxieties in relation to his wife. From time to time he felt intensely suspicious and jealous of her. In the analysis it struck me almost from the beginning that the patient's

---

[1] Compare Bychowski (1945). 'The deviation towards homosexuality was a result of a desperate search by the ego not only for his lost mother but also for his own expelled and projected virility.'

feelings lacked depth, and I observed paranoid projection mechanisms. The main part of his analysis at that time was taken up by the patient's homosexual fantasies and attitudes. After about two and a half years of analysis, he developed pleurisy, and had to go into hospital. During his stay in hospital, he developed an acute psychosis which was marked by suicidal depression and a hypochondriacal kind of paranoia. He was convinced that he was going to die, and believed that the doctors and nurses were in league against him to deceive him about this fact. I must confess that while I had realized during treatment some of the paranoid aspects of the case, my analysis of the latent paranoia had been inhibited by a theoretical consideration, namely by the teaching I had received at that time, that latent homosexuality is responsible for paranoia and paranoid character traits. I had to learn here by bitter experience that not only manifest but also latent homosexuality may cover up a latent paranoia. Many authors, particularly Federn (1943), have discussed how frequently neurotic features may hide an underlying psychotic state. Scarcely any of these cases have been described in detail presumably because the psychosis could not be approached psychoanalytically.

A famous case where both the neurosis and the underlying psychosis are described in detail is Freud's Wolf Man. Freud stressed the Wolf Man's passive homosexual traits and apparently analysed the homosexuality in great detail. However, later on a severe paranoia developed. Many authors[1] have speculated about this case and offered explanations for this occurrence. You will remember that Mack Brunswick (1929), who analysed the Wolf Man later on, found an unresolved, positive, idealized transference to Freud, which she was able to analyse by bringing to light the hidden, strongly negative transference to Freud. She did not regard the negative attitude purely from the point of defence, like Freud in his Schreber case, but analysed the hatred and the death wishes against Freud as being derived from the disappointment[2] of the patient's passive homosexual wishes in relation to Freud. She was puzzled by the fact that the patient

[1] See Harnik (1930), Melanie Klein (1932).
[2] I want to remind you here that as early as 1912, Grebelskaja showed the ambivalence in her paranoia patient. She demonstrated that the hatred against the father had been displaced on to another father figure, Dr Sch . . . who thus became the patient's greatest persecutor. The love for the patient's father was shown to be idealized.

started to improve after a dream in which his mother smashed all the ikons in his room, and she was not sure of the mechanism of the cure she had achieved. In studying her paper on the Wolf Man one has the impression that the dream represented the patient's acknowledgment of the successful work done by the analyst, namely, her smashing of the holy idealistic picture of Freud in the patient's mind.

It is Melanie Klein (1932, 1935 and 1946) in particular who has described the mechanism of idealization as a defence against persecutory figures. On the homosexual level, this means that the attraction to the idealized father is increased to ward off the fear that the father might change into an entirely bad figure, and so into a persecutor. The persecuting father is not only the disappointing love object, but also the rival father of the Oedipus situation, and in addition has all the aggressiveness and badness which is continuously being projected on to a bad object—a process which begins in earliest infancy.

Two years ago my patient returned for treatment; he was feeling physically and mentally crippled and only capable of doing part-time work. He felt that the previous treatment from me had made him ill, and it is an interesting point that he presented himself for treatment to a person whom he almost consciously, and certainly unconsciously, regarded as a deadly persecutor. The patient quickly improved during the first six to nine months of the analysis, and a great deal of interesting material appeared. Of this period, I will relate one dream to demonstrate how the patient's homosexuality was used as a defence against paranoid fears. In the dream the patient goes through an underground passage[1] until he comes to a room. There he finds a red-faced man whom he recognizes as a dangerous lunatic. Both men have revolvers. The dangerous person shoots at my patient, but his revolver does not work. My patient throws a spell over this man who is changed through this into a pale, friendly person who shoots my patient only in the arm. This is one of those dreams to which the patient returns over and over again at various stages of the analysis, when different aspects of the dream come into focus. Thus, for example, the dangerous lunatic frequently became

---

[1] The underground passage symbolizes the inside of the mother's body which the patient goes into and where he meets the father. The patient's fantasies of the father inside the mother belong to the earliest beginning of the Oedipus complex at about the sixth month of life. (See Klein, 1932.) The paranoid anxieties frequently concentrate on the sadistic persecuting penis inside mother.

identified with the insane part of the patient's personality; but at the time of the dream the red-faced man was mainly identified with the sadistic analyst, who threatened to destroy the patient. The patient omnipotently changed the persecuting analyst into a friendly man. The shooting in the arm represented the homosexual relationship with the friendly analyst, through which the patient was castrated. The castration was willingly accepted by the patient to ward off the danger of being killed. *The homosexuality appeared here as a specific defence, where the persecutor is appeased by homosexual intercourse.*

### Narcissistic Type of Homosexuality created through Projective Identification

As a fourth point I wish to discuss the relationship of certain aspects of homosexuality and the early narcissistic phase of development which I have referred to before as 'paranoid position'. I want to demonstrate this through material of the same patient. After the great initial improvement in the second analysis, the patient became increasingly detached and at times confused. A transference relationship developed which I have become accustomed to regard as typical of a paranoid schizoid form of psychosis. A great deal of oral sadistic material in relation to breast and penis appeared. For example, one day he talked about having stifled feelings about another man. When I said something to him, he replied that he could not take in what I said. My interpretations were bad and gave him indigestion. Later on, he admitted that he had been too intent on taking in every one of my words. When I interpreted that he was taking in my interpretations so greedily that he felt they were destroyed and so turned bad inside him, he suddenly complained of a fear of me attacking him homosexually, of going mad, and of a sudden severe pain in his stomach.

My interpretations seemed here directly identified with the penis which was orally incorporated and which caused the homosexual feeling. However, as it had turned bad inside him through his oral sadistic greed, it attacked him from inside and caused the fear of madness, pain and castration.

The oral sadistic attacks on his mother, and the consequent persecution by her, showed themselves for example in a dream where he bit his mother in her face and this caused a malignant naevus. (This is associated with his conviction during his psychotic illness that he had cancer.) Later on, he felt surrounded and tormented by women. He took an axe and killed one of them. Later on the dreams became more and more schizoid. For example, in one dream he studied a chart on which the fission products of the atomic bomb had been drawn. In another dream he saw many dead bodies dropping from the sky (probably from an aeroplane), and he felt that these bodies were part of himself. The patient had the greatest difficulty in differentiating himself from the analyst. For example, he had a dream where a German professor on a motor bicycle tried to split himself in two by running against a gate-post. In this dream the splitting mechanism was increased by the fact that the patient felt himself so confused with the analyst. In the transference relationship the analyst stood not only for his bad, but frequently for his good self; and the homosexual attraction to the analyst could be traced to fantasies where he projected his good self and other parts of himself, particularly his good penis, into him. In such fantasies or dreams, the analyst had generally the same profession as the patient, and achieved very high honours. He invited the patient to lunch, or otherwise had intimate relations with him.

The narcissistic type of homosexuality where the patient is attracted to a young man who represents the patient himself has been described by Freud. He defined it that a man was treating another as his own mother had treated him in the past. The mechanism involved was in Freud's description an identification with the mother. I suggest that the mechanism of the narcissistic attraction varies a great deal. In my own observation it is frequently the projection of parts of the self, particularly the penis, into another man which causes the narcissistic homosexual attraction.[1]

## The Origin of the Projective Identification

The mechanism underlying this attraction has first been described by Melanie Klein (1946) in her paper on Schizoid Mechanisms, and I used this concept in my paper on Depersonalization (chap. 1) to explain certain homosexual inclinations

[1] Weiss (1947) introduces the term extrajection for a certain form of projection which Klein (1946) described as projective identification. He connects love of the narcissistic type with extrajection and objectivation. He speaks of objectivation when a subject finds actual traits of an extraject in a real object.

in my woman patient. Anna Freud in her short communication on the subject of homosexuality stressed the projection of the good and potent penis on to other men in certain types of homosexuals. However, she related this to the phallic phase only. I feel that the observation of the projective mechanism at a certain period cannot be treated as an isolated phenomenon. Apart from the internal and external situations which may momentarily increase a need to project, it is important to trace the basis of this projection mechanism,[1] which lies in the early oral sadistic impulses of forcing the self into another object.[2]

I will now try to demonstrate the analysis of the early impulses in this patient. I noticed that the patient became particularly silent at moments when he had thoughts in his mind which he felt to be of special interest to me. It took him several hours to bring himself to tell me the name of a friend, or about a theatrical performance he had seen, or about a dream. All he could say about this difficulty was that he was afraid of my becoming too interested in him and that he had to keep me at arm's length. This was always followed by fantasies of warding off homosexual intercourse with me. For quite a long time no progress was achieved and the difficulty repeated itself over and over again, until he had the following dream. He saw a famous surgeon operating on a patient, who observed with great admiration the skill displayed by the surgeon, who seemed intensely concentrated on his work. Suddenly the surgeon lost his balance and fell right into the inside of the patient, with whom he got so entangled that he could scarcely manage to free himself. He nearly choked, and only by administering an oxygen apparatus could he manage to revive himself. With the help of this dream the patient realized his extreme fear of my getting so interested in him that I would get inside him. Apart from the depressing fear of my and his dying in this way, he also felt persecuted by the overpowering analyst inside him, by whom he felt dominated and followed everywhere. At the same time he had nightmares of being followed by men, and of men looking into his bedroom window. Only very gradually could he admit more of his own interest in me, but as there was also a reciprocal fear of his forcing himself,

[1] Compare Tausk's view, 1919. He related the persecution of his patient to a projection of part of the self, particularly the genitals. He traced the projection mechanism back to the earliest months of the infant's life.

[2] See papers by Klein, 1946; Rosenfeld, (previous chapter); Riviere (unpublished), 1948.

D

or falling into me, any expression of affection was usually followed by fears of getting entangled inside me.

At a later date of the analysis, it could be clearly established that the impulses of forcing himself into his mother, which belong to the earliest phase of infancy (Klein, 1946), were strongly present in the patient and had been reinforced later on by regression and by certain related factors—namely by the overpowering attitude of the patient's mother, who ruled the patient's life completely until his marriage, and who had virtually forced her ideas into my patient from earliest childhood. These impulses in him had been partially transferred on to the father at an early age, and constituted the most important fixation point both of his homosexuality and his paranoia. At the same time they were responsible for the great use the patient made of the projection mechanism. Clinically the homosexual fantasies and his paranoid attitude and preoccupation only gradually began to disappear after the whole early and later structure of the mother relationship was fully understood and worked through in the transference, and when his desire and need to project had considerably diminished.

In looking through the analytic literature for similar observations made by other analysts of paranoia patients, I found the following material in a paper by Grebelskaja (1912), where she described the homosexuality of a paranoid schizophrenic. She quotes the patient's words: 'First A penetrated me, he was the one who pressed within me. This penetration was so remarkable that I felt it in my whole body.' The persons who penetrated him were also his persecutors. He continues: 'When A was in me, the voices said: now he has me completely in his power, now I am no more, but A is active within.'

It seems clear to me from this description that the patient felt that the whole personality of A entered his body, and not only his penis. As a consequence he felt completely overpowered and he lost his self. (See previous chapter.) This case history shows to my mind how useful verbatim accounts of patients' statements can be to later observers, since Grebelskaja's patient obviously had similar fantasies to my own patient, but they could not be fully understood at the time.

## Summary

The purpose of this paper has been to demonstrate:

(*a*) The development of the psycho-analytical theory of paranoia in relation to homosexuality. There are several authors who suggest a primary paranoid stage of development, namely Maeder, Róheim, Pfeiffer, and particularly Klein, who described in detail the paranoid position in earliest infancy. Increased paranoid anxieties encourage the development of strong manifest or latent homosexual tendencies as a defence.

(*b*) A manifest homosexual and later a latent homosexual patient are described, who both developed a paranoia when the defensive function of the homosexuality failed. The homosexuality is related to the idealization of the good father figure, who is used to deny the existence of the persecutor. Or the homosexuality may be used by the manic defence system.

(*c*) A case is brought forward to demonstrate that, even in manifest homosexuality of a non-psychotic type, severe hidden paranoid anxieties are frequently found.

(*d*) The importance of projective processes in homosexuals is described. A narcissistic type of homosexuality is described where another man, through projection, becomes identified with the self.

(*e*) The origin of the mechanism of projective identification is traced to its root, namely to the earliest infantile impulses of forcing the self into the mother. It is suggested and demonstrated that the fixation on this early level, which has been named by Melanie Klein the 'paranoid position', may be responsible for the frequent combination of both paranoia and homosexuality.

# 3

# NOTE ON THE PSYCHOPATHOLOGY OF CONFUSIONAL STATES IN CHRONIC SCHIZOPHRENIAS[1] (1950)

DURING the last ten years I have been treating by psychoanalysis a number of schizophrenics, some of very long standing. My aim was not only to achieve a therapeutic result, but to find out more about the psychopathology of this disease group. To achieve this aim I adhered to the regular analytic situation and deviated as little as possible from the established technique employed in treating neurotics, because I felt, and still feel, that only thus may it be possible to increase our knowledge of the psycho-pathology of schizophrenia.

This paper deals with the psychopathology of confusional states which I was able to investigate during the analyses of chronic schizophrenic patients. Feelings of confusion are part of normal development[2] and they are a common feature in many pathological conditions. But in the schizophrenic process severe states of confusion seem to play an important part; I also noticed that following the confusional state there was either an improvement or a deterioration in the condition of my patients.

I shall use material from one chronic paranoid schizophrenic patient to illustrate my points. He is a painter, forty years of age (in 1948), and a manifest homosexual.[3] From 1933, he gradually developed delusions of reference and persecution. In 1946 he started psycho-analytical treatment with a male colleague, and

---

[1] Paper read at the 16th International Psycho-Analytical Congress, Zürich, August, 1949, and first published in the *Int. J. Psycho-Anal.*, **31**.

[2] We may assume that in earliest infancy the baby lives in a state of unintegration (Winnicott, 1945), where perception is incomplete and where external and internal stimuli, external and internal objects and parts of the body can often not be differentiated. This confusion due to unintegration is normal and gradually disappears during development. We also have to keep in mind here that any developmental progress may lead temporarily to some confusion until a new adjustment is made.

[3] I have given a more detailed case history of this patient in the last chapter. Here I want only to add that the patient was weaned after a fortnight and there were at first difficulties with bottle feeding.

soon felt much better. After three months sudden changes took place in his condition. He stopped treatment, and soon afterwards began to act as if he were a young homosexual prostitute. Sometimes he made himself and others believe that he was a landworker. He tried to eliminate the fact that he was a painter completely from his memory and personality. When he later started to hear voices, they discussed among other things his age and his different selves, particularly whether he was a prostitute or a painter. His voices and his confusion between reality and fantasy became so bad that in summer 1947 he had to go into a mental hospital for three months. In March 1948 he started treatment with me in my consulting room.

I shall now discuss some of the concepts to which my findings are related. Melanie Klein (e.g. 1935, 1946, 1948) has described how the child from earliest infancy projects his libidinal impulses on to a breast which he feels to be good and his aggressive impulses on to a breast which he feels to be bad. Both the good and the bad breasts are introjected and are felt to be outside and inside the infant at the same time. The good breast forms the prototype of all later good objects, while the bad breast, which is felt to be persecuting, becomes the prototype of all later persecutory objects, such as bad stool, the bad penis and so on. During the first few months of life, which Melanie Klein calls the paranoid position, the infant keeps the good breast separate from the bad breast. Occasionally states of integration occur, when love and hate can be experienced towards one and the same breast with constructive impulses mitigating and controlling the destructive ones.

I wish to make some tentative additions to these concepts, and I suggest that under certain external and internal conditions when aggressive impulses temporarily predominate, states may arise in which love and hate impulses and good and bad objects cannot be kept apart and are thus felt to be mixed up or confused. These infantile states of confusion are states of disintegration and are related to the *confusional schizophrenic states of the adult* which I am describing in this paper. The confusional state is associated with extreme anxiety, because when libidinal and destructive impulses become confused, the destructive impulses seem to threaten to destroy the libidinal impulses. Consequently the whole self is in danger of being destroyed. The only escape from this danger lies in the ability to differentiate again between love and hate. If normal differentiation cannot be achieved, splitting mechanisms become reinforced.[1]

## Confusion of Impulses

I shall first try to illustrate what I mean by confusion of impulses. In schizophrenics we frequently meet with a confusion of impulses or objects, which does not give rise to an acute confusional state but to a confusion of a more chronic kind, which may show itself in disturbances of speech or locomotion, or in severe inhibitions of other activities. When the patient began treatment with me he had become completely inhibited in his artistic activities. After some analysis with me he admitted that he blamed his first analysis for this difficulty, which was very painful to him. He explained to me that in the beginning of the first analysis he had started to paint *more*, and had shown the analyst some of the pictures. The analyst had remarked on the dark colour of the pictures, and had related this in his interpretations to the preoccupation of the patient with faeces and to his desire to smear with faeces. The patient thought that following on this interpretation he had gradually become unable to paint.

I want to explain here why I am including in this paper several of the patient's statements about his previous analysis in spite of the fact that it is quite impossible to be certain whether the previous analyst made the interpretations exactly in the way that the patient attributes them to him. Some of these interpretations sound quite feasible, but I suggest that they were inexact in a sense similar to Glover's use of this term in his paper on the therapeutic effect of inexact interpretation.[2] In the case of my

---

[1] I am concentrating in this paper mainly on the confusion of aggressive and libidinal impulses. I am only touching on the confusion of different parts of the body and the confusion of fantasy and reality. I am not discussing in this paper the confusion arising through the projection of the ego or of parts only of the ego into other objects, which is an important factor in the frequent loss of identity of the schizophrenic. In the previous chapter I discussed a paranoid patient (Case C) who had the greatest difficulty in differentiating himself from the analyst. For example, he had a dream where a German professor on a motorcycle tried to split himself in two by running against a gate post. The analysis showed that the attempt to split in two was made to escape from the state of confusion caused by the patient feeling completely mixed up with the personality of the analyst. (The analyst is of German origin and the patient had just applied for a professorship.)

[2] Glover (1931b) discusses in his paper what he means by 'inexact' interpretations: He suggests, that it would be an 'inexact' interpretation to interpret genital fantasies without attempting to uncover anal fantasies.

In the case of my patient, an inexact interpretation would be to interpret his preoccupation with faeces simply as an autoerotic activity without attempting to uncover the libidinal and aggressive anal fantasies related to objects.

patient, however, there was no therapeutic effect caused by an inexact interpretation; on the contrary, he felt intensely persecuted by it. In the treatment with me the patient tested me again and again to see whether I would make interpretations similar to those of the first analyst, so I had repeatedly to go over certain interpretations which the patient attributed to the first analysis and to seek to understand why he felt them to be so dangerous.

In the very beginning of the patient's analysis with me, I was impressed by the strong constructive impulses which were associated with his fantasies about faeces. For example, he studied various types of manure to improve the soil in his garden. The garden and soil were clearly symbols of his mother, whom both in reality and fantasy he had attacked and hurt and whom he wanted to restore. In dreams and associations the aggressive impulses related to fantasies of bad and poisonous faeces were continually confused with his libidinal fantasies about good faeces. As soon as the patient was helped through the analyst's interpretation to differentiate between fantasies and symbols of good and of bad faeces, and the libidinal and aggressive impulses related to them, he began to paint once more. The inhibition in painting seemed to be due to a confusion of good and bad faeces and libidinal and aggressive impulses in his fantasies. His blaming the first analyst for causing the inhibition in his painting meant that he accused him of not differentiating in his interpretations between good and bad faeces, which was equivalent to mixing up and confusing the good and bad faeces and the impulses related to them in the patient's mind. I will return later on to this accusation against the analyst in connexion with a dream.

## The Mechanism of Splitting Acting as Defence Against the State of Confusion

I explained before that, if normal differentiation between good and bad objects and libidinal and aggressive impulses cannot be achieved, splitting mechanisms become reinforced. For example, as a result of the confusion between the good and bad breasts, the fantasy of the good breast may be projected outside and the fantasied bad persecuting breast, identified with bad faeces, may be kept entirely within the patient. This mechanism was used by my patient to escape from a confusional state, which I now shall try to illustrate. This state occurred during a variety show. After the performance, the patient felt unreal and persecuted by his voices. Two comedians were on the stage, and one of them pretended to be attacked by severe colic. He held his stomach and ran round the stage obviously looking for an opportunity to relieve himself. Then he went into a little hut, which represented a lavatory. Anal noises were heard coming from there. When the comedian reappeared he waved a big stick of rhubarb triumphantly in his hand and shouted, 'I saved the rhubarb.' At this moment the patient became completely confused, and when he first described the performance to me, he said 'he could not see the joke, because the little hut on the stage must have been a kitchen; it could have been nothing else'. The patient had frequently had dreams, where food and faeces were confused with mouth and anus. The scene had increased his confusion of part-objects, namely the internal good breast and bad faeces. To separate the good breast again from the bad motion, he projected the good breast outside, which caused the illusion of a kitchen but which made him feel unreal; the existence of the lavatory relating to bad stool had to be denied in external reality, but his internal sense of persecution, his persecutory voices (here related to bad stool), increased.

## Confusion of Parts of the Ego

I shall now describe a dream where two parts of the patient's ego are shown to be confused. At the time of the dream, the patient was in a state of anxiety and confusion, because he was convinced that another man, whom he described as utterly selfish, greedy and dominating, was trying to overwhelm and destroy him.

In the dream the patient was in an enclosure and observed several lobsters lying side by side. Suddenly one of the lobsters crept on top of another lobster and swallowed it up completely. Soon afterwards the patient saw a perfectly horrid object, looking like a skeleton or the bones of a thorax, running across the floor. He thought the 'creature' was the two lobsters, and he chased it in order to kill it. He felt sorry for the creature, but he also thought of it as unbearably horrid.

The lobsters reminded the patient of himself, because he had frequently before identified himself with a lobster. Through other associations we began to realize that the man he felt persecuted by at the time stood for a part of his own self, which was identified with oral-sadistic impulses. His anxiety and confusion was due to his feeling that his bad self was devouring a good part of himself identified with libidinal impulses. The attempt to kill the creature in the dream represents a schizoid splitting mechanism, by which the hopelessly mixed up parts of the self are eliminated. Other associations revealed that the pieces of thorax referred not only to parts of the self, but to an object, namely, the breast, which the patient felt he had incorporated and destroyed through his oral-sadistic fantasies. There is therefore another reason why the 'creature' is so unbearably horrid, because the destroyed breast is felt to be an internal persecutor. In analysing processes of splitting the ego, one frequently realizes that the various split-off parts of the ego are identified with introjected good or bad objects.[1]

## Confusional State Arising in an Attempt at Recovery

I shall now bring forward some suggestions as to how an acute confusional state may arise in an attempt at recovery. I would remind you here that Freud (1911, 1924)[2] suggests that many schizophrenic symptoms are attempts at recovery, a concept which I found confirmed again and again. Neither of the confusional states I have described (in the lobster dream and at the variety performance) cleared up through the patient being more able to differentiate between his libidinal and aggressive impulses, but through a reinforcement of mechanisms of splitting. This implies that there was temporarily a deterioration in the patient's condition, because if mechanisms of splitting become reinforced, although the confusional states disappear, the processes of ego-disintegration increase. I had therefore to concentrate in the earlier part of the patient's treatment on the analysis of the splitting processes, which I cannot now discuss further.

Whenever splitting processes lessen, either spontaneously or through analysis, both the libidinal and the aggressive impulses become more active. The libidinal impulses assist the ego in

[1] For further details about schizoid splitting mechanisms, see Klein (1946) and Rosenfeld (chapter 1 in the present volume).

[2] Freud (1911) says in his Schreber case: 'The delusional formation, which we take to be the pathological product, is in reality an attempt at recovery, a process of reconstruction.'

In his paper on 'Neurosis and Psychosis' (1924) he says: 'In the clinical picture of the psychosis, the manifestations of the pathogenic process are often overlaid by or manifestations of an attempt at a cure or a reconstruction.'

striving for better integration and for synthesis of its internal objects. If these processes were to succeed, recovery would result. Nevertheless, at moments when libidinal and aggressive impulses are brought close together, a particular danger arises of an acute confusional state occurring, because the aggressive impulses may predominate and overwhelm the libidinal impulses and the ego.

There are two main reasons for the temporary predominance of aggressive impulses when analysis is making progress in schizoid patients.

First, a great deal of aggressive energy is expended in keeping up the splitting processes. When the splitting diminishes this aggressive energy is released and may temporarily be excessive.

Secondly, with the lessening of the splitting processes, libidinal impulses are freed and seek for immediate satisfaction. The frustration of these libidinal impulses also contributes to the increase of the aggressive impulses.

I shall try to illustrate this problem by giving some dreams from a later stage of the patient's treatment. He was making good progress at the time. At a certain point in the analysis of these dreams he appeared to be temporarily overwhelmed by his aggressive impulses and there seemed to be danger of a recurrence of the acute schizophrenic state he had experienced three years before. The dreams helped us to understand and prevent the threatening disaster.

First he dreamt that all the Christmases were stuck together, and he shook hands with a woman who was suffering from his disease, namely, schizophrenia. In the second dream a woman was boiling and mixing old and new stools in a saucepan. The patient wondered whether he could distinguish between the different stools. The analysis of these dreams went on for several weeks. In his first associations to the Christmas dream he gave a description of 'his mad year', as he called it. We now realized that the period of being the homosexual prostitute was linked to certain times in his childhood when he had good relations with his parents and to an adolescent period when he had despised them. Further he suggested that he had 'stuck his parents' into the simple people who lived in the cottages of his village. These people had in his opinion a free sexual life. At the same time he made fun of his snobbish parents in this way. The shaking hands with the paranoid woman was a friendly gesture towards her, but at the same time it meant that he made her as ill as himself by putting his illness into her. In all these associations libidinal and aggressive impulses are active, but he clearly differentiates between them. He returns to those times of his life when he was friendly and to those when he was aggressive to his parents. He allows the parents a free sexual life, but at the same time he humiliates them and makes fun of them by changing them into cottage people.[1] He is concerned about a woman who is ill, but he adds his own illness to hers by making her one with him.

Now to the dream of the woman boiling stools. The mixing of faeces in a saucepan means that faeces are treated as if they were edible food. The patient first thinks of his previous analysis. He suggested that the previous analyst had frequently interpreted his preoccupation with the breast, with parts of himself and with faeces simply as a preoccupation with faeces. He criticized the analyst for having thus muddled food and faeces and for having fed him on this mixture. The patient in the dream tries to differentiate between old and new faeces, which the woman is muddling up. This indicates a very definite improvement. In his first analysis, and during the early part of the analysis with me, the patient swallowed, so to speak, any interpretation he was given. There was never the slightest criticism from him. Now his ability to criticize begins to develop, as is indicated in this dream.

The session was followed by a week-end when he had a dream that his mother was drunk and quarrelling with his father. In the second part of this dream a woman was hanging with a rope round her neck in a lavatory, and he ran to save her. In reality his mother *never* drinks too much, while he sometimes drinks excessively, so he had projected his bad self aggressively into his mother, had made her commit suicide, and then attempted to rescue her and himself. At first he refused any associations, by saying that this dream was not worth analysing because *he had actually lived through the dream*. As in this dream he had killed his mother and himself, the statement that he had lived through the dream meant that his destructive impulses were getting out of control and he felt that the death of his mother and himself was becoming reality. If this were true the dream was no longer worth analysing, because the attempt at recovery, the rescue of the woman in the dream, would be doomed to failure. Towards the end of the interview he returned to the Christmas dream. He

---

[1] In fact, a large proportion of the patient's delusions and voices were related to the cottage people.

said, '*One receives gifts at Christmas, your interpretations are gifts to me*, but as you are doing this every day, time is eliminated, and so there is really only Christmas, and all the Christmases are one, and that is why they were all stuck together in the dream.' He added that during the Christmas following the ending of his previous analysis he was quite mad and had talked in free associations.

The patient was here confusing gifts and madness, and was indicating that he was not able to differentiate between whether I was driving him mad or making him better. The remark about free associations and being mad seemed to be related to the previous analysis, which he was confusing with the present one. I interpreted that he felt that the first analysis had driven him mad and that at this moment, in spite of the greater insight he now had, he was aggressively turning me into the woman boiling the motions in the saucepan and was confusing me with his bad self, his bad mother, and the previous analysis, which was madness to him. As a consequence he was beginning to confuse, fantasy and reality, past and present situations, and everything seemed to be turning into one. The patient replied that during the morning he thought he had seen the previous analyst everywhere; in trains, in buses, and in the street, and he had been afraid of becoming mad again.

The further analysis of this state of confusion revealed an oral-sadistic and anal attack on the patient's mother and her breast, in which she was eaten up, broken to bits and mixed up with faeces. There were attempts to repair the destroyed mother and breast and the ego parts mixed up with them, but overwhelming aggressive impulses were continuously interfering and preventing reparation. Severe paranoid anxieties were related to the situation, because the destroyed breast mixed up with bad stool became an internal persecutor and attacked and mixed up the patient from inside. This linked up with anxieties about his real mother, with his early feeding difficulties and his anxieties about his toilet training.

These factors were important for the handling of the analytic transference situation. Any inexact (Glover, 1931b) interpretation on the part of the analyst was taken by the patient as a proof that his attack on the analyst had succeeded. The analyst was felt to have been destroyed and turned into a persecutor. The patient feared that, as a retaliation against the patient, the analyst was sadistically bringing his mind, his ego, and objects together in a confused way, which meant he was going to drive the patient mad. It is possible that if many of the analyst's interpretations are in reality faulty and inexact, the patient's fantasy of the analyst as a persecutor may become completely real to him and the persecutory and confusional processes may become activated. This may be one of the ways in which an acute confusional schizophrenic state can become manifest under analysis. During and after analysis of these two dreams the voices and confusions of the patient diminished and his general contact with reality improved.

## Conclusions and Summary

I want shortly to recapitulate the main points which I have tried to bring forward in this paper. In observing confusional states during the analyses of chronic schizophrenic patients I was particularly impressed by the fact that the patients were unable to differentiate between their libidinal and aggressive impulses and their good and bad objects. Both the impulses and objects were felt by the patients to be in a state of confusion. The ego was also involved in this state of confusion. This I tried to illustrate by using a dream of my patient where the confusion of two ego parts was pictured as one part of the self eating up another part, so that they became indistinguishable.

In addition I was able to observe two ways of overcoming the state of confusion. First, the ego may regain the power of differentiation between the libidinal and the aggressive impulses. The result is better integration and clinical improvement. Secondly, the normal differentiation between aggressive and libidinal impulses fails, and subsequently new splitting mechanisms make their appearance, or the existing tendencies to split become reinforced. I have given two illustrations of splitting mechanisms following on the confusion. After the splitting becomes activated, the confusion and anxiety disappears, but there is clinically a deterioration in the patient's state, since the splitting causes progressive disintegration of the ego. An acute confusional state is apt to occur when splitting processes lessen, either spontaneously or through analysis, and both libidinal and aggressive impulses become more active as the aggressive impulses may temporarily predominate and interfere with the attempt at recovery.

I will state briefly my hypothesis about the state of confusion which may occur when the attempt at recovery fails.

Melanie Klein has shown that the splitting of objects and the ego is characteristic for the paranoid position, while the depressive position is introduced through a lessening of splitting mechanisms, so that libidinal and aggressive impulses can be brought closer together. Thus the libidinal impulses can help to modify and control the danger of the aggressive impulses, and feelings of reparation can begin to develop.

When the schizophrenic patient is making progress his reparative tendencies show themselves more openly. His libidinal impulses become related to fantasies of repairing his ego and his external and internal objects, which he has attacked and destroyed in his aggressive fantasies and which are felt to be in pieces. In the successful attempt at recovery the libidinal impulses achieve the restoration of the ego and its objects by connecting the various pieces correctly.

However, when aggressive impulses become temporarily predominant, the reparative process may be interfered with in a particular way. The libidinal impulses succeed in bringing the pieces of the objects and the ego together, nevertheless the aggressive impulses prevent the pieces from being sorted out and put together correctly. In the worst instance, the objects and the ego become pieced together but in a completely mixed up and faulty way. The result is a state of confusion, which may be either described by the patient himself or diagnosed only by an observer, who finds the patient confused and disorientated and without insight.

I have tried to illustrate this faulty reparative process and the severe persecutory anxieties related to it in my schizophrenic patient. The analysis seemed to prevent the manifestation of an acute psychotic confusional state, which was threatening at the time.

4

# NOTES ON THE PSYCHO-ANALYSIS OF THE SUPEREGO CONFLICT IN AN ACUTE SCHIZOPHRENIC PATIENT[1] (1952)

IN analysing a number of acute and chronic schizophrenic patients during the last ten years, I have become increasingly aware of the importance of the superego in schizophrenia. In this paper I shall present details of the psycho-analysis of one acute catatonic patient in order to throw some light on the structure of the schizophrenic superego and its relation to schizophrenic ego-disturbances. I also wish to discuss the controversy about methods of approach to acute schizophrenic patients.

*The Controversy concerning the approach to Schizophrenic Patients by Psycho-analysis*

In discussing the value of the psycho-analytic approach to schizophrenia, we have to remember that psychotherapists with widely different theories and equally different techniques claim success in helping the schizophrenic in the acute states of the disease. The attempt to concentrate on producing a quick therapeutic result in the acute schizophrenic state, irrespective of the method of approach, may be temporarily valuable to the individual patient and gratifying to the therapist; but these 'cures' are generally not lasting and the therapists often neglect the importance of continuing the treatment during the chronic mute phase of the disease which follows the acute state.[2] The psycho-analytic method can be used for both the acute and the chronic phase of the disease. I have found that when used in the acute phase it can be

---

[1] Published in *Int. J. Psycho-Anal*, **33** and also in *New Directions in Psycho-Analysis*, ed. M. Klein, P. Heimann, and R. E. Money-Kyrle (London, Tavistock, 1955).

[2] Eissler (1951) suggested the terms: 'acute or (first) and mute or (second) phase of schizophrenia'. He pointed out that the acute phase may last many years and the illness may take its course entirely either in the first or in the second phase. Eissler's contention is that the whole question of the psycho-analysis of schizophrenia can be decided only in the second phase.

carried on in the chronic phase without any fundamental change in technique; in fact, the use of the analytic technique in the acute phase prepares and assists the psycho-analytic treatment of the mute phase. The ultimate success of the treatment seems to depend on the handling of the mute phase. But, if a non-analytic method of forcible suggestion or of reassurance is used in the acute phase, psycho-analysis has been found to be exceedingly difficult in the chronic phase and its ultimate success may be prejudiced. Therefore if analysis is to be used at all in the treatment of schizophrenia, it is advisable to start with it in the acute phase.

There are many who would disagree with this view that the psycho-analytic technique can be used in the treatment of acute schizophrenia. Most American psycho-analytic workers on schizophrenia, for example, H. S. Sullivan, Fromm-Reichmann, Federn, Knight, Wexler, Eissler, and Rosen, have changed their method of approach so considerably that it can no longer be called psycho-analysis. They all seem agreed that it is futile to regard the psycho-analytic method as useful for acute psychosis. They all find re-education and reassurance absolutely necessary; some workers like Federn have gone so far as to say that the positive transference must be fostered and the negative one avoided altogether. He has also warned us against interpreting unconscious material. Rosen seems to interpret unconscious material in the positive and negative transference, but he also uses a great deal of reassurance, a problem which I shall discuss later on in greater detail. But a number of English[1] psycho-analysts, stimulated by Melanie Klein's research on the early stages of infantile development, claim to have been successful in treating acute and chronic schizophrenics by a method which retains the essential features of psycho-analysis. Psycho-analysis in this sense can be defined as a method which comprises interpretation of the positive and negative transference without the use of reassurance or educative measures, and the recognition and interpretation of the unconscious material produced by the patient. The experience of child analysts may help us here to define in more detail the psycho-analytic approach to acute schizophrenics, because the technical problems arising in the

[1] There may be a number of workers in the U.S.A. and South America such as Kaufmann and Pichon-Riviere who have treated schizophrenic patients by psycho-analysis. They have, however, not described their clinical approach. (Pichon-Riviere's papers on schizophrenia are only theoretical.)

analysis of acute psychotics are similar to those encountered in the analysis of small children. In discussing the analysis of children from the age of two years and nine months onwards, Melanie Klein has pointed out that by interpreting the positive and negative transference from the beginning of the analysis, the transference neurosis develops. She regards any attempts to produce a positive transference by non-analytic means, such as advice or presents or reassurance of various kinds, not only as unnecessary but as positively detrimental to the analysis. She found certain modifications of the adult analysis necessary in analysing children. Children are not expected to lie on the couch, and not only their words but their play is used as analytical material. Cooperation between the child's parents and the analyst is desirable, as the child has to be brought to his sessions and the parents supply the infantile history and keep the analyst informed about real events. In the analysis of children as described by Melanie Klein, however, the fundamental principles of psycho-analysis are fully retained.

All the experience thus gained has been used as guiding principles in the analysis of psychotics, particularly acute schizophrenic patients. If we avoid attempts to produce a positive transference by direct reassurance or expressions of love, and simply interpret the positive and negative transference, the psychotic manifestations attach themselves to the transference, and, in the same way as a transference neurosis develops in the neurotic, so, in the analysis of psychotics, there develops what may be called a 'transference psychosis'. The success of the analysis depends on our understanding of the psychotic manifestations in the transference situation.

There are some technical points which should be mentioned here. I never ask an acute schizophrenic patient to lie down on the analytic couch. After the acute schizophrenic condition has passed, one has to consider very carefully when the lying position should be introduced. This decision is by no means an easy one, as I have found that there are many chronic schizophrenic patients who are better treated in the sitting-up position. Schizophrenic patients frequently change their position in the consulting-room during any one session and also from one session to another, and this behaviour is significant as an expression of the patient's unconscious fantasies. I use as analytic material the whole of the patient's behaviour, his gestures and actions of various sorts, to a far greater extent than with neurotic patients. Close cooperation by parents and nurses is essential, particularly if the patient has to be seen in a mental hospital or nursing home or has to be brought to the analyst by a nurse or relative. Another important question is how often and how long at a time the patient should be seen. I have found that acute schizophrenic patients have to be seen at least six times a week, and often the usual fifty minutes' session has seemed to be insufficient. In my own experience it is better not to vary the length of time of any one session, but to give the patient, if necessary, longer sessions (ninety minutes) while the acute phase persists. It is also unwise to interrupt the treatment for more than a few days while the patient is still in the acute state, since it may cause a prolonged setback in his clinical condition and in the analysis.

The analysis of schizophrenic patients has many pitfalls, since the nature of the schizophrenic process makes the analytic task exceedingly difficult. The analyst has to cope with disturbing counter-transference reactions in himself and is often tempted to change or abandon his analytic technique. This may be one of the reasons for the controversy about the possibility of an analytic approach. The solution of the controversy can only be found in practice: namely, by showing that a transference analysis of acute schizophrenic patients is possible; and by examining the nature of the schizophrenic transference and other central schizophrenic problems and anxieties.

I have the impression that the need to use controlling and re-assuring methods is related to the difficulty of dealing with the schizophrenic superego by psycho-analysis. Wexler (1951) has contributed to the understanding of this point in his paper 'The Structural Problem in Schizophrenia'. In criticizing the view of Alexander, who denies the existence of a superego in schizo-phrenics, Wexler says: 'To explain the schizophrenic's conflicts (hallucinations and illusions) wholly as expressions of disorgan-ized instinctual demands that have lost their inter-connexion, is a travesty of the clinical picture of schizophrenia, which often reflects some of the most brutal morality I have ever encoun-tered. Certainly we are not dealing with a superego intact in all its functions, but a primitive, archaic structure in which the primal identification (incorporated figure of the mother) holds forth only the promise of condemnation, abandonment and con-sequent death. Though this structure may only be the forerunner of the superego which emerges with complete resolution of the Oedipus situation, its outline and dynamic force may be felt both in young children and schizophrenic patients, and if we do not see it (the superego), I suspect it is because we have not yet learned to recognize the most archaic aspects of its development.'

While fully recognizing the importance of the archaic superego, Wexler has, however, deviated considerably from psychoanalysis in his clinical approach. Apparently he did not attempt to analyse the transference situation. He tried to identify himself deliberately with the superego of his patient by agreeing with the patient's most cruel, moral self-accusations. In this way he established contact with his patient which he had failed to do before. The treatment continued while the therapist was taking over the role of a controlling and forbidding person (for example, he forbade the patient any sexual or aggressive provocations which threatened to disturb the therapeutic relationship). Wexler made it quite clear that he also acted in a very friendly, reassuring manner towards his patient. The theoretical background of his approach is his attempt as a therapist to identify himself with the superego of the patient. As soon as he has made contact with the patient in this way he feels that he has succeeded in his first task, and he (the therapist) then begins to act as a controlling but friendly superego. He claims that in this manner a satisfactory superego and ego-control is gradually established which brings the acute phase of schizophrenia to an end. The patient who had been distinctly helped by Wexler's method was a schizophrenic woman who had been in a mental hospital for five years.

Rosen (1946) described a technique in approaching acute, excited, catatonic patients who felt pursued by frightening figures. He established contact by 'deliberately assuming the identity, or the identities, of the figures which appeared to be threatening the patient and reassured the latter that, far from threatening him, they would love and protect him'. In another case, Rosen (1950) directly assumed the role of a controlling person by telling his woman patient to drop a cigarette which she had grabbed. He also controlled her physically and told her to lie still on the couch and not to move. But towards the end of the session described, he changed his attitude by saying, 'I am your mother now and I will permit you to do whatever you want.' In Wexler's and Rosen's case it is clear that the particular approach aims at a modification of the schizophrenic superego by direct control and reassurance.

Wexler suggests that Knight's and Hayward's success in the treatment of their schizophrenic patients must have been also due to their taking over superego control. It seems likely that all these methods which use friendly reassurance have a similar aim, i.e. the modification of the superego.

Indeed, from this critical survey, it would seem that all these psychotherapeutic methods are aimed at a direct modification of the superego. But I should add that none of the workers I have quoted have so far made clear whether they tried to approach the acute schizophrenic patient by a psycho-analytic technique and, if so, why they failed.

### Some Psycho-analytic Views about the Superego in Schizophrenia

Freud (1924) said: 'Transference neuroses correspond to a conflict between the ego and the id, narcissistic neuroses to a conflict between the ego and the superego, and psychoses, to one between the ego and the external world.' Freud did not explicitly discuss schizophrenia in this paper; but this formula seems to suggest that he did not think the superego could play any significant role in schizophrenia (dementia praecox). But earlier, in 1914, he pointed to a parallel between delusions of observation such as the hearing of voices in paranoid disorders, and the manifestations of conscience. He suggested that 'Delusions of being watched present (the conscience), in a regressive form, thereby revealing its genesis'. He then proceeded to link the ego-ideal with homosexuality and the influence of parental criticism. Later on in the same paper he said that in paranoid disorders the origin or 'evolution of the conscience is reproduced regressively'. These statements of Freud (1914b) imply that he did appreciate the importance of the superego in schizophrenia. He seems also to hint that the analysis of regressed schizophrenics suffering from auditory hallucinations might help to explain the origin of the superego.

E. Pichon-Riviere (1947) stressed the importance of the superego in schizophrenia. He suggested that the psychoses (including schizophrenia) as well as the neuroses are the outcome of a conflict between the id on the one hand and the ego at the service of the superego on the other. He says: 'In the process of regression there arises a dissociation of the instincts, and that of aggression is channelled both by the ego and the superego, thus determining the masochistic attitude of the former and the sadistic attitude of the latter. Tension between the two instincts originates anxiety, guilt feelings and the need for punishment. . . .'

Pious (1949) stated that he 'became convinced that the fundamental structural pathology in schizophrenia most probably lies in the formation of the superego'. He believes in the early development of the superego, but only stresses its positive aspects. He says: 'The superego develops from several loci, the earliest of which is the introjection of the loving and protecting mother-image. I believe that the development is jeopardized by prolonged privation and by hostility in the mother.' In his opinion the schizophrenic has a defective superego, but the structure of this defective superego is not explained.

Nunberg expressed his views on the superego in schizophrenia in 1920. His patient, who suffered from an extremely severe feeling of guilt, claimed that he had destroyed the world; and it became clear that he believed he had done so by eating it. Nunberg says: 'In his cannibalistic fantasies the patient identified the beloved person with the food and with himself. To the infant the mother's breast is the only loved object, and this love, at that stage, bears a predominantly oral and cannibalistic character. There cannot yet exist a feeling of guilt.' Nunberg, however, suggests that certain feelings and sensations of the oral and anal zone, which cannot yet find expression in speech, 'form the emotional basis for the development of that ideational complex known as guilt-feeling'. Reading Nunberg's description of his patient, we are surprised at his statement that 'there cannot yet exist a feeling of guilt' at the oral stage. For his case suggests that guilt-feelings and a superego exist at a preverbal period and seems to show that the sensations of the oral tract to which he refers are related to fantasies of consuming objects.

Melanie Klein[1] has contributed most to our understanding of the early origins of the superego. She has found that, by projecting his libidinal and aggressive impulses on to an external object which at first is his mother's breast, the infant creates images of a good and a bad breast. These two aspects of the breast are introjected and contribute both to the ego and the superego. She has

---

[1] I do not attempt to present here a detailed description of Melanie Klein's views; I only try to concentrate on those points which are relevant to the theme of my paper.

also described two early developmental stages corresponding to two predominant early anxieties of the infant; 'the paranoid-schizoid position', which extends over the first three to four months of life, and 'the depressive position', which follows and extends over most of the remaining months of the first year. If, during the paranoid-schizoid phase, aggression and therefore paranoid anxieties become increased through internal and external causes, fantasies of persecutory objects predominate and disturb the ability to maintain good objects inside on which normal ego and superego development depend.

She has emphasized that 'if persecutory fear and, correspondingly, schizoid mechanisms are too strong, the ego is not capable of working through the depressive position. This in turn forces the ego to regress to the paranoid-schizoid position and reinforces the earlier persecutory fears and schizoid phenomena' (Klein, 1946). In such cases the internal objects, including the superego, will be only slightly modified by the later development, and so will retain many of the characteristics of the early paranoid-schizoid position, i.e. objects are split into good and bad ones. There is an inter-relationship between these good and bad objects in that, if the bad objects are extremely bad and persecutory, the good objects as a reaction-formation will become extremely good and highly idealized. Both the ideal objects and the persecutory objects contribute to the early superego and in patients who have regressed to the paranoid position we can observe that some idealized and also some persecutory objects have superego functions. In the analysis of many acute schizophrenic patients we have difficulty in detecting the ideal objects functioning as the superego and we are impressed only by the persecutory quality of the superego. This may be due partly to the extreme demands of idealized objects, which make it so difficult to differentiate them from the demands of the persecutory objects.

Generally speaking, in schizophrenic patients the capacity to introject and maintain good objects inside is severely disturbed. However, even in acute schizophrenic patients we can occasionally observe attempts, which coincide clinically with the appearance of depressive anxieties, to introject good objects. As the infant during his normal development moves towards the depressive position, the persecutory anxiety and the splitting of objects diminishes, and the anxiety begins to centre round the fear of losing the good object outside and inside. After the first three or four months of life, the emphasis shifts from the fear that the self will be destroyed by a persecuting object, to the fear that the good object will be destroyed. Concurrently there is a greater wish to preserve it inside. The anxiety and guilt about the inability to restore this object inside, and secondly outside, then come more to the fore and constitute the superego conflict of the depressive position. The normal outcome of the depressive position is the strengthening of the capacity to love and repair the good object inside and outside.

In schizophrenic patients there has been a failure of normal working-through of the depressive position, and regression to the paranoid phase has taken place. The process does not become stationary at this point and frequent fluctuations involving progression and regression take place (Klein, 1946).

This may explain why in an acutely regressed schizophrenic patient one often observes a superego which shows a mixture of persecutory and depressive features. Clinically the patient may be observed to be in a 'struggle' with objects inside, which attack him by criticizing and punishing him, and which seem to represent a persecutory superego. But often quite suddenly the nature of the internal objects seems to change and they assume a more complaining character and make insistent demands for reparation, features which are more characteristic of what might be called a 'depressive' superego.[1] The conflict can rarely be maintained on the depressive level for any length of time and persecution increases again.

In the following description of the struggle of a patient with his internal objects I have purposely concentrated on those internal objects which go to form the superego. The contribution of internalized objects to the ego and their relation to the id are also of vital importance, but I have not discussed them in detail in this paper.

The investigation of the psychopathology of schizophrenia has also shown the importance of certain mechanisms such as splitting of both the ego and its objects, which were named by Melanie Klein 'schizoid mechanisms'. For example, she described, among others, the splitting of the ego caused by aggression turning against the self and by the projection of the whole or parts of the

[1] In Melanie Klein's view, the superego of the depressive position, among other features, accuses, complains, suffers and makes demands for reparation, but, while still persecutory, is less harsh than the superego of the paranoid position.

self into external and internal objects–a process which she has called 'projective identification'.[1]

In previous papers I have drawn attention to the importance of projective identification in schizophrenia. In the transference analysis of acute schizophrenic patients it is often possible to trace the mechanism of projective identification to its origin. I have observed that whenever the acute schizophrenic patient approaches an object in love or hate he seems to become confused with this object. This confusion seems to be due not only to fantasies of oral incorporation leading to *introjective* identification, but at the same time to impulses and fantasies in the patient of entering inside the object with the whole or parts of his self, leading to '*projective* identification'. This situation may be regarded as the most primitive object relationship, starting from birth. In my opinion the schizophrenic has never completely outgrown the earliest phase of development to which this object relationship belongs and in the acute schizophrenic state he regresses to this early level. While projective identification is based primarily on an object relationship, it can also be used as a mechanism of defence: for example, to split off and project good and bad parts of the ego into external objects, which then become identified with the projected parts of the self. The chronic schizophrenic patient makes ample use of this type of projective identification as a defence. If, however, projection as a defence becomes too extensive, the ego, instead of being strengthened, loses its own capacity to function and an acute schizophrenic state of disintegration may result. In neurotic patients the severe superego often causes the projection of impulses unbearable to it into the outside world, or in mania the superego is projected into the outside world to rid the ego of its internal tormentor. In acute schizophrenia I found that not only internal objects, including the superego, are often projected into external objects, but the projection of the superego was accompanied by massive projection of parts of the self into external objects, which caused severe splitting and disintegration of the ego.

I cannot discuss in this paper all the mechanisms of ego-splitting, but shall draw attention to ways in which the superego is responsible for *ego-splitting*. I also wish to show that a primitive superego exists in the acute schizophrenic patient, that the origin

---

[1] For the more detailed study of these mechanisms I refer to Melanie Klein (1946) and to my paper on depersonalization (chap. 1).

of this superego goes back to the first year of life, and that this early superego is of a particularly severe character, owing to the predominance of persecutory features.

## Discussion of Certain Aspects from the Psycho-analysis of an acute Schizophrenic Patient

### DIAGNOSIS

When I saw the patient for the first time he had been suffering from acute schizophrenia for about three years. He had always responded for a short time to electric shock or insulin comas, of which he had had at least ninety. There was a query whether he was hebephrenic, because of his frequent silly giggling, but, in spite of some hebephrenic features, practically all the psychiatrists who saw him diagnosed a catatonic type of schizophrenia of bad prognosis. Leucotomy had been suggested to diminish his violence and to help the nursing problem, but at the last minute his father decided to try psycho-analysis.

### HISTORY OF PATIENT

The patient, who was twenty-one, was born abroad, after a difficult forceps delivery. He was the eldest child (a brother was born four years later). He did not do well at the breast and after four weeks was changed over to the bottle. He cried for hours as a baby because his parents were advised not to pick him up. Difficulties over taking food were present throughout childhood and the latency period. A change occurred several years before the beginning of his illness, when he suddenly developed an enormous appetite. He had frequent attacks of nervous vomiting from childhood onwards. Other symptoms were disturbing sensations like deadness and stiffness in his arms and legs, and a feeling in his tongue that it got twisted. He could never stand being hurt, and when he had pain he often tried to pinch his mother as if he were angry with her about it. He was popular at school and had a number of friends. There was a period of exhibitionism between nine and eleven years of age. When he was about sixteen an incident occurred which frightened the parents and made them aware that there was something seriously wrong with the patient. He and his brother occupied a bedroom next door to that of their parents during holidays. His mother saw the patient on the parapet of the balcony, which was on the fourth floor, and thought he was about to commit suicide by throwing himself to the ground below. She managed to stop him and he 'broke down' and accused his father of not telling him the facts of life. Apparently the patient had had a period of intense masturbation before this episode. At seventeen he fell in love with a ballet dancer. She jilted him and soon afterwards he had his first schizophrenic breakdown.

## PARENTS OF THE PATIENT

His mother had not felt well during her pregnancy, and, after her confinement, developed asthma and could not look after the baby, who was handed over to a nurse. It is very difficult to assess clearly her relationship to him, but it seems that she preferred the younger boy.[1] When the patient grew up he frequently quarrelled with her, and got on much better with his father. When he fell ill, she would not have him at home and later on she was strongly opposed to his having psycho-analytic treatment. His father was an emotional man, very fond of his eldest boy, but undecided and unreliable.

## THE TREATMENT

At the time when I first saw the patient he was socially withdrawn, suffered from hallucinations and was almost mute, and sometimes he was impulsive. The first fortnight he was brought by car from the mental nursing home where he was looked after. Later I saw him there and he had two private male nurses. For the first four to five weeks of the treatment he was at times dangerously violent. From then on the violence lessened a good deal and he became much easier to handle. This changed again at a time when the nurses and I began to realize that his parents, particularly his mother, intended to stop the treatment. I had the strong impression that, although the patient had not been directly informed about this, he must have sensed it through his surround-

[1] In some papers on schizophrenia, particularly by American writers like Pious and Fromm-Reichmann, the mother's hostile and 'schizophrenogenic' attitude has been stressed. The mother in this case seems to have been unconsciously hostile to the patient and the patient's illness increased her guilty feelings. But we ought not to forget that in all mental disturbances there is a close inter-relationship between external factors acting as trauma and internal ones which are determined mostly by heredity. In our analytic approach we know that it is futile and even harmful to the progress of an analysis to accept uncritically the patient's attempts to blame the external environment for his illness. We generally find that there exists a great deal of distortion of external factors through projection and we have to help the patient to understand his fantasies and reactions to external situations until he becomes able to differentiate between his fantasies and external reality.

ings. I was driven to this assumption because from that moment he became progressively more violent, though even then he never attempted to attack me. Till then he had cooperated with me in negative and positive states.

TECHNIQUE

I saw him regularly for about one hour and twenty minutes every day, with the exception of Sundays. When he spoke he rarely used whole sentences. He nearly always said only a few words, expecting me to understand. He frequently acknowledged interpretations which he felt were correct, and he could show clearly how pleased he was to understand. When he felt resistance against interpretations, or when they aroused anxiety, he very often said 'No' and 'Yes' afterwards, expressing both rejection and acceptance. Sometimes he showed his understanding by the clarity and coherence of the material he produced after an interpretation. At times he had great difficulty in formulating words and he showed what he meant by gestures. At other times, in connexion with certain anxieties, he altogether lost his capacity to speak (for example, when he felt that everything had turned into faeces inside him), but this capacity improved in response to relevant interpretations. Later on in the course of treatment he began to play in a dramatic way, illustrating in this manner his fantasies, particularly about his internal world.

## The Problem of Case Presentation

In presenting certain aspects of an analysis like this, it is impossible to reproduce all the material given by the patient and all the interpretations. It has also to be remembered that, with such a severely ill patient, the analyst cannot understand everything the patient says or tries to say.

However, I hope that I shall be able to show that this deeply regressed patient, who had great difficulty in verbalizing his experiences, conveyed his problems to me not only clearly enough to make a continuous relationship possible, but also in a manner which gave a fairly detailed picture of his guilt conflict in the transference situation, and the ways and means by which he was trying to *deal with it.*

Since some analysts, such as Eissler, deny the importance of interpretations in acute schizophrenia, it is necessary to discuss the significance of verbal interpretations. Eissler stressed the schizophrenic's awareness of the primary processes in the analyst's mind, and it is these primary processes on which, in his opinion, the result of treatment depends and not on the interpretations. I understand this to mean that the schizophrenic is extremely intuitive and seems to be able to get help from a therapist who *unconsciously* is in tune with his patient. Eissler seems to regard it as unimportant and leading to self-deception to consider whether or not the psychotherapist consciously understands the schizophrenic patient. He writes: 'I did not get the impression that in instances in which interpretations were used during the acute phase there was a specific relationship between interpretation and clinical recovery. It may be assumed that another set of interpretations might have achieved a similar result' (Eissler, 1951).

In my opinion the unconscious intuitive understanding by the psycho-analyst of what a patient is conveying to him is an essential factor in *all* analyses, and depends on the analyst's capacity to use his counter-transference[1] as a kind of sensitive 'receiving set'. In treating schizophrenics who have such great verbal difficulties, the unconscious intuitive understanding of the analyst through the counter-transference is even more important, for it helps him to determine what it is that really matters at the moment.

But the analyst should also be able to formulate consciously what he has unconsciously recognized, and to convey it to the patient in a form that he can understand. This after all is the essence of all psycho-analysis, but it is especially important in the treatment of schizophrenics, who have lost a great deal of their capacity for conscious functioning, so that, without help, they cannot consciously understand their unconscious experiences which are at times so vivid. In presenting the following material, I would therefore ask the reader to remember that I had continuously to watch for the patient's reactions to my interpretations, and often to feel my way until I could be sure of giving them in a form that he could use. For example, I was surprised to find that he could follow without much difficulty the interpretation of complicated mechanisms if I used simple words.

Even so, it was at times obvious that he was unable to under-

---

[1] Cf. Paula Heimann (1950): 'On Counter-Transference'.—'My thesis is that the analyst's emotional response to his patient within the analytic situation represents one of the most important tools for his work. The analyst's counter-transference is an instrument of research into the patient's unconscious.'

stand verbal communication, or at least that he misunderstood what was said. We know from the treatment of neurotics that the analyst's words may become symbols of particular situations, for example, a feeding or a homosexual relationship; and this has to be understood and interpreted. But with the schizophrenic, the difficulty seems to go much further. Sometimes he takes everything the analyst says quite concretely. Hanna Segal (1950) has shown that if we interpret a castration fantasy to the schizophrenic he takes the interpretation itself as a castration. She suggested that he has a difficulty either in forming symbols or in using them, since they become equivalents instead of symbols. In my experience I found that most schizophrenics are only temporarily unable to use symbols, and the analysis of the patient under discussion contributed to my understanding of the deeper causes of this problem. This patient had certainly formed symbols, for instance his symbolic description of internalized objects was striking. But whenever *verbal* contact was disturbed, through the patient's difficulty in understanding words as symbols, I observed that his fantasies of going into me and being inside me had become intensified, and had led to his inability to differentiate between himself and me (projective identification). This confusion between self and object, which also led to confusion of reality and fantasy, was accompanied by a difficulty in differentiating between the real object and its symbolic representation. Projections of self and internalized objects were always found to some extent, but did not necessarily disturb verbal communication. For it is the *quantity* of the self involved in the process of projective identification that determines whether the real object and its symbolic representation can be differentiated. Analysis of the impulses underlying projective identification may also explain why the schizophrenic so often treats fantasies as concrete real situations and real situations as if they were fantasies. Whenever I saw that projective identification had increased, I then interpreted his impulses of entering inside myself in the transference, whereupon his capacity to understand symbols, and therefore words and interpretations, improved.

## The Progress of Treatment

Before describing certain stages of the treatment which gave me some detailed and inter-related material about my patient's superego problem, I will sketch briefly the first four weeks of treatment, during which time he cooperated particularly well. In the first few sessions he showed clear signs of both positive and negative transference. His predominant anxieties were his fear of losing himself and me, and his difficulty in differentiating between himself and me, between reality and fantasy, and also between inside and outside. He talked about his fear of losing and having lost his penis: 'Somebody has taken the fork away'; 'Silly woman.' He was preoccupied with being a woman, and he had a wish to be re-born a girl:[1] '*Prince* Ann.' By analysing material like 'The Virgin Mary was killed', or 'One half was eaten',[2] and 'Bib (penis) was killed', we began to realize that he attributed his dangerous, murderous feelings against his mother, and against women in general, to his male half and his penis. We also understood that his fantasies of being a woman were greatly reinforced by his desire to get rid of his aggression. When he began to understand this method of dealing with his aggression, his wish to be a woman lessened and he became more aggressive.

Sometimes his aggression turned outward and he attacked the nurses, but frequently it turned against himself. He then spoke of 'Soul being killed', or 'Soul committing suicide', or 'Soul being dead': 'Soul' being clearly a good part of himself. Once when we discussed these feelings of deadness, he illustrated this turning of his aggression against himself by saying 'I want to go on–I don't want to go on–vacuum–Soul is dead', and later astonished me by stating clearly, 'The problem is–how to prevent disintegration.' (The turning of the aggression against the self has been described as part of the splitting process causing disintegration in schizophrenia by Melanie Klein, 1946, and H. Rosenfeld, chap. 1.)

A predominant anxiety in the analytic situation, which the patient on rare occasions was able to formulate, related to his need for me. My not being with him on Sundays seemed at times unbearable, and once on a Saturday he said, 'What shall I do in the meantime, I'd better find someone in the hospital.' On

---

[1] Compare Rosen who described the frequent re-birth fantasies of schizophrenic women wanting to be re-born as boys.

[2] During the analysis it became clear that the patient felt he had split off or killed those parts of himself which were felt by him to be bad and dangerous to his good objects. In attributing the dangerous aggressive impulses to his penis, he felt that his penis was to be killed, to be eaten or destroyed, and consequently lost, which greatly increased his castration anxiety.

another occasion he said, 'I don't know what to do without you.' He gave me repeatedly to understand that all his problems were related to 'Time', and when he felt he wanted something from me, it had to be given 'instantly'.

Whenever he attacked somebody physically, he reacted with depression, guilt, and anxiety; and it gradually became clear that when his aggression did not turn against himself, but against external or internal objects, a guilt and anxiety problem arose which in fact occupied most of the time in the analysis.

I will now give some detailed material which followed an attack on Sister X four weeks after the beginning of his treatment. A few days before the attack, he seemed preoccupied with fantasies of attacking and biting breasts and with fear of women ('witchcraft'). He was inarticulate and difficult to understand. He talked about 'three buns', which probably meant three breasts, but it was not clear at the time why there were three. He attacked Sister X suddenly, while he was having tea with her and his father, hitting her hard on the temple. She was affectionately putting her arms round his shoulders at the time. The attack occurred on a Saturday, and I found him silent and defensive on Monday and Tuesday. On Wednesday he talked a little more. He said that he had destroyed the whole world and later on he said, 'Afraid.' He added 'Eli' (God) several times. When he spoke he looked very dejected and his head drooped on his chest. I interpreted that when he attacked Sister X he felt he had destroyed the whole world and he felt only Eli could put right what he had done. He remained silent. After continuing my interpretations by saying that he felt not only guilty but afraid of being attacked inside and outside, he became a little more communicative. He said, 'I can't stand it any more.' Then he stared at the table and said, 'It is all broadened out, what are all the men going to feel?'[1] I said that he could no longer stand the guilt and anxiety inside himself and had put his depression, anxiety, and feelings, and also himself, into the outer world. As a result of this he felt broadened out, split up into many men, and he wondered what all the different parts of himself were going to feel. He then looked at a finger of his which is bent and said, 'I can't do any more, I can't do it all.' After that he pointed to one of

---

[1] 'It is all broadened out' refers also to the world which is destroyed; but his ego is included in the destroyed world and this seemed to be the relevant factor to recognize.

my fingers which is also slightly bent and said, 'I am afraid of this finger.' His own bent finger had often stood for his illness, and had become the representative of his own damaged self, but he also indicated that it represented the destroyed world inside him, about which he felt he could do no more. In saying that he can't do it all, he implied a search for an object outside. But what kind of object relations do we find in the transference situation? I immediately seemed to become like him and was frightening. I interpreted to him that he put himself and the problems he could not deal with inside me, and feared that he had changed me into himself, and also that he was now afraid of what I would give back to him. He replied with a remark which showed his anxiety that I might stop treatment and he added explicitly that he wished that I should continue seeing him.

I shall now examine this material from the theoretical point of view. After his attack on the sister, the patient felt depressed and anxious. His behaviour, gestures, and the few sentences and words he uttered, showed that he felt he had destroyed the whole world outside, and he also felt the destroyed world inside himself. He makes this clearer later on in the analysis; but it is very important to realize at this stage that he felt he had taken the destroyed world into himself and then felt he had to restore it. To this task he was driven by an overpowering superego, and his omnipotence failed him. He also felt persecuted by the destroyed world and was afraid. Under the pressure of both overwhelming guilt and persecution anxiety, which were caused by the super-ego, his ego began to go to pieces: he could not stand it any more and he projected the inner destroyed world, and himself, outside. After this everything seemed broadened out and his self was split up into many men who all felt his guilt and anxiety. The pressure of the superego is here too great for the ego to bear: the ego tries to deal with the unbearable anxiety by projection, but in this way ego-splitting, and in this case ego-disintegration, takes place.[1] This is, of course, a very serious process, but if we are able to analyse these mechanisms in the transference situation, it is possible to cope analytically with the disastrous results of the splitting process.

The patient himself gave the clue to the transference situation, and showed that he had projected his damaged self containing

---

[1] See the more detailed discussion of the relation of ego-splitting and ego-disintegration which follows.

the destroyed world, not only into all the other patients, but into
me, and had changed me in this way. But instead of becoming
relieved by this projection he became more anxious, because he
was afraid of what I was then putting back into him, whereupon
his introjective processes became severely disturbed. One would
therefore expect a severe deterioration in his condition, and in
fact his clinical state during the next ten days became very precarious. He began to get more and more suspicious about food,
and finally refused to eat and drink anything. He became violent,
and appeared to have visual hallucinations and also hallucinations of taste. In the transference he was suspicious of me, but
not violent, and in spite of the fact that he was practically mute
we never lost contact entirely. He sometimes said 'Yes' or 'No' to
interpretations. In these I made ample use of previous material
and related it to his present gestures and behaviour. It seemed to
me that the relevant point had been his inability to deal with his
guilt and anxiety. After projecting his bad, damaged self into me,
he continuously saw himself everywhere outside. At the same
time, everything he took inside seemed to him bad, damaged, and
poisonous (like faeces), so there was no point in eating anything.
We know that projection leads again to re-introjection, so that
he also felt as if he had inside himself all the destroyed and bad
objects which he had projected into the outer world: and he indicated by coughing, retching, and movements of his mouth and
fingers that he was preoccupied with this problem. The first
obvious improvement occurred after ten days when the male
nurse had left some orange juice on the table which he (the
patient) viewed with great suspicion. I went over previous
material and showed him that the present difficult situation had
arisen through his attempt to rid himself of guilt and anxiety
inside by putting it outside himself. I told him that he was not
only afraid of getting something bad inside him, but that he was
also afraid of taking good things, the good orange juice and good
interpretations, inside since he was afraid that these would make
him feel guilty again. When I said this, a kind of shock went
right through his body; he gave a groan of understanding, and
his facial expression changed. By the end of the hour he had
emptied the glass of orange juice, the first food or drink he had
taken for two days. There was a distinct general improvement in
his taking food from that time, and I felt it was significant that
a patient, in this very hallucinated state, was able to benefit by

F

an interpretation which showed him the relationship of the acute hallucinated state to his guilt problem.

The analytic material and the mechanisms I have described here are not an isolated observation. They seem to be typical of the way an acute schizophrenic state develops. I have stressed that it is the inability of the schizophrenic patient to stand the anxiety and guilt caused by his introjected object or objects, including the superego, which causes the projection of the self, or parts of the self containing the internalized object, into external objects. This results in ego-splitting, loss of the self and loss of feelings.[1] At the same time a new danger and anxiety situation develops which leads to a vicious circle and further disintegration. Through the projection of the bad self and all it contains into an object, this object is perceived by the patient to have changed and become bad and persecuting, as the clinical material above indicated. The persecution expected after this form of projection is a forceful aggressive re-entry[2] of the object into the ego. During this phase therefore introjection may become inhibited in an attempt to prevent the persecuting object from entering.

Thus a most important defence against the re-entry of the objects into which projection has taken place is negativism, which may show itself as a refusal to have anything to do with the world outside including the refusal of food. Such a defence is, however, rarely successful, since almost simultaneously with the projection of the self into an external object, the external object containing the self is also introjected. This implies that the object exists in fantasy externally and internally at the same time. In the process the ego is in danger of being completely overwhelmed, almost squeezed out of existence. In addition, we have to remember that the whole process is not stationary, because as soon as the object containing parts of the self is re-introjected, there is again the tendency to project which leads to further introjection of a most disturbing and disintegrating nature. This means that we are dealing not just with one act of splitting, projection and introjection, but with a process where multiple projections and introjections can take place in a very short time.

[1] In my paper 'Analysis of a Schizophrenic State with Depersonalization' (chap. 1 in this volume) I have dealt in greater detail with the problem of ego-splitting, loss of self and loss of feelings.

[2] This process has been described by Melanie Klein, 'Notes on some Schizoid Mechanisms' (1946).

Clinically and theoretically it is important to consider the process from at least two angles: first the projection takes place to safeguard the ego from destruction, and may therefore be considered a defensive process which is unsuccessful and even dangerous because ego-splitting, and therefore ego-disintegration, takes place; secondly, there is also an object relation of an extremely primitive nature connected with the projection, because the introjected objects and parts of the self are projected *into an object*. This is important to understand because the strength of the persecutory fears about the re-entry of the object depends on the strength of the aggressive impulses pertaining to this primitive object relationship. In a previous paper (chap. 3) I described this object relationship in greater detail, so I only want to repeat here that there is evidence that, in addition to the relation to the breast, the infant from birth onwards has libidinal and aggressive impulses and fantasies of entering into the mother's body with parts of himself.[1] When there are fantasies of the self entering the mother's body aggressively, to overwhelm and to take complete possession, we have to expect anxiety, not only about the mother and the entering self being destroyed, but also about the mother turning into a persecutor who is expected to force herself back into the ego to take possession in a revengeful way. When this persecutory mother figure is introjected, the most primitive superego figure arises which represents a terrible overwhelming danger to the ego from within. It is most likely that the inability of the schizophrenic ego to deal with introjected figures arises from the nature of this early object relationship.

In the clinical material described above I have not explained why the patient attacked Sister X. I wish to add here that at a later date I had more material about the incident and I understood that at the moment when Sister X put her arms round him he became afraid that she was going to force herself into him in order to take possession of him. As I interpreted this, he shuddered and raised his arm as if to ward off an assault.

A FORTNIGHT LATER

I shall now report material which was obtained about a fortnight later. On a Monday, before I saw the patient I learnt from the male nurse that on the previous Sunday he seemed tense and had

[1] These impulses and mechanisms have been described by Melanie Klein, 'Notes on some Schizoid Mechanisms' (1946).

been about to make an attack on him. The attack did not materialize, but the patient turned very pale and said 'Hiroshima'.

When I approached him on the Monday, he received me by saying 'You are too late.' His limbs were trembling and he jumped in fright when the nurse sneezed in the room next door. He later said 'I cannot look,' and he repeated several times, 'I can't do anything.' He mentioned death several times and then became silent. He opened his mouth as if to speak but no words came out. I said that he could not speak because he was afraid of what he felt inside and what would come out of him. He replied 'Blood'. In my interpretations I told him that he had missed me over the week-end and had felt very impatient. He felt that he had killed me inside himself, and thought that as an external person I was too late now to do anything to help him and to help myself inside him. He was afraid to look at the destruction inside, and his difficulty in speaking, and his fear that blood might come out of him, showed how real this murderous inner attack had felt to him.

On the Tuesday, he said, 'We have to stop, I can't do it any more.' He again showed his bent finger, mentioned death and blood, and shrugged his shoulders. After I had again stressed how real and concrete his inner, killing attack on me had been, and that he could do nothing to make me alive, he pointed to a certain part of the hospital and said, 'I want to have shock treatment.' When I asked him what shock treatment meant to him, he replied without the slightest hesitation, 'Death.' I said that having killed me, he now felt that he ought to be killed as a punishment, to which he agreed.

What is significant in these two interviews is that he was more aware of having made an attack on me as an internal object. By greeting me on my arrival with the words: 'You are too late,' he was recognizing me as an external object and had to some degree differentiated this external me from the internal murdered me (blood). He was struggling to repair the damage he had done, but felt quite unable to do so. He felt less persecuted and more guilty, and his desire to have shock treatment expressed his need for punishment to relieve his guilt. However, the process did not stop here. As before, under the pressure of guilt, the splitting process temporarily increased. When I saw him on Wednesday, he looked very confused. He asked, 'Can I help you?' He looked round all over the floor as if he were searching for something he had lost, and he picked up imaginary bits and pieces. I interpreted that he felt himself to be confused with me as a helpful person, that he had put himself inside me for help because he could not deal with his inner problems any more, but that he now felt split and all over the place, and was therefore trying to collect himself. He made a movement with his shoulders as if he wanted to say, 'Of course, what else can I do?' After this he made eating movements and I interpreted that he felt he was eating me up to get something good inside himself, and also to swallow back the self he had put into me. He immediately stopped and said, 'One can't go on eating. What can I do?'

The patient's response to my interpretation gives the impression that he took my interpretation that he was eating me up as a reproach. In schizophrenic patients the misunderstanding of interpretations is generally due to their attribution of concreteness to their thought-content and thought-processes, i.e. whatever they think of exists in actual concrete form. On this occasion the patient reacts to what the analyst said with the thought that he is in fact actually eating the analyst up, therefore he must not do it. From the technical point of view one may attempt to interpret to the patient that he has taken the interpretation simply as a reproach and that he felt attacked by this interpretation. This may be sometimes helpful but a more effective approach is to understand the deeper causes for the misunderstanding. When I discussed the temporary inability of the schizophrenic to use symbols (on p. 77), I suggested that when projective identification is reinforced the patient loses some of his capacity to understand symbols and therefore words, and he takes interpretations very concretely. I felt that the projection of the internal object (the superego) into me, leading to projective identification, was in this instance the essential factor, on which I concentrated in my interpretations. So I again explained to the patient that he had put himself into me as an external object because he could not deal with his guilt about having killed me inside himself. As a result of this interpretation, he said, 'Blood and death', which seemed to indicate that he had reversed the process of projection and reintrojected the damaged object, and then he talked about Eli in an attempt to find an omnipotent solution of the conflict which we had previously discussed. Then he looked more relaxed and said, 'My son, my son', in a friendly, loving way, and added, 'Memory.' I showed him that he had been able to revive the memory of a good relationship with his father and so with me, and that he had begun to realize that the good feelings and memories about his father and myself were helping him to deal with his hatred and guilt. During this interview the patient had repeated a method of dealing with his guilt by projecting himself into an external object—a process which I have already described in discussing earlier sessions (after the attack on Sister X). The projective identification was on both occasions accompanied by confusion and splitting, but this time, after the interpretation, he was able to reverse the process and attempted other means of dealing with his guilt.

I will attempt to explain some of the differences between these two guilt situations, which both ended in projecting the guilt and parts of the self into an external object. In the first instance the patient did attack an external object, Sister X, and he felt he had destroyed the whole world. It appeared that he felt the destruction outside and inside. After the projection of the guilt situation into me he felt that I had been changed and had become persecuting. In the second instance (when the patient said 'Hiroshima') he must have felt violently aggressive and his description afterwards of what he experienced inside himself emphasized that he felt he had killed an object inside (blood, death), but at the time of the violent anger he managed to control himself and did not attack a real person. Later, when he projected his guilt and his self into me, he did not think that he had changed me into his bad self, but he felt that he had changed into me and so had become the helpful person whom, on this occasion, he felt me to be.

A FEW DAYS LATER

The following interview showed another variation of the patient's attempts to deal with his superego. At the beginning of the interview he touched my hand several times, looking at me anxiously. I interpreted that he wanted to see if I was all right. He then asked me directly, 'Are you all right?' I pointed out that he was afraid of having hurt me, and that he was now more able to admit his concern about me as an external person. He then said 'Chicken'–'heat'–'diarrhoea'. I replied that he liked chicken and that he felt he had eaten me like a chicken and his diarrhoea made him feel that he had destroyed me as an inner object in the process of eating me up. This increased his fear that he had also destroyed or injured me as an external object. He now became more concerned about his inside. At first he said 'movement' and 'breath' which I interpreted as a hope that I was alive inside him. But afterwards he kept his leg rigidly stiff for several minutes and on being asked what this implied, he said 'Dead'. This I interpreted as a feeling that I was dead inside him. He then said, 'Impossible'–'God'–'Direct', which I interpreted as meaning that he felt I should be all-powerful like God and do something directly to make this impossible inner situation better. He then said, several times, 'frightened', and he looked very frightened indeed. Suddenly he said 'No war'. He got up and shook hands with me in the most amiable manner, but while he was doing so he said 'Bluff'. I said that he felt at war with me inside after having had the fantasy of eating me up and killing me, and that he was now afraid of my revenge from inside and outside. He wanted to be at peace with me outside and inside, but he felt no real peace was possible, that it was only 'bluff'. I related this to his past life, to his feeling that his good relationship with people outside had been built on bluff, but also that he had felt that his coming to terms with his guilt and anxiety had often been based on bluff and deception.

In considering this session I suggest that my patient tried to make it clear that his guilt and fear were related to an introjected object which he believed he had killed by devouring. He showed that his relationship to this internalized object was a mixture of concern and persecution; when the fear of the persecution by the dead internal object increased, the only solution, apart from an omnipotent one, seemed to be to appease the persecutors, which also represented his superego. This he felt to be bluff.

In the following session the patient discovered a different method of helping me to understand his inner relationship to me, and so his superego conflict. When I approached him he was sitting very quietly on a chair, looking intently at his hand, at first examining it from the outside. Afterwards he stared fixedly at the inside: it looked as if he imagined that he was holding something there. I asked him what he saw, and he replied 'Crater'. I then asked whether there was anything inside the crater. He replied, as if to put me off, 'Nothing–empty'. I now interpreted that he was afraid that I was in the crater, and that

I was dead. Later he closed his hand and squeezed it tightly. I interpreted that he felt that he imprisoned me inside his hand and that he was crushing me. He continued squeezing his hand for some time, looking withdrawn. Suddenly he got up, looked round in a frightened way, and escaped from the treatment room, which was not locked. The nurses brought him back, and he sat down again without any struggle. I pointed out to him that, while he was fantasying holding and squeezing me inside himself, the room had suddenly turned, for him, into a dangerous prison from which he tried to escape. I interpreted also that he had identified himself with me, because he felt guilty about what he was doing to me inside him. While I was interpreting the fear of the room, his anxiety seemed to lessen, and he returned to squeezing his hand.

The next day the nurses reported that the patient had become very frightened during a walk. He had suddenly stopped, staring at the ground. He would not go any further. On questioning him the nurses found that he heard voices threatening to punish him with death. He stopped walking because he saw an abyss in front of him. After some time he calmed down. Later on he had what seemed to be two cataleptic attacks in which he suddenly fell forward as if dead. The nurses were sure that he was not unconscious during this attack. I used this information next day with the patient, although he made no reference to it himself, and I explained this frightening experience as a continuation of what we had been discussing during the previous session. I related the abyss to the crater and interpreted that not only did he feel that he had killed and destroyed me in the crater, but also that he felt he had changed me into a retaliating object which was threatening him with punishment and death. The cataleptic fits represented both his own and my death. The striking feature about this experience is the distinct connexion between the threatening superego voices and his own aggressive fantasies against me. The superego is here again persecuting and threatening him according to the talion principle.

So far we have seen that the patient was mainly preoccupied with me as an internal object, which he had killed with his oral sadistic impulses. In surveying these sessions it seems that he felt guilty and persecuted by this internal object which, particularly in its persecutory form, had a superego function.

He showed various methods of dealing with this frightening

superego. He attempted to expel it by projecting it into an external object. But this did not lead to a clinical improvement, because in projecting the superego he also projected parts of his self. In the first instance (after the attack on Sister X), where he projected his bad self into an external object in an aggressive manner, not only the splitting but also the persecution from without increased. In the second instance of projection (Can I help you?), the superego was also projected, but here the emphasis was on projecting the good side of the self and the object which needed to be restored into an external object, the analyst. This did not create a feeling of external persecution. But the projection of goodness produced a splitting of the ego which is felt as a depletion of goodness in the self. In this case it led to an increased oral greed in an attempt to recapture the good self and a good object by eating it up in fantasy.

These two instances illustrate the relation of the superego to ego splitting, and I suggest that, as methods of dealing with the superego, they commonly occur in acute schizophrenic states with confusion.

The other methods shown by the patient in this material are the desire for punishment and the appeasement of persecutors: the two cataleptic fits[1] seem to imply a complete masochistic[2] submission to the killing superego, and the same explanation applies to the need for punishment in asking for electric shock (death) treatment. In the latter case the masochistic submission, however, was not to the internal superego, but to an external object. This, incidentally, throws some light on the psychological importance of electric shock treatment[3] which subjects a patient to the experience of death without actually killing him. The appeasement of the persecutory superego by bluff, as illustrated by my patient, is a very common mechanism, particularly in chronic schizophrenics. It also plays a considerable part as a defence against an acute schizophrenic state. Moreover, the strengthening of the appeasement mechanisms may bring about

[1] These attacks resembled a catatonic stupor. The pathology suggested here may also contribute to our understanding of the catatonic stupor.

[2] Cf. Garma's (1932) and Pichon-Riviere's (1947) theory of the masochistic ego and the sadistic superego in schizophrenia.

[3] If the patient had been submited to electric shock treatment at the time when he asked for it, his guilt conflict would have been temporarily alleviated, and very likely he might have had a remission of the acute state which still persisted, but this would have meant abandoning further psycho-analytic understanding of his conflict.

a remission of an acute attack; but recovery by this means is unsatisfactory, because it completely stifles any development of personality.

## THE 'HELPFUL' SUPEREGO

In the following session, which I shall refer to as (a), we came to understand more of the positive relationship of the patient to his superego. In the beginning of the session he was looking for something in his pocket. He could not find it and it turned out that it was his handkerchief he wanted. I interpreted that he was not only looking for his handkerchief but also for the part of himself which helped him to control himself, but which he could not find. I pointed out to him that he had frequently lost himself and his inner control because he felt he could not stand anxiety and guilt.[1] He then looked me straight in the face and said, 'The problem is how to feel the fear.' I interpreted that he wanted to feel the fear which meant anxiety and guilt inside because he realized his need of control. He then looked out of the window where a man was trimming the hedges.[2] He was watching him in a fascinated way, without apparent fear. I pointed out that this man was trimming the hedges, and was in this way keeping them in shape, and in control, without damaging them. That was the relationship he wanted to feel with me inside himself; a helpful control without feeling damaged. The patient's remark 'The problem is how to feel the fear' is significant because it implies his realization that he had avoided the experience of guilt and anxiety and so was without an inner means of control. The nurses reported that after this session he was rational for the first time since he had been in hospital. He was able to converse with doctors and nurses. This state lasted for several hours, and recurred almost every day for about three weeks. The improvement coincided with a greater capacity to acknowledge the need for an internal object as a helpful, controlling figure, and a lessening of his persecutory anxiety. During the next session (b) he became more able to verbalize his superego conflict. I found him sitting in a rigid position. It took

[1] From the patient's whole attitude I felt that this interpretation was needed at that moment, but I do not want to give the impression that looking for a handkerchief in an acute schizophrenic patient always has this particular meaning. One has always to consider a multitude of factors to understand the meaning of schizophrenic actions.

[2] One might of course think that the man with the shears aroused his castration anxiety. But I think this aspect was not in the foreground at that moment.

more than twenty minutes before the rigidity lessened. He then said, 'No energy'–'Struggle', and later on 'I am wrong'. He sighed and continued, 'Worn out.' 'Hercules.' Later during the session he said 'I can only do my best, I cannot do any more.' (He was looking very tired.) He also said 'Religion', but was not able to discuss in detail what he meant. I interpreted that he was trying to face his sense of guilt which was a struggle, that the demands of his conscience were so enormous that he felt quite worn out, and that he thought he would have to be a Hercules to do all that he felt he ought to do. At the end of the session he opened a black box which stood in a corner of the room where I was treating him. This box contained human bones, used for teaching students and nurses.[1] Almost every time from now on he opened the box once or twice during or at the end of a session, until, at a later date, he gave a full illustration of what this skeleton in the box (his superego) seemed to be like.

I suggest that we may view this analytical material from two angles: (a) The patient was in this hour willing to face and accept his destroyed internal world. This experience was accompanied by greater depression. It seemed to me that his opening of the box symbolized his looking inside himself. The contents of the box were actually bones of a skeleton, and from his previous remarks it can be assumed that the object he felt he had inside was a destroyed one. (b) This destroyed object had previously threatened him with destruction, but during this session it seemed that there were internal demands for its reparation, which were felt by him to be overwhelming and made him feel worn out. It would appear that either this internal destroyed object itself had a superego function or that another object having this function made demands for the reparation of this destroyed object.

PRIMARY ENVY

During the next session (c) the patient was preoccupied with envy and how to get rid of it. In the session after that (d) he sat silently on a chair, looking anxiously at the outside and inside

[1] The hospital unfortunately had no proper consulting rooms. I had several times to change the room where I treated the patient, and in the end the superintendent thought that I would be least disturbed in the lecture room. One day the patient discovered the black box with the bones. I had no knowledge of its presence beforehand. I decided not to have the box removed but to analyse the patient's interest in it. But I want to stress that I was in this room only by force of external circumstances, not by my own choice.

of his hand. I asked, 'What are you afraid of?' He replied, 'I am afraid of everything.' I then said he was afraid of the world outside and inside, and of himself. He replied 'Let's go back,' which I took to mean that he wanted to understand the early infantile situation in the transference. He stretched out his hands towards me on the table, and I pointed out that he was trying to direct his feelings towards me. He then touched the table tentatively, withdrew his hands and put them into his pockets, and leaned back in his chair. I said that he was afraid of his contact with me, who represented the external world, and that, out of fear, he withdrew from the outer world. He listened carefully to what I said and again took his hands out of his pockets. He then said, 'The world is round', and continued clearly and deliberately, 'I hate it because it makes me feel burnt up inside'. And later he added, as if to explain this further, 'Yellow'–'envy'. I interpreted to him that the round world represented me felt as a good breast, and that he hated the external me for arousing his envy, because his envy made him feel he wanted to kill and burn me inside himself. So he could not keep me good and alive himself, and felt he had a bad and burning inside. This increased his envy and his wish to be inside me, because he felt I had a good inside. At the end of the session (d) he touched the burning hot radiators in the treatment room and the wooden shelf over them.

This session (d) is particularly significant because it throws some light on the patient's fundamental conflict with the world, and his deep-seated envy of the good mother and breast.

In the analysis of neurotic and pre-psychotic patients this early envy has frequently been described. It is, however, interesting that this inarticulate, regressed patient should so stress his envy and jealousy in his earliest infantile object relationship with his mother. Sometimes he referred it to the beginning of life, repeatedly stressing birth and envy, and it was clear that the jealousy of his brother, which was also frequently discussed, was not the problem he had most in his mind. It seems that some of the earliest aggression, starting from the separation of the infant from his mother at birth, is experienced as envy, because everything that makes the infant feel comfortable seems to belong to the outer world–the mother.

This conflict became manifest in the transference situation when I was equated with the good mother and the good breast.

Historically the patient had had a short, unsatisfactory time at the breast, and his mother was unable to look after him because of her asthma. Previously he had shown that he hated me when I was absent, but in this session (d) it is his envy of me which makes it difficult for him to take good things from me.

The envy of the good mother and her good inside also increases the greedy impulses to force the self inside the mother, because, if the mother has all the goodness, the child wants to be inside her. But the envy and jealousy with which in fantasy the child enters the mother's body create images of a destroyed mother. At the end of the hour, the patient touched the hot radiators which burned his hand, and afterwards he touched the wooden shelf, which may have meant that he feared that by entering me he changed me, so that my inside was as burning as his own.

Another interesting feature is the way the patient, through the gestures of his hands, showed whether his cathexes were directed to external or internal objects. If he turned his instinctual impulses towards an external object, he took his hands out of his pockets, and indicated by the movement of his fingers that he was trying to make contact with the external world. When he withdrew the cathexis from the outer world, and directed it towards what was going on inside him, he put both his hands back into his pockets. When his feelings were directed outside and inside simultaneously, he kept one hand in his pocket and laid the other one on the table.[1]

During the following session (e) he looked inside the box with the bones and again touched the radiators. Then he took some crumpled-up paper out of his pocket and tried to straighten it out, but soon he looked frightened again. He walked past me and looked out of the window. At the next session (f) he emphatically said, 'My own birth.' He kept looking inside his hand and repeated several times, 'Birth, Time and Jealousy.'

I suggest that he was trying to indicate the connexion of birth and envy. It is the birth situation which starts the envy of the mother and her good inside. The patient's looking out of the window was probably an expression of his feeling that he was inside me.[2] I pointed out before that when an object is introjected, which through projective identification has been identified

[1] I do not want the reader to think that I would always interpret the play with hands in this way, but at this point I was convinced that this was its meaning.

[2] In my experience with other schizophrenic patients looking out of the window frequently meant that the patient felt he was inside the analyst.

with parts of the ego, a particularly complicated situation arises: here the patient was trying to deal with an internal object, but he also felt himself to be inside this object.

During this period he again seemed to misunderstand my interpretations. For example: When I interpreted to him during session (g) that he felt envious of me, he suddenly got up and moved away from me. He then went to the box and took a bone from it, showed it to me and put it back again. After this he seemed to get more frightened of me, and tried to get out of the room. Then he sat on the radiator, at a distance, and laughed at me in an aggressive and challenging manner. Afterwards he walked about the room, ignoring me, and looking contemptuous; he made movements with his legs as if he were dancing. His attitude to me had changed after my interpretation of his envy. It seemed that he felt that by my interpretation I had made an attack on him, blaming him for his impulse. His taking a bone from the box here emphasized the concreteness of his experiences: namely, that he identified me with whatever the bone meant to him, probably a threatening superego. His dancing suggested that he had killed me and that he felt triumph and contempt. He was treating me like dirt. This concreteness of the patient's experiences continued after the session. The nurses reported that after I had left he had a large bowel motion, and used at least five times as much toilet paper as usual to cover it up.

When I arrived the next time (session h), he sat in his usual chair. In front of him on the table were two little heaps: one little heap of half-burnt cigarette tobacco and cigarette paper was on one side, next to it there was a little heap of grey ashes. The tobacco and the paper looked like a miniature faecal mess and paper. The patient kept his eyes fixed on the heaps for some time. He came very close to it with his mouth, then he moved away again. He repeated this several times. He did not show that he noticed my presence. I interpreted that the heap which looked like a bowel motion represented me. I added that he felt he had changed me into a motion last time. The little heap of ashes seemed to represent those parts of himself mixed up with me, which he also felt were burnt up and destroyed. He continued staring at the heaps, making eating movements. I interpreted that he had both burnt up and destroyed me and himself, and that he wanted to take me and himself back again by eating.

He was now picking up different bits and pieces and trying to sort them out, but they all dropped again into the mess. After the looking and mouthing, the touching and playing with the heap became much more intense. His playing with the mess seemed to be an unsuccessful attempt both to differentiate himself from me and to restore us. After the play he looked first at his hands, which were dirty, and then for a little time at a whitish spot on the table. I pointed out that he seemed to get mixed up between playing with his faeces and playing with his penis, because the glistening spot on the table seemed to be connected with masturbation (emission). When his confused look lessened I gave him a more detailed interpretation, showing him in detail how the present situation had arisen. I also linked it with the past, particularly with the earliest relations to his mother.

From the material presented, it may be difficult to see why I referred here to my patient's masturbation fantasies, but as I explained before, it is not always possible in an analysis such as this to show all the reasons for giving an interpretation. My patient had never during his breakdown really played with faeces or eaten faeces, but he masturbated a great deal. He seemed to me confused, and he probably felt that he himself actually was the concrete mess that he had shown me in his play. So the interpretations had to be given in a way that helped him to recognize that his impulses differed from one another, and also to differentiate between himself and the objects with which he felt confused.

These last two sessions (g and h) are related to the earlier sessions (after the attack on Sister X and 'Can I help you?') in which the patient had projected his self and his superego into me as the representative of the external world. In the earlier instance he had refused food, and he probably at that time had fantasies that he was forced to eat faeces–poison–representing his own bad self and persecuting objects. In the later one he had tried to recapture himself and me as a lost good object through eating. In the present instance (g and h) he illustrated his experience in play, and made it clear that the faeces represented me as the accusing superego which he tried to expel and destroy. When the persecutory anxiety relating to objects inside, including the superego, increased, he expelled the superego, but his fantasy of eating the heap of faeces and his playing with and sorting out the heap seemed to me to point to fantasies of regaining and restoring a good object, which would imply that he was attempting here to deal with his conflict on the depressive level.

I would like to refer to Abraham's (1924) observation on coprophagic fantasies in melancholia. Abraham suggested that the coprophagic fantasies of his patient turned out to be the expression of a desire to take back into his body the love object which he had expelled from it in the form of excrement. Abraham thought that 'the tendency to coprophagia seems to contain a symbolism which is typical for melancholia'. He described impulses of expelling (in an anal sense) and of destroying (murdering): 'The product of such a murder–the dead body–became identified with the product of expulsion–with excrement.'

My experience with this schizophrenic patient would seem to confirm the view that the coprophagic fantasy can represent a depressive mechanism of re-incorporating a lost object identified with faeces. But then the question has still to be answered: Why is coprophagia and playing with faeces in the adult typical for schizophrenia? I would like to suggest a tentative answer: The schizophrenic is trying to take back not only the object he has lost but also the parts of his ego which are mixed up with the object. Moreover, the actual eating of faeces is a sign not only of regression but also of having lost the capacity for symbolic representation. It depends on the degree to which his (mental) experiences actually have a concrete character for him, whether the schizophrenic can differentiate between fantasies of faeces as a destroyed object and faeces themselves.

In his experience during this session the patient came dangerously near to losing his ability to differentiate between symbol and actual object, because of the intensification of the projective identification process, which I had not sufficiently interpreted in session (g) in which his envy was again so strong. In session (h) where he played with the heap, I took care to help him to differentiate again.

During the same session (h) the patient had difficulty in talking, but the nurses reported that afterwards he talked rationally and did not seem confused. But it must be remembered that these rational periods never lasted more than a few hours.

In the next session (i) he began looking away from me and remaining silent; but he looked eager and less confused, so I decided to go over the last sessions with him, showing him in detail in what way he was repeating experiences and fantasies of his early relationship with his mother and her breasts. I connected his silence with his anger and with his envy of the breast. I spoke of the roundness which at first represented the world to him, and of his difficulties in feeding from the breast because of his anger and his feelings of being burnt up inside. I reminded him of his feelings that the breast inside him had turned into faeces, and was threatening him; that, as we had seen last time, he wanted to free himself from this inner persecution, but that he could not bear to lose this internal breast even if it had turned into faeces, and that he was preoccupied with taking it back as he wanted an object he could love. I said he refused to have anything to do with me because of his fear of attacking me as an external object representing the breast, and that he was so angry and envious because I was separate from him and not his own possession, his own self. After this interpretation he held his head in his hands. I interpreted to him that he wanted to hold me and have a good relationship with me outside and inside himself. He agreed, but very soon withdrew his hands into his pockets, which seemed here to indicate a withdrawal of libidinal cathexis from the outside. I interpreted that the aggressive feelings had become stirred up in him against me as an external object representing the breast, and that he was afraid of his aggressive biting mouth. That was the reason why he had turned away from me. He at first said, 'I can't do anything.' Then he got up and went slowly to the black box and looked into it intently. He then took out a lower jaw bone (mandible). I asked him whether he knew what kind of bone this was. He did not answer but turned to me and held the bone in the position of his lower jaw to show me that he knew. He then put the bone back into the box and repeated the behaviour of session (g), only this time he showed more clearly that he was frightened of me, and he walked quickly away from me. I interpreted that he was afraid that I would attack and bite him, because he thought that I had changed into an attacking mouth. Then he came towards me and gave me a very slight punch (which obviously was not meant to hurt but was part of the dramatization of the situation). After this he walked up and down the very large room in a most peculiar manner, with hunched-up shoulders, and a fierce expression. He moved his legs as if he had hallucinations that bodies were lying on the floor and that he had to step over them. He looked so much like a wolf, who was running up and down in a cage, that I called out to him, 'You behave like a wolf in a cage.' He agreed with loud laughter, and went on running up and down and twice he tried to get out of the room.

During the next session (*k*) he was much more rational. He asked me how all this related to the past, to fears at night, and to me, which we discussed in detail. Then he said again, 'I am wrong', which suggested to me that he felt that all we had been working over together during the last sessions (*g* to *k*) was related to his guilt feelings. He said, 'Lupus', 'Brown cow', 'Yellow cow'. After this he took a match out of his pocket which he broke into three pieces. He asked, 'How are there three parts?' I said that he showed me that at present he felt his conscience was divided into three pieces: 'Lupus', 'Brown cow', and 'Yellow cow'. And I explained to him that he had shown this to me during the last few days. He had dramatized 'Lupus', the wolf, last time, after taking the lower jaw bone from the black box. The jaw bone represented the internalized breast which he had attacked like an aggressive, hungry wolf, and which in his fantasies had turned into an aggressive, biting mouth. The brown cow seemed to be the breast he felt he had destroyed and changed into faeces; while the yellow cow seemed to be a breast which he had changed through envious and urinary attacks, and which had also become bad and threatening. The three pieces of the match seemed here to correspond to three aspects of his superego. The number three had previously appeared when he talked about three buns, which seemed to represent three breasts. But he also sometimes talked about the third penis and at a later date he referred to the third man. It is quite likely that further analysis would have revealed that the third man and the third penis did not only refer to his real brother or father but also to three male aspects of his superego.

It is, of course, impossible to clarify all these details, but I thought it was clear enough that the patient used the box containing the bones to illustrate in a concrete way fantasies and sensations of internal objects also representing his superego. In particular, these were dramatically represented by 'brown cow', the destroyed breast which had turned into faeces, and 'lupus' representing the persecuting, internalized, attacking mouth (the biting conscience). 'Yellow cow' referred to the times when he talked about envy, birth and yellow, which I had linked with fantasies of entering the mother. But these fantasies were probably more difficult to represent in a dramatic way.

During the next few weeks the patient was more depressed, and seemed less manic and persecuted. He was eager during the sessions, showed in words and actions that he was trying to bring things together inside, and felt he wanted to give the good things up to God and the analyst. There was sometimes a distinct desire to be guided by me, but there was also a fear of giving everything back to me lest he should have nothing left himself. To guard against this he played a game in which he kept something hidden from me. For example, he held something in one hand while he allowed me to see only the other one. During this period he once said to the nurse that he had a great deal to worry about, but he felt it would be all right in the end. At times he again projected his depression with parts of himself into me; and at such times he was more preoccupied with losing his self and being inside an object than with objects inside himself. When he smoked a cigarette, he seemed to identify the ashes with a projected part of his own self. This seemed to me the explanation of the fact that he got anxious and disturbed when he dropped the ashes to the ground. His looking for the ashes seemed to symbolize that he was attempting to recapture this lost self. Once he said: 'How can I get out of the tomb?' I felt here that he implied that in projecting his self, his depression, into me, he felt enclosed by me and so I became a tomb from which he wanted my help to be released. At other times, when in his depressed state, he seemed entirely preoccupied with attempts to restore a good, idealized object inside. He sat quietly and thoughtfully, and when I asked him what he was doing, he replied that he was rebuilding heaven. During this period the depressions lasted longer and the periods of excitement were shorter.

About the time of the arrival in England of the patient's mother, he ceased to cooperate as well as he had done hitherto, and it was obvious that there were considerable difficulties to overcome. It is very hard to assess how far the expected arrival of the mother was related to the worsening in the patient's cooperation, which might be considered a temporary difficulty. But it is quite clear that when she did arrive, and showed her disapproval of psycho-analysis, asked for further opinions, and considered leucotomy, he became rapidly violent and uncontrollable. We have to remember that, in treating acute psychotic patients, we are in the same position as the child analyst treating a young child. There is no way of preventing parents from interfering with or stopping the treatment, should they so wish.

However, before this problem arose, he had cooperated with me so well, in spite of the severity of his condition, that I regard the progress made in the analysis, and the understanding derived from it, as deserving of consideration in its own right.

After the three months of treatment preceding the arrival of the patient's mother, the nurses, the hospital doctors, and myself were agreed that there had been a distinct improvement in the patient's condition which had gradually come about since the beginning of the analysis when he had been acutely excited and had refused food altogether. After such a short treatment improvement could not of course in any case be considered stable. It seemed, however, that the analysis had at times distinctly diminished the patient's persecutory fears and had also affected to some extent the process of splitting the ego. As a result of this work the depression was coming more clearly to the surface, which coincided with a lessening of the persecutory character of the superego.

I wish to stress here that in treating severe schizophrenics by psycho-analysis one has to keep in mind that the tendency to fluctuations in their clinical state is to be expected to a far greater extent than in neurotic patients, even when the analysis is making good progress. But nevertheless the points just now discussed can be considered as criteria by which the progress in the psycho-analysis of a schizophrenic patient may be judged over *prolonged* periods: stable improvement depends on a gradual lessening of persecutory anxiety and ego splitting, and greater capacity to deal with conflicts on the depressive level, which would imply a greater capacity to maintain good objects outside and inside. These changes also affect the superego so that positive features of the superego become more noticeable.

## Conclusion

In this paper I have approached the problem of the superego in schizophrenia by illustrations from the analysis of an acute schizophrenic patient. My findings in this case are not an isolated observation, as in other schizophrenics I also encountered a particularly severe superego of a persecutory nature.

In neurotic cases it takes a long and deep analysis to follow the development of a superego of this kind to its source into early infancy. In treating an acute regressed schizophrenic patient, however, we get an insight into early infantile processes near the beginning of the analysis, which may give us a certain amount of confirmation of the theories and concepts which have gradually been built up from the deep analysis of neurotic and psychotic adults and children. I found Melanie Klein's concept of the early infantile development, including her view of the early origin of the superego, most valuable because it enabled me to understand the varying and difficult problems which one meets in such cases, and my experience fully confirmed her views.

Analysts who are anxious to treat schizophrenics must remember that they will be faced with a great number of difficulties which may at first appear insurmountable but which yield to deeper psycho-analytic understanding. If we abandon the psycho-analytic approach because of these difficulties, we give up the hope of further psycho-analytic insight. In watching the development of the superego conflict during an analysis such as I have described, one may often be tempted to change one's approach. Some American workers may argue: Why not cut right across the superego death-theme by saying to the patient, 'I am not dead, I am not going to kill you, I love and protect and control you.' Rosen has shown that such an approach often works, though it is not sufficiently clear how it works. Nevertheless, I should like to refer to the session where my patient said 'No war' and where he most amicably shook hands with me, saying 'Bluff'. Was his previous adjustment based on successful bluff? If so, a forceful reassurance may again build up a more stable bluff situation. I have had the opportunity of analysing a chronic schizophrenic who had an acute schizophrenia many years ago. During the acute state and afterwards for about twelve years, he was treated by a great deal of reassurance and friendliness by a therapist who was very interested in him. The patient had made a better adjustment, but had developed other very disturbing symptoms. When we analysed the superstructure of his illness, it became clear that his improvement and cooperation were due to a terror of the outer world, and that he was continually appeasing fantasied persecutors. The friendly doctor was a persecuting figure to him, and the previous treatment and the first part of the treatment with me were dominated by continuous appeasement and bluffing. It took several years of analytic work to modify this attitude which had been reinforced by reassurance.

I do not think there is a central bluff situation in all schizophrenics, but I think it is very common. In judging the success of reassurance methods one has also to remember that every schizophrenic patient keeps on projecting his self and his internal objects, including his superego, into the therapist. The fact that the therapist does not alter, and remains friendly, is important both for the psycho-analytic and the psychotherapeutic situation. The psychotherapist who uses reassurance relieves the patient's anxiety temporarily about his dangerous superego and his dangerous self. When the therapist says: 'I love you and will look after you', he implies: 'You are not bad and I will not retaliate', and also: 'You can put all your badness into me; I will deal with it for you.' This may help, but it is the therapist's unconscious understanding and acceptance of the feelings of his patient which causes the reassurance to be effective, and it is doubtful whether such a patient can ever become independent of the therapist and whether he can ever develop his personality. In the psycho-analysis of schizophrenia, we are also confronted with and accept the schizophrenic's projection of his internalized objects, including his superego and himself, continuously into the analyst; but the analyst interprets this situation and the problems connected with it, until the patient is gradually able to acknowledge and retain both his love and hate and his superego as belonging to himself. Only then can we consider that the analysis of a schizophrenic has been successful.

I have recorded a fragment of the analysis of this severely ill patient in order to contribute to the research into the psychopathology of schizophrenia. The problem of the superego and its development and origins is not only important for schizophrenia, but for all the neuroses and psychoses. Melanie Klein's research on the early origins of the superego, and the earliest anxieties, has been accepted by many but by no means all analysts. Some of the doubts they have about her view that these origins are to be found in earliest infancy arise from their difficulties in assessing the developmental period to which certain material belongs. It has frequently been suggested that the analysis of very young children, and of severely regressed schizophrenics, will help to throw further light on this problem.

My aim here has been to show that a transference analysis of a deeply regressed schizophrenic is possible, and that it can throw light on the earliest introjected objects and on their superego functions.

# 5

# TRANSFERENCE-PHENOMENA AND TRANSFERENCE-ANALYSIS IN AN ACUTE CATATONIC SCHIZOPHRENIC PATIENT[1] (1952)

MOST analysts have until recently refrained from treating schizophrenic patients, in the belief that the schizophrenic is incapable of forming a transference. My own experience has shown me that we are dealing here not with an absence of transference, but with the difficult problem of recognizing and interpreting schizophrenic transference-phenomena. It may be valuable to examine first the findings of other analysts.

Both Freud (1911 and 1914b) and Abraham (1908a) made it quite clear that in their opinion the schizophrenic is incapable of forming a transference, owing to his regression to the auto-erotic level of development. They explained this by stating that on the earliest infantile level, which they called the auto-erotic phase, there was as yet no awareness of an object. But there are several statements of Freud's which seem to contradict the concept of an auto-erotic phase, in which there is no relation to an object, such as that in *The Ego and the Id* (1923) where Freud says: 'At the very beginning, in the individual's primitive oral phase, object cathexis and identification are no doubt indistinguishable from each other.' From this later opinion of his we may conclude that he recognized the existence of object cathexis in earliest infancy. Freud however never gave any indication that he changed his view about the lack of transference in schizophrenia (perhaps because he had no later experience with such patients).

Nunberg (1920) had the opportunity of observing a schizophrenic patient over a long period. Nunberg's description is most illuminating and his patient himself relates most of his experiences to the transference. Nunberg states that the transference

[1] First published in the *Int. J. Psycho-Anal.*, 32.

was mostly on the homosexual anal level, but the paper also gives a clear description of object-relations on the oral level. At the height of the oral sadistic transference the patient lost interest in the analyst as an external object; the internal object-relation, however, was apparently retained. Nunberg himself suggested that the patient was able to regain his object occasionally by consuming it, and he gives a lucid description of the symptoms and experiences of the patient after 'consuming the analyst in fantasy'.

O'Malley (1923) described both positive and negative transference reactions in her psychotic patients. Barkas (1924) stated that in psychotic patients the negative and positive transference are of a violent nature. Laforgue (1936) discussed the successful analysis of a schizophrenic girl. In the beginning of the analysis the patient developed such extreme anxiety that she was unable to stay with the analyst for more than a few minutes before escaping to the waiting room. By the persistent analysis of the negative transference the patient's anxiety gradually diminished and she talked freely, obviously developing a positive transference. Federn (1943) pointed out that schizophrenics develop both a negative and a positive transference. He stressed that schizophrenic patients can be treated only in the positive transference, which has to be fostered all the time. He does not interpret either the positive or the negative transference and discontinues treatment when a negative transference appears. Rosen (1946, 1947, 1950) stated that all his schizophrenic patients showed both a strong positive and negative transference which he deals with both by reassurance and interpretation. Other American workers on schizophrenia, such as H. S. Sullivan, Fromm-Reichmann, R. P. Knight and their collaborators, have described the importance of the transference in schizophrenia and concluded that the infant is capable of an object-relation from birth onward. Eissler (1951) has emphasized that the schizophrenic responds to almost any sympathetic psychotherapeutic approach – a factor which in his opinion is due to the schizophrenic's acute awareness of the 'primary process' in other people's minds. He has, however, not recognized that this peculiarity of the schizophrenic is a transference phenomenon which may be related to a particular primitive object-relationship.

In England Melanie Klein's research on the earliest phases of infantile development has greatly encouraged analysts to study psychotic conditions of varying severity. She has found evidence that the infant develops an object-relationship from birth onward both to external objects and through introjection to internal ones. She acknowledges the importance of auto-erotisn and narcissism, but she has added a great deal to the understanding of these phenomena by her hypothesis that they include the love for the internalized object. In her paper 'Note on Schizoid Mechanisms' she has contributed to the psychopathology of schizophrenia. There she describes schizoid mechanisms used by the infant as a defence against anxiety which on the earliest level of development is of a paranoid type. This period she named the 'paranoid-schizoid position'. Klein agrees with Freud that the schizophrenic regresses to the earliest infantile level, the first few months of life, but her views on this period differ from his.

My aim in this paper is (*a*) to illustrate that an acute schizophrenic patient is capable of forming a positive and a negative transference, (*b*) that it is possible to interpret these transference phenomena to a schizophrenic patient, and (*c*) that the schizophrenic's response to interpretations can at times be clearly noticed. In addition I wish to draw attention to my observation that the schizophrenic patient whom I am discussing here and all the schizophrenics I have investigated show one particular form of object-relationship very clearly; namely, as soon as the schizophrenic approaches *any* object in love or hate he seems to become confused with this object, and this is due not only to identification by introjection, but to impulses and fantasies of entering inside the object with the whole or parts of himself in order to control it. Melanie Klein has suggested the term 'projective identification' for these processes. Projective identification, which is complementary to introjection of the object, throws some light on the infant's difficulty in distinguishing between the '*me*' and the '*not me*', and it explains a number of phenomena which are commonly called auto-erotic or narcissistic. It is also related to processes of ego-splitting, which were described by Melanie Klein (1946) and by myself in 1947 (chap. 1). The impulses and fantasies of forcing the self into an object may be regarded as the most primitive type of object-relationship, starting from birth. They may colour the oral, anal, urethral and genital impulses, and in this way influence the earlier and even later relations to objects. In my opinion the schizophrenic has never completely outgrown the earliest phase of development to which this object-relation belongs, and in the acute schizophrenic state he regresses to this early level. The severity of the process depends on a quantitive factor, namely, how much of the ego as well as of the instinctual forces are involved in the regression.

The defences of the ego against the impulses to force itself into other objects are also of great importance in schizophrenia; they are, however, not discussed in detail in this paper. One of such defences is for example negativism. In my chapter 'Analysis of a Schizophrenic State with Depersonalization', I refer to a woman patient whose negative attitude towards everything concerning the analyst lessened when we began to understand the patient's paranoid fear of the analyst forcing himself into her, so that she would lose her identity. Through her negative attitude she was defending herself against her active love wishes because they were related to impulses and fantasies to force herself into the analyst to rob and empty him. She was also defending herself against her fear of losing herself inside him. Very similar clinical material was described by Anna Freud in her paper, 'Negativism and Emotional Surrender' (1951). She found that her patient's negativism was connected with the fear of experiencing feelings of love for the analyst because this meant to the patient that she was surrendering to, and would therefore be 'invaded' by, the analyst. She would thereby turn into the analyst. Anna Freud suggested that these processes might go back to the first few months of life, were possibly linked with introjection, and might have a connexion with schizophrenia.[1]

The clinical material I shall bring here is taken from a very ill schizophrenic man, aged twenty, whom I treated by psychoanalysis for four months.

The patient had been ill for three years when I saw him first. He suffered from hallucinations and was confused and at times violent. He had had altogether 90 insulin comas and many electric shocks. The superintendent of the mental hospital where

---

[1] These observations and suggestions by Anna Freud, which are virtually identical with some aspects of Melanie Klein's concept of 'Projective Identification' are one of the indications of the growing corroboration – coming from various psycho-analytic quarters – of Melanie Klein's concept of early introjective and projective processes, paranoid anxieties and schizoid mechanisms, which is an integral part of her contributions to the theory of the earliest stages of development.

the patient was living described him as one of the worst cases of schizophrenia he had had to deal with. He was said to be dangerously impulsive, withdrawn, and at times almost mute. Neither doctors nor nurses had been able to make contact with him. However, when two analytic colleagues saw him for consultation, they were able to make some contact, and they felt that psycho-analysis could be attempted. I then started the analysis at the beginning of 1952. For a fortnight he was brought to my consulting room by car; after that I saw him in the private mental hospital where he was looked after. The analysis was interrupted after four months–by the parents, who lived abroad –which was unfortunate, as a great deal of analytic work had been done. From the beginning of the third month the patient had rational periods lasting for several hours outside the analytic sessions; but it was clear that it would still take many months before a stable improvement could be expected.

The most important and striking feature in the analysis of this apparently entirely unapproachable and withdrawn patient was the interest he was able to show from the first moment in the analyst and the analytical procedure. From the very first session there were clear signs of a positive transference, and by the third session a violent negative transference had come to the surface. My own approach was analytic, in so far as a great deal of what I was able to understand of the patient's words and behaviour was interpreted to him, and whenever possible, and that was frequently, the analytical material was related to the transference situation. The patient often showed a striking response to interpretations, either of relief or anxiety; he often confirmed what I said directly or indirectly, and at times corrected me. One may say that the analytic procedure in this case was in all essentials the same as in neurotic cases. However, I did not make use of the couch. Some slight adjustments of technique which sometimes became necessary, for example, the use I made of the nurses' reports, are discussed in chapter 6. Here I will only emphasize that I never used any direct reassurance in my approach. However, the material presented by this patient was more difficult to understand than in the neurotic cases, and I had at times to understand and interpret quickly with very little material. At a later stage the analysis became similar to a play-analysis with children.

In order to give a clearer picture of the patient's behaviour, of his way of talking and his response to interpretations, I will report in some detail the greater part of the first four sessions and one later session. Before the first session the patient had been informed by a colleague that he would be seen by me regularly every day, with the exception of Sunday.

When the patient was alone with me for the first time, he sat down in a chair looking very puzzled and confused. After a few minutes he managed to say one word, 'RESURRECTION'. After that he again looked confused. I said, 'Resurrection means to become alive.' He looked straight at me and said, 'Are you Jesus?' I said that Jesus could do miracles and that he hoped I would make him well in a miraculous way. He then looked distressed and uncertain, and after a considerable silence he mentioned the name of Dr A. who had treated him by physical methods for over a year. After another long pause, he said, 'Catholicism.' I interpreted that he had believed in Dr A. and he felt disappointed because the treatment had failed. He then replied with emphasis, 'The Russians *were* our allies.' I replied that he felt that Dr A. had been an ally and had now turned against him, and he was afraid that I also would turn from an ally into an enemy. He then said clearly, 'This is true.' He became now more rational and talkative and mentioned a number of his sexual problems, for example, circumcision, which he thought was a form of revenge, and he said, 'I do not understand love and hate.' Later on he said, 'There was a boy at school'; after a pause, he continued, 'He sat beside me, the trouble was--a boy was sitting on the other side of him.' I interpreted that he began to like me as he liked the boy at school; but he wanted me to himself, and he realized I had other friends and patients. He agreed, but soon after this he became restless and got up from his chair and said, 'One must get out at once--I better go now', and later he mumbled, 'I must have a saw.' I thought he was afraid of his jealousy of other patients and that he wanted to get away to prevent himself from hating and attacking me. After pointing this out to him, he still remained restless until the end of the hour.

To recapitulate the striking features of this session: this very ill and confused patient almost at once tried to relate his present experience with me to a previous one in terms of a personal relationship. The doctor who had stopped treatment with him had turned from a friend and an ally into an enemy in his mind.

In asking me whether I am Jesus, he apparently thinks of me as of an omnipotent figure; later he shows signs of forming a transference on a homosexual level. The anxiety about leaving me and the need for a saw was not sufficiently understood in the first session, but it implied his inability to separate parts of himself from me. Altogether his interest in me as an object is unmistakable.

At the beginning of the second session, the patient looked considerably more confused than at the first and seemed preoccupied with hallucinations. He took no notice of me and looked round the room in a puzzled way, trying to fix his eyes on one spot and then another. He seemed completely out of touch with me. After some time I interpreted that he had lost me and that he was trying to find me again. He said distinctly, 'Not true', and continued his search round the room. Remembering his remark about the saw on leaving last time, I interpreted that he felt he had lost himself and that he was looking for himself in my room. His expression became almost immediately *less* confused and he looked straight at me, saying, 'One has to find one's own roots.' A little later he said, 'I do not know whether it is right liking you *too* much.' I interpreted that he was afraid that by liking me too much he would get right inside me and lose his own roots and himself. He replied, 'I want to go on peacefully in *my own* way.' After that he became absolutely still and did not move again for ten minutes. When I questioned him, he said he was afraid to move. After a pause he continued, saying that there was a heavy burden on his shoulder, and added quickly, looking at me, 'It is lighter now.' I pointed out that he implied that he wanted to rid himself quickly of the burden.

In the first part of this session, the patient seemed completely withdrawn in a world of his own, oblivious of me and occupied only with visual hallucinations. He corrected one transference interpretation, referring to losing me; but he responded to an interpretation that he had lost himself. This later interpretation is of course also a transference interpretation, taking into account that the patient felt that in loving me too much he had lost himself in my room, which was a symbol of me. The apparently narcissistic withdrawn state was clearly related to projective identification. What the burden on his shoulder meant and how it got lighter so quickly was not clear to me, but the expression of the patient's face indicated that the burden had something to do with me, namely, that through introjection I had become an inner burden to him.

In the beginning of the third session, the patient was very restless and laughed a great deal in an aggressive challenging manner. He also was preoccupied with hallucinations and, when he was not laughing *at* me, he ignored me. At first no contact with the patient seemed possible and he said nothing. In observing his behaviour I noticed that he made movements with his hands, as if he was brushing me aside. I then interpreted that he wanted to show me that the treatment was no longer any good; he said immediately, increasing his aggressive laughter, 'No good at all—' making movements with his hands as if everything had come to an end. I pointed out to him that he had expected a miraculously quick cure, and in disappointment and anger he felt he had destroyed me and had made me and the treatment no good. After this his facial expression changed, he looked frightened and suspicious, and when I spoke he jumped in his seat, as if I had attacked him. I interpreted that he felt muddled and confused, and that he blamed me for feeling so bad. He felt frightened when I spoke because he believed that I was putting words aggressively into him to muddle him. This was the reason why he was shutting himself off from me and why he tried to take no notice of me. I had to repeat interpretations of a similar kind several times, speaking very clearly and quietly. After some time he became less frightened and talked about colour schemes. Then he pointed to my blue diary and said it was brown. I took this to be a cooperative gesture, showing me more clearly what he felt, namely, that his attack had changed me into faeces and that as a revenge I was putting the muddle (faeces) back into him.

The striking feature of this session was the violent negative transference which came to the surface so soon after the beginning of treatment. His laughter expressed both a sadistic attack on me and a triumph over me. His anal attack had changed me into a persecutor. This persecutory situation was frequently repeated in different ways, and later on it became evident that one could not think of the attack as merely anal. I mentioned that at the end of the last session he talked about the burden on his shoulders. In later sessions he illustrated that the burden on his shoulders represented all the problems inside him, his introjected objects, anxieties, depressions, persecutions and his own bad self;

and his fantasies of putting this burden on to me or into me were always felt by him to be a violent attack on me, in which I was not only changed into faeces, but into his own bad self.[1] Another point, which I can only touch upon, is the fact that whenever the patient felt he had got rid of his burden, he not only felt persecuted by me, but it seemed to him that he had put his burden into innumerable people, and so he felt split and divided into many men, who all turned into persecutors. Apart from the persecutions, he then complained of losing parts of his self.

Another important feature of this hour was the patient's withdrawal of interest. The schizophrenic's lack of interest and his withdrawal is frequently attributed only to his auto-erotism; in this session, however, and at later times it became clear that the withdrawal from the external world was related to his fear of persecution. When the external object representing the world had been attacked, the world was not only felt to be destroyed, but the external world and the objects representing the world outside became changed into persecutors. So the withdrawal of interest from the outside world was used as a defence against persecutors outside.

It was a very illuminating experience for me to realize that this patient, who in the beginning of the session was quite unapproachable, seemed to understand and respond to the interpretations of his persecutory fears in the transference situation. By the end of the session his laughter had completely ceased and he looked much less hallucinated.

In the fourth session he seemed to be better; however, he confused me at first with Dr A. He said several times, 'That happened before,' or 'That was last time.' I interpreted his anxiety that everything would repeat itself and that I also would leave him, like Dr A., which meant for him that I would turn against him. Then I linked the persecutory anxieties of the previous hour to the reality situation. I explained to him that when Dr A. stopped treatment with him he thought Dr A. had aggressively left him in a muddle. He felt this was a retaliation, because he thought he had made Dr A.'s treatment no good in the same

---

[1] At one time when the patient felt he had got rid of his bad self as well as his guilt and anxiety, and had projected it into the analyst, he also became very *negativistic* for several days and refused food and drink. I have discussed this part of the analysis and the mechanisms used by the patient in greater detail in my paper 'Notes on the Psycho-analysis of the Superego Conflict of an Acute Schizophrenic Patient' (chap. 4 in the present volume).

way as he had shown me the previous day that my treatment had become no good. The patient indicated several times that he understood and towards the end of the hour he said, 'I want to do everything to help.'

You will remember that in the very first session the patient had warned me of his persecutory fears, and when he said, 'The Russians *were* our allies.' In this session the patient's suspicions could be connected with the earlier experience of the treatment he had had before. The patient's persecutory anxieties relating to his being left were later on connected with earlier reality experiences, particularly with his mother, who had left him crying for hours when he was a baby.

We may sum up that in this hour the patient continued to work through his negative transference. The fear of repeating earlier experiences and the actual repetition of earlier experiences in the transference is of course one of the most important factors in any transference analysis.

I will now bring one later session (five weeks after the start of treatment) to illustrate in greater detail some of the aspects of the patient's object-relation which he repeated in the transference. I explained in the beginning that the patient's home was abroad; his father had brought him to England for treatment. Two days before this session, the father had left again for home. In the beginning of the session the patient looked a little confused but, without waiting for any comment or help from me, he said clearly, 'Confused', and, when I questioned him, he added, 'with father'. After a struggle for words, he said, '*I should* have stayed longer.'[1] I pointed out that he showed how 'confused' he felt with his father, because he obviously meant that his *father* should have stayed longer. He immediately went on

---

[1] Nunberg's patient felt sometimes confused with Nunberg. On such occasions he talked about Nunberg as if he and the analyst were one and the same person. For instance, the patient said: 'I want *myself* to go,' instead of 'I want *you* to go.' Nunberg came to the conclusion that a narcissistic identification had taken place. He states that it is the *desire for the object* which in this phase led to the disappearance of the distance between the ego and the object. The patient had taken possession of the object and had incorporated it into the ego.

In my opinion the introjection of an external object does not by itself lead to confusion with the object. In all the cases of confusion of subject and object I have observed so far, projective identification, in addition to identification by introjection, had taken place. The desire to enter into an object is not only determined by an omnipotent wish to eliminate the distance between subject and object, but also to get rid of 'time' as this schizophrenic patient later on explained. The distance from the object or separation from the object is intimately linked with the awareness of the passing of time, because as soon as an object is desired, *instant* gratification of this wish is demanded.

to say, 'Dr A. committed suicide, through psychiatry, I mean.'
I pointed out to him that he also confused Dr A. with himself.
When Dr A. stopped treatment he, the patient, was depressed
and suicidal, but he felt he had put his depressed and suicidal
self into Dr A. I related this to his father's departure and I
reminded him how often he had shown his fear that I too would
leave him. He then said, 'Atheism.' I said he wanted to tell me
he could not believe in anybody any more after his disappointment about his father leaving him now and earlier too in his life.
He became however gradually much more interested and lively
and looked very friendly and confidentially at me, as if he
wanted to explain everything. He said, 'If one goes all the way
one cannot retake everything.' I then interpreted that when he
loved somebody and believed in him or her, he wanted to go all
the way, which meant to him that he went inside the other
person and so he got mixed up and confused. He also felt that
when he put himself into people he had difficulty in taking
himself out again. I said it was very important to him that I
should understand how much he put himself into me, and that
this was one of the reasons why he was so afraid to be left, as he
feared he would not only lose me but himself. He agreed whole-
heartedly and again looked at me in a confiding way and said,
'A big-boned man eats a lot' and he made chewing movements.
I said he was warning me of his greed and he showed me that,
in his loving wish to get inside me, he was eating me up. He then
uttered a great number of words, referring to the country of his
birth, and he talked about colours. It was clear here that he felt
a need to stress his separateness, and that the different colours
represented different aspects of himself, a fact which we had
understood before. He then asked, 'How is pink related to all
this?' As pink had become the code-word for oral wishes towards
the penis, which we had analysed and discussed repeatedly, it
was clear that the impulses to get inside me were stimulating his
homosexual oral wishes. He got up and, finding a jug full of
water, he drank from it; then he leaned back making sucking
and chewing movements. While he was doing so, he seemed quite
withdrawn. I interpreted that when he was drinking, he had a
fantasy of drinking from my penis and chewing it up. I suggested
that the wishes to get inside me stimulated his wishes towards
my penis. In his withdrawn state he felt confused with me,
because he not only felt that he was inside me, but that he was

eating me and my penis at the same time. He again became more attentive, he seemed to listen carefully and he agreed several times.

In this session, the patient illustrated more distinctly the object-relationship which he had begun to understand in the second session. He now showed that *it is* oral feelings which predominate in his impulses to enter an object, which in his own words the patient called 'his going all the way'. This led here to a state of confusion, which the patient was able to describe himself. When the state of confusion and the state of splitting was more severe, the patient was unable to speak and other ego-functions like coordination of movements were severely disturbed.

One important transference aspect which was dealt with in this session was the tendency to leave parts of the self in the analyst. This is important for the analyst to understand, because the interpretations of the processes of projective identification and splitting enable the patient gradually–to use my patient's words–'to retake himself', which is necessary for the process of ego-integration.

Another interesting point is the apparently auto-erotic state the patient went into towards the end of the hour. The whole material of the session suggested that in the withdrawn state he was introjecting me and my penis, and at the same time was projecting himself into me. So here again I suggest that it is sometimes possible to detect the object-relation in an apparently auto-erotic state.

In later sessions the patient often differentiated more clearly between objects within himself and parts of himself which were entering or being inside his object, in other words only at a later stage of treatment was it possible to distinguish between the mechanisms of introjection of objects and projective identification, which so frequently go on simultaneously.

## *Summary*

In this paper I have concentrated on certain aspects only of this case. I wished to illustrate that a severely ill withdrawn schizophrenic patient is capable of forming a positive and negative transference, that the transference can be observed and interpreted to the patient, and that the patient responded both to interpretations of the positive and negative transference. I also endeavoured to illustrate that the withdrawn state of the schizophrenic patient cannot be considered simply as an auto-erotic regression. The withdrawal of the schizophrenic may be a defence against external persecutors, or it may be due to identification with an object by both introjection and projection. In the state of identification which may be experienced by the patient as a confusion, the patient is aware of being mixed up with someone else (his object). Another purpose of this paper is to illustrate the regression of this schizophrenic patient to a stage of earliest infancy for which Melanie Klein has suggested the term 'paranoid-schizophrenic position'. The patient shows signs of an object-relation, in which he has impulses and fantasies of forcing himself or parts of himself inside the object, which leads to states of confusion, to splitting of the self, to a loss of the self and to states of persecution in which visual and auditory hallucinations are pronounced.

This object-relation and the mechanisms developed from it and connected with it have an important bearing on many other neuroses and psychoses; they have a particular significance, however, for the whole group of the schizophrenias.

I suggest that the greater understanding of projective identification is beginning to open up a new field of research and in this paper I have attempted to show how this made it possible to understand and interpret the transference phenomena of this schizophrenic patient.

# 6

# CONSIDERATIONS REGARDING THE PSYCHO-ANALYTIC APPROACH TO ACUTE AND CHRONIC SCHIZOPHRENIA[1]

## (1954)

I PROPOSE to discuss the psycho-analytic approach to the treatment of schizophrenia, as it is being developed by a number of psycho-analysts in England, including myself. This work derives from Melanie Klein's researches into the early stages of infantile development and from the technique she uses, both in adult neurotic and borderline psychotic patients and in the analysis of children.

In our approach to schizophrenia we retain the essential features of psycho-analysis: namely, detailed interpretations of the positive and negative transference without the use of reassurance or educative measures; the recognition and interpretation of the patient's unconscious material; and, above all, the focusing of interpretations on the patient's manifest and latent anxieties. It has been found that the psychotic manifestations attach themselves to the transference in both acute and chronic conditions, so that what one may call a 'transference-psychosis' develops. The analyst's main task in both acute and chronic schizophrenias is the recognition of the relevant transference phenomena and its communication to the patient. Particularly in the analysis of acute schizophrenia, certain practical problems arise as to the management of the patient in the consulting-room; these will be described later.

## The Management and Treatment of Acute Schizophrenic States

The first difficulty in managing an acute schizophrenic patient outside the analysis is the question whether he should be kept

[1] Paper read in the symposium 'Therapy of Schizophrenia' at the 18th International Psycho-Analytical Congress in London, 28 July, 1953. First published in the *Int. J. Psycho-Anal.*, **35**.

at home or in a mental hospital or nursing home. Some of such difficulties may increase during the analysis, for the changes in the patient's condition are often so quick and dramatic that the relatives are completely at a loss in responding to his behaviour and cannot cope for long with these problems. Again, if we arrange for the patient to stay in a mental nursing home and to come from there with a nurse by car to our consulting-room, there may be aggravations in his condition when it is impossible for him to travel. So in any treatment of acute schizophrenia we may sooner or later be faced with having to visit the patient in a nursing home, which may involve a great deal of time travelling. It is not possible to treat an acute schizophrenic patient unless one has the fullest support of the environment. For example, the nurses or relatives have to inform one every day about the patient's talk and behaviour.[1] The ideal background for an analysis of an acute schizophrenic would be a hospital with a trained staff easily accessible to the analyst. This does not exist in London as yet because it requires financial means beyond our capacity. Therefore the psycho-analysis of acute schizophrenics has often to be carried out under most unsatisfactory conditions.

### The Actual Treatment of Acute Schizophrenia

In the analysis of acute schizophrenic patients the whole of the patient's behaviour, his gestures and actions are to be used as analytic material to a far greater degree than is usual in the analysis of neurotics. The patient often has difficulty in talking and may be confused, negativistic, or withdrawn. In almost all the cases of acute schizophrenia I have seen in consultation or have treated by analysis such typical schizophrenic behaviour was being used as a cover for overwhelming anxieties. The patient may not be able to respond to any ordinary conversation, but if we use interpretations to approach him and if our interpretations touch upon his anxieties, we shall get some response. There will either be a change in his behaviour or he will talk.

[1] The analyst has often to discuss with the nurses the main trend of the patient's fantasies in order to enable them to handle the patient without force. While avoiding reassurance myself in order not to obscure the analytic situation, I encourage the relatives and nurses to use reassurance. For example, when a patient refuses to eat because of overwhelming greed, I advise the nurse that the patient may be helped to eat by being told 'I will see that you will not eat too much'; or if he feels too guilty to eat, the nurse is told to say, 'You deserve to eat.'

With acute schizophrenic patients, these severe anxieties become related to the transference-situation. I will report some material of the analysis of an acute schizophrenic girl of seventeen, not so much for the purpose of substantiating the correctness of my interpretations, but in order to illustrate that an acute confused schizophrenic can be approached by transference-interpretations and that a response to interpretations can often be clearly observed.

Anne is in her third acute schizophrenic phase, which had lasted for over six months when I started the treatment at the end of May, 1953. The first attack occurred at the age of thirteen. She had had electric shock treatments and insulin comas at various times, but they had to be stopped because she had become too excited. The mother had been unable to breast-feed the child and had left her almost entirely in charge of a nannie from the beginning, while she herself went out to business. The father was away during most of the war, so there was considerable deprivation of parental love in early childhood. Anne is often confused and hallucinated, at other times obstinate and negativistic. She is capable of strong emotions of love and hate, which quickly change from one extreme to the other, making the management at home very difficult. At the beginning of the treatment she was brought to my consulting-room by her mother and a nurse. She exhibited acute signs of anxiety and would not part from her mother, so that I had to give interpretations in the presence of the mother for the first five sessions. This is a great disadvantage, because of the suspicions it arouses in the patient; also the analyst has to be more careful in his interpretations in order not to stir up the mother's anxieties. At the beginning of each session Anne seemed to take no notice of me, but it was soon clear that she was trying to use the presence of the mother to re-enact some aspects of the oedipal situation, in particular to accuse her and devalue her in my eyes. She said, for example, that the mother was a murderess, had sold her for £5, and had made her have the disgusting electric shock treatments and injections.

In one of the next sessions Anne changed her attitude and said her mother was wonderful, there was nobody like her in the world. She asked mother for cigarettes, smoked them excitedly and turned her back on me completely, allying herself with her mother against me. Later in the session she took more interest in me, touching my hands and kissing them before leaving the room.

In the fifth interview there was a stormy scene. For Anne threw a brooch contemptuously at her mother and said to her 'You obviously want to be alone with him. I am nothing, I feel terrible, I had better go off by myself.' Later in the session after she had tried to get out of my house, she said to her mother: 'What did you say? You said something very rude.' The patient had obviously heard an inner voice saying something to her. When I interpreted that the voice she heard was the voice of an inner mother with whom she was quarrelling and that this mother wanted to take all the credit and make her (Anne) feel stupid in front of me, she replied emphatically, 'That is exactly what she is trying to do.' After this I gave the mother a sign and Anne allowed her to leave the room for the first time. After this period of the analysis there was a change in the patient's behaviour at home. While she had ignored her father previously she now became very interested in him and often sat on his knee. At night she would not stay in her room and was very excitable and often tried to run into her parents' bedroom. In the analysis she complained of being hot and sick and of feeling closed in. The heat and sickness referred to her omnipotent sexual wishes to make me feel hot and excited and to incorporate me in this way, which led to her feeling persecuted by me inside her. She illustrated this by greedily smoking a cigarette, then turning the burning end towards her lip, and after this complaining of sickness and trying to run out of the house in a very determined way. I interpreted at the door to her while I was preventing her from getting out that she thought that I was making her feel hot and sexual and sick inside. She replied after some time, 'I know you do. Don't talk about sex', and she covered her ears with her hands. I interpreted that she felt that I was putting the hot sexual feelings into her when I talked about sex and she answered, 'Why do you?' But soon she gave up struggling to go and asked for a cigarette and returned to the consulting-room, where I was able to give her a more detailed interpretation of the situation. Her wish to have a cigarette was then not so much an admission of her sexual wishes towards me, but the acknowledgement of her desire to receive a good interpretation representing a good penis from me. The effect of the interpretation at the door had temporarily lessened her sense of persecution and enabled her to introject something good from me.

Up to this time the nurse had reported that the patient was unable to sleep in spite of large doses of nembutal.[1] Shortly after the interview described above I was told that she slept very much better, which seemed to me the result of the analysis of some of her sexual fantasies in the analytic setting. Her behaviour changed a little at home; while she had some lucid periods, she was at times more confused. She complained to the parents of not knowing *where* she was and of feeling shut in; she became very negativistic and did not want to come to the sessions, and when she came she remained silent. It became possible to understand some of the reasons for her negativism, confusion and her feeling shut in in the transference-situation. At one session when I went into the waiting-room the patient looked confused and did not seem to know me. While waiting in the waiting-room she had said to her mother and brother who had brought her that she wanted to get out, to be free, and I interpreted that she felt imprisoned by me and that she needed her relatives as protection against me. After ten to fifteen minutes I managed to see the patient by herself. She did not talk, but I noticed that she was looking at the ceiling in a confused and frightened manner. I interpreted that she felt shut in somewhere, but she was not sure whether she was inside me or in somebody else. When I said this she looked much more frightened at first, but her attempts to escape from my consulting-room lessened. I repeated my interpretations in slightly different ways. After some time she did not look quite so confused and made some attempts to speak. She then asked me whether my room was the same and later she said she was very mixed up and she did not know how she got into my room. She became more confiding, and said: 'I want to tell you something. I was walking along in the park and I was quite cool. Suddenly I had a blackout and then I was in somebody else's coat.' I pointed out to her that she had suddenly gone into somebody else and consequently felt mixed up with somebody else. I also explained in some detail that she was experiencing the same situation with me. She then looked at me for quite a time and said: 'Why do you imitate me?' I interpreted that she had put herself into me and that she felt that I was her and had to talk and think for her. I explained

[1] Anne complained at night of feeling hot and she got up very frequently.

to her that this was the reason why she felt so shut in when she came to my house and why she had to escape from me. She was now looking much more comfortable and trusting, and said: 'You are the world's best person.' I interpreted that because she felt I was so good she wanted to be inside me and have my goodness.

After some time she replied that I was making myself dry by talking and that she did not *mean* to come to me. Suddenly she looked frightened and asked whether I was phoning the police; she also mentioned a hospital and tried to escape from my room. I pointed out to her that she felt she had taken all the goodness out of me, and that I was now sending for the police to get rid of her and punish her by shutting her up in a hospital. She then expressed concern for having hurt me, kissed me affectionately on the cheek, while I remained of course quite passive, and told me that she saw me in the faces of all the people in the street. I interpreted that she wanted to take me with her as a good and helpful person but she was afraid of making me dry and losing me inside herself. So she put me for my protection in all the people in the outside world and that was the reason why she saw me there. She left in a friendly mood at the end of the session.

This interview illustrates some dynamics of the acute schizophrenic process and the way it is influenced by interpretations. Following the interpretations that the patient felt she was inside me, she was able to extricate herself out of me which lessened her confusion. She then became more aware of me as an external object and was able to talk. She also could express strong positive feelings towards me, because after taking the intruding part of herself out of me which she felt was bad, I changed from being *bad* into the world's best person. After this her feelings underwent several rapid changes, each of which was interpreted and these interpretations assisted the process of integration.

When I became a good object, the patient became able to experience her greed and wished to rob me of my goodness, because at that moment I had become an object apart from her. This greed quickly produced persecutory fear as well as guilt and concern at having hurt me. Her affectionate kiss was not only a desire to restore me, but was an attempt to introject me as a good object. This transference experience revives the earliest relationship to her mother, because the infant intrudes in fantasy into her out of a number of motives of which the desire to rob her of the good contents of her body predominates, producing feelings of persecution and guilt. During the next three weeks certain aspects of this situation appeared in the transference as the main focus of the patient's resistance. She refused to come to my consulting-room because coming to see me meant for her an admission of her desire to put herself into me. In the end I was forced to visit the patient at home. She said she did not wish to come to see me and she asked why I was keeping her under my jacket and why I was playing about with her. But while saying this she put her hand playfully into the pocket of my jacket, showing me that she had reversed the situation and that it was she who put herself under my jacket and was playing about with me. It appeared that by such reversal she not only wanted to deny her own desire to intrude into me, but that after the intrusion all her experiences appeared to be reversed, which made her feel shut in and interfered with by me.

When the patient realized through consecutive interpretations the connexion between her impulses to intrude and her reversal of this, her negativism lessened and she could experience a positive relationship without forcing herself into me so completely.[1] The analysis of this transference-situation was followed by marked clinical improvement, which has continued up to the date of publication of this paper. She coped well with the interruption of the analysis during the summer holidays in August, 1953, and was able to attend my consulting-room by herself after the holidays.

In the acute schizophrenic state the patient tends to put his self so completely into objects that there is very little of the self left outside the object. This interferes with most ego-functions, including speaking and understanding words. It inhibits the capacity to experience relations with external objects and it also disturbs the introjective processes.

In earlier papers I have described the schizophrenic impulses to intrude into the analyst with positive and negative feelings, and the defences against this object-relationship, as typical of the transference-relation of most schizophrenic patients. This early object-relationship relates to processes of ego-splitting and has been called by Melanie Klein 'projective identification'.

---

[1] I am grateful to Miss Evans who in a discussion drew my attention to the importance of the patient's experiencing her impulses in reverse.

## The Management and Treatment of Chronic Schizophrenic Conditions

The chronic schizophrenic patients I have analysed so far can be roughly divided into two groups. In the first group there is a history of very gradual deterioration over a period of years, but often no history of an acute state. They lack feelings and are out of touch with their surroundings, but they often retain a certain amount of insight into their condition. I found that some of these patients attend analysis regularly over many years and their condition often shows gradual but distinct improvement in the course of analysis. There is sometimes a danger of an acute attack during the analysis, particularly at moments when the patient is making progress, but mostly this can be avoided. They seldom require any particular management and behave during the analysis almost like neurotic patients; for example, they do not object to lying on the couch and are able to associate.

If an acute schizophrenic attack develops during an analysis, it is of course important that the analysis should be continued during the acute phase. But here again we are faced with the management problem, which often causes a breakdown of the analysis at this vital stage.

The patients of the second group are those who have had one or more severe attacks of acute schizophrenia from which they have only partially recovered. They no longer talk about their delusions; they often maintain that they are all right; but they remain unable to work, and detailed observation often reveals that some delusional system still persists. These patients rarely ask for treatment on their own initiative, but they come on the suggestion of a friend or relative. Once they agree to come, they often come regularly by themselves, but the treatment may be exceedingly difficult. They have the tendency not to discuss their symptoms lest their delusions should come up, and one may find that they have very little or no insight. In addition, they may not discuss reality problems, and when these are referred to they are presented from the patient's particular angle, which means that they may be grossly distorted. If the patient is of the chronic paranoid type, he often insists that we should not discuss his problems with any friend or relative. If we have any contact with relatives or friends of a chronic paranoid patient we cannot use the information we gather for our interpretations, as we can often do with an acute schizophrenic. But it may confirm our awareness of the extent to which we remain excluded from the real events of the patient's life. Relatives of chronic paranoid schizophrenic patients may go through periods of great suffering and worry, and they often make demands for help and advice from the analyst which the analyst is in no position to give. I have found it best to advise the relatives to discuss their problems regularly with a colleague who is co-operating closely with the analyst.

Some of these chronic schizophrenic conditions seem often quite inaccessible until the relevant facts of the transference-psychosis are understood and interpreted. To illustrate this shortly, I will take the patient Charles who had had an acute paranoid breakdown several years before and was still unable to work. His main conscious attitude towards me could be summarized by his constantly trying to convince me that he was quite well. He blamed the psychiatrists who had seen him when he was acutely ill for trying to make him ill by introducing the idea of a serious psychotic breakdown by their very presence. Almost any interpretation aroused serious paranoid anxieties in him. When I interpreted that he was afraid of realizing that he was ill, he immediately reacted by saying that I was trying to make him ill, and at once became excited and aggressive. He refused to discuss the relationships he had with his parents or other people, and when I made a transference-interpretation and related it to the parents he got angry and said his relations to his parents were quite normal. For some time I felt there was no interpretation I could make which did not increase his acute feeling of being attacked by me. It was also obvious that for the first few months of treatment he got worse and he accused me of making him worse by introducing the notion of his being ill. Gradually I became aware of the importance of his feeling that his illness had existed *only* in the psychiatrist's mind and that it was this which was now appearing in the transference. He felt that the notion of his being ill existed *now* very concretely in *my* mind. He was not aware of having put it there, but he sometimes explained that I had to be careful because there were certain powers who projected sadistic notions into me which were very dangerous, and I might inadvertently introduce them into him. It became gradually possible to discuss with him how he believed he was being made ill and there was not always the need to prove to me continuously that he was all right. The patient was a doctor himself; and in spite of feeling persecuted by the treatment, he sometimes emphasized that psycho-analysts should be allowed to go on with their work. However, he immediately became paranoid if I took this to mean that he appreciated what I was doing for him; but he accepted interpretations in which I showed him that the psycho-analyst who should be allowed to do his work was representing his good self, which he felt had a right to exist and to work. He gradually became able to bear interpretations that I was representing also his bad and dangerous self when he tried to show me how I could misuse my powers by being omnipotent, sadistic and selfishly pursuing my own ideas. The inability of this patient to accept any interpretations during the first three months of his treatment was related to his feeling that whenever I made an interpretation I put myself, containing his sadistic omnipotent self, into his mind, and he felt this so concretely that he sometimes threatened to inform the police about what I was doing to him. Since almost anything I was saying was felt by the patient to be a real attack, it was absolutely necessary to analyse the basis of this concrete experience in order to make any progress. When I concentrated in the analysis entirely on interpreting the projection of his good and bad self into me and the persecution related to this, *without of course using any analytic terms*, which he was very suspicious of, there was not only some improvement in the patient's clinical condition, but he seemed more able to listen to me without feeling so intensely persecuted. This patient frequently discussed the concreteness of his experiences without any awareness that they were paranoid fantasies or delusional.[1] The transference analysis of the processes of projective identification, namely, of projecting the bad self and the good self into the analyst, diminished the concreteness of the patient's experiences, and seemed to be responsible for the slight improvement in the patient's condition.

The difficulty for the analyst to make the exact interpretation which the schizophrenic needs at any particular time is often very great and this applies as much to the chronic as to the acute patients. Our counter-transference is frequently the only guide.

[1] Psychiatrists like Goldstein and Vigotsky have studied the disturbances of thought in schizophrenia and have stressed that schizophrenics have lost the power of abstract thinking and are only capable of *concrete* thinking processes.

By this I do not mean that we should reveal our feelings to the patient even if he appears to demand this, but we should be sensitive to whatever the patient projects into us by non-verbal and verbal means and become able to verbalize what we unconsciously perceive. I cannot, however, discuss the detailed use of the counter-transference as a therapeutic instrument in the frame of this paper.

## Conclusions and Summary

The aim of this paper is to illustrate that in the analysis of acute and chronic schizophrenics the psychotic manifestations attach themselves to the transference and a transference-psychosis develops. The relevant transference phenomena can be interpreted to the patient and his response to interpretations can often be clearly observed.

At this state of our research we shall not over-estimate the therapeutic possibilities of psycho-analysis in severe acute and chronic schizophrenic conditions, because the analysis, particularly of acute schizophrenia, however promising, is a very difficult and strenuous task and the management also still presents almost unsurmountable difficulties. At present therefore we can only hope to be successful in a minority of cases. However, this does not invalidate the psycho-analytic approach. Every acute or chronic schizophrenic patient, even if he is being treated for a short time only, enriches our understanding of the psychopathology and makes the analysis of subsequent patients easier.

I have discussed the many difficulties which we encounter in this work. But we should remember that there are acute and chronic schizophrenic patients who respond more easily to our analytic approach. They gain insight, cooperate in the analysis and seem to improve from the beginning. In these cases there seems to be a part of the personality not completely involved in the psychosis. So in spite of their severe psychotic manifestations they do not completely lose touch with reality once the analysis is going ahead. The information gained from these less-difficult schizophrenic patients has been of great value in understanding the more serious ones; for we need a great deal of knowledge of the psychopathology in order to gain access, for instance, to a silent schizophrenic patient, or in order to understand and utilize the sometimes very scanty information which some schizophrenics are able to give us.

# 7

# ON DRUG ADDICTION[1] (1960)

IN scrutinizing the literature of drug addiction and alcoholism it becomes apparent that the great majority of psycho-analytic papers on that subject were written before 1945. One of the reasons for the scarcity of psycho-analytic contributions during the last twenty years may be the recognition that the treatment of drug addiction in psycho-analytic practice is a very difficult problem.

## The Management of the Addict

I suggest that the drug addict is a particularly difficult patient to manage because the analyst has not only to deal with a psychologically determined state but is confronted with the combination of a mental state and the intoxication and confusion caused by drugs. As a severely intoxicated patient is not accessible to analysis, an attempt has to be made from the beginning of the treatment, or when the drug addiction is diagnosed while the patient is under analysis, to get the severe drugging under control, and the patient has to accept either private nursing or residence in a nursing home or hospital. If the patient accepts the condition of control of the drugging, analysis can proceed. Nevertheless, excessive acting out, which can lead to crises in the treatment, occurs when the patient periodically breaks through the control. The control cannot be too severe and absolute because this would amount virtually to imprisonment of the patient, a situation which he would experience as punishment and not as help in his attempt to give up the drugs. The difficulties in treating these patients have been stressed by Bychowski (1952) who warned every therapeutic enthusiast against the treatment of any drug addict in private practice. He adds: 'This is possible only in exceptional cases and puts an extraordinary strain on the psychiatrist and the

[1] Read at the 21st Congress of the International Psycho-Analytical Association, Copenhagen, July 1959, and first published with extended introductory paragraphs, in the *Int. J. Psycho-Anal.* **41**.

patient's environment.' My own psycho-analytic investigation of drug addicts has been limited to a few patients, but I found it unnecessary to modify my usual psycho-analytic approach. As in my earlier experiences in investigating psychotic conditions, like schizophrenia and manic-depressive states, I feel that progress in understanding the specific psychopathology of drug addiction must come through the understanding of the transference neurosis or the transference psychosis, however difficult this may be, but not by giving up the psycho-analytic approach.

## The Psychopathology of Drug Addiction

In investigating drug addicts psycho-analytically I found that drug addiction is closely related to the manic-depressive illness, but not identical with it. The drug addict uses manic-depressive mechanisms which are reinforced by drugs and consequently altered by the drugging. The ego of the drug addict is weak and has not the strength to bear the pain of depression and easily resorts to manic mechanisms, but the manic reaction can only be achieved with the help of drugs, because some ego strength is necessary for the production of mania. One has also to consider the symbolic meaning of the drug, which is related to the unconscious fantasies attached to the drug and drugging and the pharmacotoxic effect which increases the omnipotence both of the impulses and of the mechanisms used.

As I mentioned before the relation of mania and depression to drug addiction has been noticed by previous writers, but the detailed meaning of this relation has not been elaborated.

In this paper I shall first attempt to describe in some detail the depressive and manic mechanisms which I was able to observe in the drug addict and to relate them to the drugs and drugging.

The manic defences have their origin in earliest infancy, at a phase which Melanie Klein (1940) has called the paranoid-schizoid position. They become modified later in the depressive position. For this reason the manic defences are related both to paranoid and depressive anxieties and mechanisms.

I shall first describe the manic mechanisms which are mainly used by the drug addict to control paranoid anxieties, such as idealization, identification with an ideal object, and the omnipotent control of the objects which may be part or whole objects. Under the dominance of these mechanisms all frustration, anxiety, particularly persecutory anxiety, is denied, and the bad aggressive part of the self is split off. The drug symbolizes an ideal object, which can be concretely incorporated, and the pharmacotoxic effect is used to reinforce the omnipotence of the mechanisms of denial and splitting. This can be clearly observed when the drug addict uses drugs to produce states of drowsiness leading to sleep. He is then blissfully hallucinating an ideal object and feels united or identified with it. He does not appear to regress to the state of satisfaction of the infant at the breast as Rádo (1926) suggested, but to a phase of infancy where the infant uses hallucinatory wish-fulfilment fantasies in dealing with his anxieties. This state is closely related to the manic mechanisms and defences, the drug effect being used as an artificial physical aid in the production of the hallucination, in the same way as the infant uses his fingers or thumb as an aid to hallucinating the ideal breast. Thus the drug is used to help in the annihilation of any frustrating and persecuting object or situation. In addition to the use of drugs for strengthening the mechanisms of defence against persecutory anxieties, drugs and drugging are more directly related to persecutory anxieties and sadistic impulses. The drug is then felt to be a bad destructive substance, incorporation of which symbolizes an identification with bad destructive objects which are felt to be persecutory both to good objects and the good self. The pharmacotoxic effect is used to increase the omnipotent power of the destructive drive. When drugging occurs under the dominance of sadistic impulses the patient splits-off and denies his good self and his good internal objects and his concern for them. He is thus able to act out his destructive drives without any anxiety and concern but also without any control which implies that the controlling power of the internal object, his superego, has also been lost. The patient can now give himself up to an orgy of destruction which is directed against the external object but which also includes his internal objects and himself. This destructive drugging represents a severe danger to the patient and a great anxiety to his relatives. It is also a major difficulty in dealing with him analytically, because during such states all progress and insight is denied and seems to be lost. I would suggest that this omnipotent destructive drugging is also closely allied to mania.

Abraham (1924), Róheim (1923), Weiss (1926), Alexander (1929), Eddison (1934), Fenichel (1945c), Federn (1953), Rochlin (1953), and particularly Klein (1957) have drawn attention to the importance of destructive impulses breaking through in mania. Melanie Klein (1940) suggested that the triumph in mania was related to destructive omnipotence, and in 1957 she defined the destructive omnipotent element in elation as primary oral envy, a view she illustrated by case material from a manic-depressive patient.

I have so far been discussing the relation of drug addiction and mania. I want now to add a note about its relation to depression. Rádo emphasized the primary 'tense' depression as a basis for a need to take drugs. Simmel (1928) suggested that the periods of hospitalization and withdrawal treatment in drug addiction were analogous to periodic depression in so far as the patient appeared to provoke the painful withdrawal treatment which to him had the meaning of masochistic self-punishment by excessive drugging. I would agree with the importance of Simmel's point but would consider it as *only one* of the factors in the relation of depression to drug addiction. In my view, the essential factor of the relation of drug addiction to depression is the identification with an ill or dead object. The drug in such cases stands for such an object and the drugging implies a very concrete incorporation of this object. The pharmacotoxic effect is used to reinforce the reality both of the introjection of the object and of the identification with it.

I want finally to add a note about the relation of drug addiction to ego splitting. It has been pointed out by several writers, for example Federn (1953), that the drug addict is unable to cope with pain and frustration. This is in my opinion not only due to oral regression of the drug addict but to the excessive splitting of his ego and his objects which is bound up with the ego weakness. In the analytic transference situation it becomes apparent that excessive splitting of objects into idealized and denigrated ones plays an important part; simultaneously external objects are used extensively for the purpose of projecting into them split-off good and bad parts of the self. This splitting of the self drives the patient to behave both in his external life and in analysis as if he were two or more different people. This factor also contributes to his acting out excessively during psycho-analytic treatment. In addition the ego splitting may lead on the one hand to attempts to control in an elaborate way the people into whom the patient has projected his self, but on the other hand the projective process has the effect of making the patient over-dependent on and over-sensitive to the same people.

The above observations may throw some light on the behaviour and on the ego of the drug addict, but there is a further more direct link between drug addiction and ego splitting. The drug appears frequently as the symbol of the split-off bad part of the self, and drugging occurs when this bad self is projected into external objects or when the projected bad self is taken back into the ego. During the analysis it can be observed that the pharmacotoxic effect of the drug is used to increase the omnipotence of the mechanism of projection and the omnipotence of the destructive drives which are directed against the analysis and against the objects which are used for the projective process.

From the discussion so far, it seems clear that the drug addict is fixated at an early infantile phase which Melanie Klein (1940) has called the paranoid-schizoid position, in spite of the fact that he has partially reached the depressive position. This I believe to be of fundamental importance for the understanding of drug addiction. It is particularly the ego of the drug addict and the defence mechanisms of the ego which have regressed to this early position. As far as the drug addict's object relations and the libidinal levels of development are concerned the regression is not always so marked, except when there is a complete withdrawal from external objects in the drugged state. In the cases I have observed the hunger for external objects was still very marked, and while oral impulses seemed to play their part, the oedipal problems were often more in the foreground.

I shall now select a few points from the analysis of a woman patient who had been a barbiturate addict for ten years when she began treatment with me. From the history of the patient I only want to mention that she was breast-fed for a time, but as a baby she apparently never cried for her feed. She was an intense finger sucker and biter from early on. Many methods were used to rid her of this habit but they were unsuccessful. The patient turned to her father at an early age. She idealized him, admired his success and learning, and apparently he also was fond and proud of her. He developed severe asthma when the patient was about seventeen and died six years later from this complaint. The patient looked after him devotedly and he talked to her for hours about the problems which preoccupied him at the time of his illness, particularly the conflict with his own brother. After the father's death, the patient was not unusually depressed, and as the mother, who had been very dependent on her husband, was shaken, the patient took charge of the situation and seemed to have been quite efficient. The patient had a sister three years older and a brother two years younger than herself, to whom she was very attached. This brother developed a severe depression after the father's death, began drinking heavily, and finally committed suicide by taking an overdose of a sleeping drug. He left only one letter, which was addressed to my patient. This touched her very deeply. The first night after the brother's death, the patient was given a sleeping pill and this seems to have started off the addiction, which gradually became very severe. As a consequence of the addiction, the patient often became emaciated and her mother put her into mental institutions many times for withdrawal treatment. Psychotherapy was attempted several times but it proved unsuccessful and it was given up because she became too hostile and persecuted.

When I first saw the patient in consultation, she was intoxicated and confused apparently through a mixture of hypnotic and exciting drugs, and she appeared both physically and mentally very ill. She had to be put into a nursing home for the control of the drugging and for her physical condition. It gradually emerged that she was keen to have psycho-analytic treatment. She felt persecuted by the psychiatric treatment including shock therapy which she had received previously, and she put all her hopes and idealizations into psycho-analysis. Her drug addiction was very complex and over-determined.

The psycho-analytic treatment revealed a strong identification with the brother who had committed suicide by taking drugs, but there was also a deep sense of union with him and the father, as idealized objects, which was experienced as an omnipotent sexual possessing of both of them, a fantasy which often led to compulsive drugging and sleeping. The drugging had here a manic and a depressive meaning: the identification with the dead brother and father implying a depressive reaction, while the omnipotent sexual union seemed to have a manic meaning, namely that of idealizing both the father and brother and denying the persecutory anxieties related to them. When these feelings attached themselves to the transference, these aspects could be seen in the following dream. In this dream she joined me in being sent to a concentration camp to be killed, but before death she had a very satisfactory sexual relation with me. For several days before this dream she had been feeling anxious and had dreams of men persecuting her. Following the dream of joining me in death, she went through a stage of acute anxiety, when she felt shut in and pursued by monsters. At times the anxiety was so severe that she complained of hallucinating these monsters during the daytime, and she wanted to drug herself to change the frightening situation back again into the pleasurable dream. As during this period she was prevented from using drugs, her persecutory anxieties were less split-off and denied and appeared almost simultaneously with the idealization. Drugging frequently had the meaning of omnipotently controlling the penis as an idealized part-object. She became sexually excited and anxious after taking sleeping drugs at night-time in the nursing home, which prevented her from sleeping so that she had to take more drugs to go to sleep. She then had dreams that her mouth was swelling up, leading to emissions in her mouth. The anxiety seemed due not only to sexual excitement but to a feeling of persecution because the drug symbolized the idealized penis. But as she felt she had bitten off the penis out of envy it soon became persecuting inside her, so that more drugs had to be taken to allay the persecution and reinforce the idealization of the omni-potently controlled penis. The drug was often experienced as representing an idealized internal breast. After a session where the analysis represented the good breast and the patient had reacted with anger and envy because she felt that the analyst controlled the analysis, standing for the good breast, she would stay in the nursing home when her session was due, take a sleep-ing pill and go to bed. In this way she repeated the early situation with her mother as a baby when she did not cry and sucked her fingers or went to sleep instead of feeding. The drugging also represented a reinforcement of her omnipotent destructive self because when she first became aware of her envy of my possessing the analysis as a good breast, she told me of her anxiety after seeing a film of Stevenson's *Dr Jekyll and Mr Hyde*. She felt identified with Jekyll who, through drugging, could turn himself completely into his bad self, the Mr Hyde. This division of herself into a good self and a hidden bad self, a 'Mr Hyde self', was of particular importance in relation to her father, whom consciously she had only loved and admired. For example, she had a thinly disguised transference dream where I, standing for her father, had a friendly daughter in her who worked hard for me in the garden, but there was also a hostile daughter of the same age who completely ignored me. The bad aggressive part of herself was related on the one hand to her intense jealousy which was mainly connected with the oedipal situation, and on the other hand to her extreme envy of women and particularly of men, the envy of both her brother and her father having been almost completely split-off and denied. This split-off envious part of herself became projected during the analysis into both women and men friends of her environment, which led to intense acting out. At such times she almost desperately tried to prove to me the reality of the bad envious characteristics of these friends, some of whom in fact were unselfishly attempting to help her. The brother and father had had a difficult relationship, and it had been apparent that the brother had not been able to deal with his own rivalry and envy of the father after the latter's death. The analysis revealed that the patient felt that she had split off her own envious aggressive relationship to the father on to the brother, who had to carry for her the bad part of her relation to her father while she managed to appear to the father only in a good light. It was this projection that led to such intense guilt feelings and a need to identify with her brother after the latter's death. This identification was in turn expressed by her need to drug herself immediately after the brother's death, the drug representing the dead brother, and her bad self, which she had projected into him and which she felt compelled to take back after the brother's death. Identification with the father and projection into him of a bad part of herself also played an important role, and I shall illustrate this by some case material from the seventeenth month of the patient's analysis. The material refers to four consecutive sessions, starting with a Thursday.

During this Thursday session I noticed that the patient had started to take more drugs, and she confirmed this. She made an attack on a woman friend more viciously than usual, trying to prove to me that this friend was full of envy and jealousy of her and me. She accused this friend, in addition, of not seeing her own envy and needing analysis from me. There were references to her father's illness. I tried to show her that she was denying her own envy and jealousy of me standing for the father and that she was projecting this envy and jealousy into her friend. This projection made her feel not only that her friend was envious and jealous, but also that she had attacked her friend and made her ill so that she needed treatment. Her friend seemed here to stand for the ill father. I also pointed out that she used her drug in this present situation to make herself and me believe that her friend was in reality bad. On Friday she said that she wanted to stop drugging and she realized that there was an impulse in her to destroy. She said: 'When I am drugging I can't understand your interpretations, because while I am drugging I am giving the drugs an omnipotent power to destroy.' She also admitted that she wanted to put all her own viciousness and envy into her friend and make out that her friend was the bad one and she was the good one. Here it seemed confirmed that I had become the good father and she had, by her drugging, omnipotently put her own bad destructive feelings against me into her friend, to make her the bad one. Over the weekend the patient felt depressed and lonely, but she stopped taking drugs. She saw her woman friend in the latter's flat, but on returning to her room in the nursing home she thought it was over-full and felt asphyxiated by all the rubbish in it—it seemed 'just full of old newspapers'. I pointed out to her that it was the taking back into herself of the bad self which she had previously projected into her friend which made her feel so asphyxiated, so small and full of rubbish like her room. She then complained of a bad headache, which had started during a dream. In the first part of the dream a man and the patient's woman friend were sitting in a bar. The patient herself was lying down on a couch. The man offered the patient a drink, saying to her: 'Here is a very nice new drink which you can have, but when you drink it you have to swallow what is at the bottom of it.' When the patient looked into the glass she saw on the bottom the phlegm of her own catarrhs and felt disgusted. In the second part a friendly aunt had sent her daughter, who has the same first name as the patient, to London for a throat operation. The patient knew it was cancer. The aunt told the patient in the dream that she herself had something wrong with her eyes which caused her to have a headache. She wanted to consult a specialist. At that moment the patient developed a severe headache in the dream and wanted to take a aspirin tablet, but when she tried to swallow it, it turned into her drug. In her associations the disgusting phlegm reminded her of her drug and the disgust she experienced when she met another drug addict in the nursing home. She related the aunt to her woman friend, who the day before had complained about the same trouble with her eyes. I was now able to show her that the nice new drink stood for the treatment which forced her to take back into herself her own problems, the phlegm of her catarrhs, which she had projected into her woman friend so often before but particularly again on Thursday. I showed her also that her own projected problems, the phlegm, representing her jealousy and envy, was identified with drugs and drugging. The identification of her projected problems with bodily substances like urine and faeces had become clear in the early part of the analysis. There was, in addition, out of a sense of guilt, a need to identify herself with her woman friend as the ill person which was shown by the headache, but instead of being able to find some relief by taking aspirin she experienced the identification as a punishment. This seemed to be the reason why the aspirin changed into her drug in the dream. The woman friend, during the whole week, appeared to represent mainly the ill father, whom she had attacked with her projections, but this became fully confirmed only in the next session. On Tuesday she said she felt sick with depression. She had become aware of a disturbing feeling in her throat. She wondered whether her tonsils should be taken out. She mentioned her many throat illnesses and catarrhs during her childhood. Suddenly she remembered that her father had had a throat operation at the beginning of his serious illness and he once took a large dose of aspirin to relieve his pain, but took so much that he developed a severe haemorrhage. The patient looked after him at that time but felt disgusted. She explained that she had despised her father during his illness, because he was so disturbed about the envy of his brother. Whenever her father talked about his brother an attack of asthma developed and the patient realized that the father could not cope with envy himself. I interpreted to her that she triumphed over her father because of his weakness in not being able to cope with envy which also implied to her that he was castrated. At the same time she used the weakness of the father to project into him her own envy and her inability to deal with it. Out of guilt she had to take back into herself the envy and jealousy which she had projected into her father, and out of guilt also she had to identify with the father's illness, his throat trouble, and his asphyxiation and his inability to see his problems, all of which in the dream was represented by the aspirin which turned into her drug. I was thus able to show to the patient how the transference situation and her acting out by her projecting into her woman friend related to the past. Her woman friend stood both for the despised ill father into whom she had projected her own bad envious self, while I had remained the good father representing the nice new drink. In the following sessions the patient reported that she felt very relieved through her having recognized and understood the identification with her ill father. She also felt more confident in being able to accept and to deal with that part of herself which she was constantly projecting, her envy and jealousy.

There is another point I would like to consider. One might wonder why the splitting and projection of the patient seemed predominantly to relate to the father and brother, and the envy of the penis, while there was evidence of the origin of her problems in early infancy in relation to the mother and the breast. One link was given in a dream where the patient was hiding a dish full of nice food in a place called 'daddy'. There were other suggestions that a great deal of the good and bad mother relationship had been put into the father relationship. After the analysis of the identification with the father the analysis turned predominantly to the relation with the mother.

The interrelationship of the patient's earliest experiences, fantasies and mechanisms and her later development was to some extent noticeable from the beginning of the treatment, but it came clearly into the open during such episodes, which the patient called her '*crises*'. At such times the patient indulged in some kind of orgy of drinking and drugging which generally ended in her taking an overdose of a sleeping drug. I shall attempt to throw some light on the psychopathology of these crises and shall use case material from the sixth month of the analysis.

I have come to the conclusion that the crises formed part of a negative therapeutic reaction. Negative therapeutic reactions are a common occurrence in manic-depressive patients, and they are equally common or even more frequent during the treatment of drug addictions. Joan Riviere has described the relationship of the negative therapeutic reaction to mania, while Melanie

Klein has added to our understanding of this reaction by relating it to envy, which is mobilized by some successful analytic work. Both these factors could be observed in analysing the patient's crises. The manic reaction seemed on the one hand to be produced by the patient's feeling that she had gained much from the analysis, but that she wanted to take it away from me to triumph over me; on the other hand she found herself overwhelmed by feelings of guilt and depression as the result of the deeper insight gained by the analytic work and therefore took flight into a manic reaction. But it was also clear that the progress in the analysis reduced the patient's tendency to split off a highly envious negative part of her personality, which came to the surface during the crises, overwhelmed the rest of her personality and caused the dangerous acting out. Once she had consumed either a great deal of alcohol or stimulating drugs, the destructive part of her personality became reinforced by the stimulants, as I have pointed out earlier. The positive part of her personality had no chance to control the situation once the crisis had started.

Before the first Christmas holidays, six months after the beginning of treatment, the patient felt so much better that she risked moving from the nursing home to the flat of her woman friend. During the Christmas holidays she suffered a great deal of anxiety and depression, but she managed to cope without taking more than the prescribed drugs. She began to feel very guilty after Christmas, having spent a lot of money on presents and on herself. She realized that the overspending was not only a denial of having very little money herself and wanting to show off and be popular, but it also implied a desire to rob her mother who was paying all her expenses. She became increasingly aware that a great deal of sexual excitement was linked with taking sleeping drugs at night. She began to feel guilty about holding on to her sleeping drugs and she realized that overspending and drugging both had the meaning of stealing from her mother, the drugs and the money symbolizing father's penis. She seriously thought of taking a step in the direction of health and normality by reducing her expenses; she also made up her mind to cut down the amount of sleeping drugs. The day following this decision she told me that she had tried to go to sleep on $1\frac{1}{2}$ grains of sodium amytal, instead of $4\frac{1}{2}$ grains, but she had stayed awake until after midnight and had been feeling lonely and miserable, longing to be with her mother, with whom she had been on bad terms most of the time. In returning from this particular interview she went home to the flat of her woman friend and found her unwell. Her friend asked her to help her and make some food for her, but the patient felt that she could not bear to stay with her ill friend, representing the robbed and damaged mother. She rang up a boy friend who went out with her. She first went to a pub with him, had four drinks and then went on with him to a party and spent most of the night drinking and taking both stimulating and soothing drugs. She came home to the flat late at night, took 9 grains of sodium amytal, and was found next morning by her woman friend in a comatose condition. A doctor was called in who sent her to a hospital to have her stomach washed out, because he could not rule out her having taken a large overdose. The patient spent twenty-four hours in the hospital and had to miss one of her interviews, but she appeared the following day for her usual session,[1] feeling very guilty about this episode but also furious about having been sent to the hospital. She particularly remembered waking up in hospital and feeling intensely humiliated to be without shoes. This related to an identification with the castrated brother. There had been an important incident in childhood, which she often talked about, where her father had punished her brother by taking away his shoes. She had felt intensely sorry for him and very angry with her father for humiliating him in such manner. She also told me that she felt very guilty because in the last interview before her drugging she had withheld a dream from me. In the dream her hands were made partially of diamonds and of gold. She felt thrilled at the idea that she was rich. She thought this did not only apply to money, but to being full of beautiful and interesting things. The dream expressed clearly that she felt that she had a lot of good things, which were part of her and belonged to her, but as in fact she had been overspending her mother's money and had also in fact received a great deal of help from her analysis, the dream represented both an inability to acknowledge what she had received from her mother and the analysis and a denial of her stealing; she did not have to receive or to steal anything from anyone because she had so many good and valuable things herself.

However in her withholding of the dream from me the stealing

[1] After this incident she returned to the nursing home.

was acted out, and she began to feel guilty about this after leaving me. On seeing her ill woman friend her guilt increased, but she denied concern and need for reparation and a manic reaction set in. Her ringing up a boy friend was consciously related to a desire to make her woman friend envious and to triumph over her. In this way she had attempted to project the envy coming to the surface in the analysis into her woman friend. As she confessed to me in the same hour that on her wedding night she told her husband that she had lost her sexual interest in him and belittled his potency, her withholding of the dream and the consequent drugging implied in part an acting out of her castrating wishes towards me, but it took some time to understand the complex nature of this crisis.

A few days later she had the following dream. It was morning, and she was going to bathe in the sea. The weather was very nice and she was preparing to take the plunge, but at the last moment she suddenly decided that she wanted to go to sleep and so she took some drugs. In her dream she went into a drugged sleep, in which she had another dream. There she dreamt that she had not needed to take any drugs to go to sleep and that she was very pleased with herself that she was well enough to go back to her home town, cured of her addiction. In the dream she said: 'Now I am no longer in need of Dr Rosenfeld to give me analysis, there is another doctor at home who can give me treatment.' Her associations closely linked up with the manifest content of the dream. Her trying to take the plunge into the sea implied a recognition of the opportunity which the treatment gave her to take the plunge and start her life again, which had been completely spoilt by her drug addiction, but just at the moment when she was ready to do so, she decided against going forward and returned to her drugged sleep. In the manifest dream the purpose of the drugged sleep is to create the illusion of being cured of the drugging, so that she could be independent of her analysis. I am suggesting that the dream illustrates that aspect of the patient's negative therapeutic reaction which was due to envy being mobilized by the analysis as a result of her having experienced some improvement. The envious feelings prevented her acknowledgement of her increased need and greed for what the analysis has to offer. The drug is used by her omnipotently to hallucinate sleep and a state of being cured, representing an omnipotently created internal breast which makes her independent of the analyst standing for the real mother and her breast.

This analytic experience is a repetition of the very early situation when as a baby the patient felt hungry and in need of her mother but refused to cry and turned away from the mother and breast to her fingers which she sucked until she went to sleep.

Earlier in the paper I have related the early infantile experiences of the baby in turning to the thumb to hallucinatory wishfulfilment and mania. I want to add that early envy of the breast plays an important role in the early turning away from the breast to the thumb which is an important factor in the predisposition to drug addiction.

On the surface the crisis seemed to have been produced by the patient's envious castrating wishes being stirred up by the father transference, but I have come to the conclusion that even at those times when the acting out predominantly expressed the negative father or brother transference, the early aggressive impulses against the mother and her breast had been mobilized in the transference.

The analysis was prematurely interrupted after twenty-two months against the patient's conscious and unconscious wishes by the patient's family. As I mentioned before, the relation to the mother and the breast had by then appeared more openly in the analysis. At times her addiction to drugs had changed into an addiction to food, for example a compulsion to eat oranges.

It is interesting that analysts from early on have been perceptive in looking for the main psychopathological basis of drug addiction in orality and the very early sadistic impulses, which they related to the progressive defusion of instincts.

This view is largely confirmed by this investigation, which stresses not only the importance of manic depressive mechanisms, but the importance of the early splitting of the ego in addiction.

## Summary

It is suggested in this paper that drug addiction is closely related to the manic-depressive illness, but not identical with it. The drug addict uses certain manic and depressive mechanisms which are reinforced and consequently altered by the drugs. The drug has both a symbolic meaning which relates to the unconscious fantasies attached to it and the drugging and also a pharmacotoxic effect which increases the omnipotence of the mechanisms used and the omnipotence of the impulses.

The use of the mechanisms of idealization, identification with ideal objects, and denial of persecutory and depressive anxieties is related to a positive or defensive aspect of mania.

The destructive phases in drug addiction are closely allied to the destructive aspect of mania. Drugging often has a depressive meaning also, the drug symbolizing a dead or ill object which the patient feels compelled to incorporate out of guilt. An important part in drug addiction is played by the mechanisms of ego splitting and projection of good and particularly bad parts of the self, mechanisms which are more pronounced than in the manic-depressive states. The bad part of the patient's personality often becomes identified with a drug and during the drugged state is projected into objects in the environment which often leads to severe acting out. Drugging also occurs when the bad self is taken back into the ego. I am suggesting that the weakness of the addict's ego is related to the severity of the process of ego splitting and that the prognosis of the psycho-analytic treatment of a drug addict depends on the extent to which the analysis is able to help the patient to integrate the split-off parts of the self, a process which implies a strengthening of the patient's ego.

Crises of severe drugging may occur when the analysis is making progress and the splitting of the ego diminishes, which leads to aggressive acting out. This reaction may be regarded as a negative therapeutic reaction.

On the surface the oedipal conflict and homosexuality play an important part in the psycho-pathology of the drug addict, but during analysis it becomes apparent that the overwhelming force of his conflicts can only be understood by examining their basis in the very earliest conflicts and mechanisms of the infant.

# 8

# THE SUPEREGO AND THE
# EGO-IDEAL [1] (1962)

SINCE the aim of this symposium is to discuss both the ego-ideal and the superego, I shall first attempt to clarify the way in which these terms have been employed by Freud, and then discuss my own understanding of the terminology and how it is used in this paper. The term 'superego' was introduced as an alternative to the term 'ego-ideal' by Freud in 1923 with the implication that the ego-ideal and the superego were identical. On the other hand, the term 'ego-ideal' which Freud originally introduced (1914b) had an entirely different meaning. At that time he differentiated the ego-ideal from a special psychical agency, the conscience, relating the ego-ideal to the 'narcissistic perfection of childhood' and suggesting that this ideal was a substitute for the lost narcissism in which we were our own ideal. This explanation would suggest a connexion between the ego-ideal and omnipotent fantasies of early infancy when the baby fantasies himself in the role of an omnipotent ideal figure, or as possessing an ideal object or part-object, often the breast or the penis. We frequently find that narcissistic patients have a highly idealized omnipotent picture of themselves which is in contrast to their real self. I am not in favour of using the term 'ego-ideal' for these specific narcissistic idealized fantasies.

In the *New Introductory Lectures* (1933) Freud introduced a distinction between the two terms and a different meaning for the term ego-ideal. He describes the superego as a vehicle of the ego-ideal by which the ego measures itself and whose demand for perfection it is striving always to fulfil. He added: 'No doubt the ego-ideal is the precipitation of the old idea of the parents, an expression of the admiration which the child felt for the perfection which it at that time ascribed to them.' I shall here

---

[1] Read as part of a Symposium at the 22nd International Psycho-Analytical Congress, Edinburgh, July–August 1961, and first published in the *Int. J. Psycho-Anal.*, **43**.

use the term 'ego-ideal' to describe the aspect of the superego which arises from the identification with idealized objects.

In discussing the superego, I shall distinguish between the early and the later superego. The later superego begins in the latency period and undergoes changes during adolescence until the superego of the adult finally emerges. In using the term 'early superego' I am indicating that I am following Klein's work on the early superego (1933). In her view the earliest beginnings of the superego contain mainly idealized and persecutory aspects of the breast, soon including aspects of the penis and, with the beginnings of the early Oedipus conflict in the middle of the first year, aspects of the oedipal parental figures. Freud thought that the superego develops at the end of the classical oedipal situation through the introjection of the parental images, a view which he seemed to modify in 1933 when he stressed the identification with the superego of the parents rather than the parents themselves. As far as can be seen from the literature few writers would now actually agree that there is no superego formation before the latency period, but opinions differ about the origin, the content, and the development of the early superego which is discussed under various terms (Beres, 1958; Fraiberg, 1952; A. Reich, 1954; Spitz, 1958; Weissman, 1954) such as 'archaic', 'pre-oedipal', 'precursors of the superego', etc. There seems to be as yet no detailed psycho-analytic investigation, and certainly no agreement amongst analysts, as to how the early and the later superego are related. In my view the superego, as it emerges in the latency period, is essentially a continuation of the early superego, but it is also interrelated with it: the changes that appear at latency are not fundamental changes in content, but changes in the method of dealing with the anxieties of the early superego. In this development external objects play a prominent part.

In the first part of this paper my aim is to discuss the relation of the later superego to the early superego. I am suggesting that in the latency period, internal anxieties deriving from the early superego exert pressure on the individual to identify more closely with external objects, and that the greater the inner persecutory anxieties, the greater is the need to make complete and uncritical identifications with external objects. There is some projection of idealized and persecutory aspects of the early superego into external objects, but the projections are denied in favour of the real qualities of the external objects. The ensuing unmodified identifications with the external real objects imply an attempt on the ego's part to split off the persecutory and highly idealized aspects of the early superego. In adolescence these split-off aspects of the early superego normally come to the surface again and are projected on to external objects, but to aid the externalization there is a need to deny the real aspects of external objects. In the second part of the paper I shall examine the factors which enable the analyst to bring about a change in the structure of the superego: I shall especially discuss the view that the superego cannot be understood and successfully treated without its very earliest aspects being brought into the analytic situation.

I shall now bring some case material to illustrate the interrelationship between the early and the later superego situation. The patient I am going to discuss was an attractive-looking single woman in the middle thirties. She had apparently been quite well until her early twenties when, after some small disappointment with a boy friend, she developed neurotic symptoms, and by the time she came for treatment she had been suffering for a long time from sleeplessness, difficulties in swallowing, and severe anxiety and depression. From her early history it was known that she had turned away from her mother very early, apparently after weaning, and had attached herself to her father who was very fond of her. Her mother was a quiet, affectionate woman who liked looking after the household: she was somewhat despised by my patient. The father was very ambitious and demanded that the patient should do well in her studies at school and at the University. He was irritable, quickly lost his temper, and was a difficult man to please, but the patient fitted in with most of his demands. She also formed a good relationship with some of her male teachers, and whenever she could admire and idealize them she worked extremely well for them. The father was also strict about her going out and meeting friends, believing that none of them were good enough for her. However, when the patient was about seventeen or eighteen, she managed to become more independent and able to tolerate her father's disapproval. She formed an idealized friendship with a man of her own age which lasted for several years. He seemed to have taken the relationship very seriously, but when once he failed to see her for a fortnight, the patient refused to see him again. She felt let down and remembers that she turned back to a mental image of her father, thinking 'father is right after all, one should not trust anybody'.

It seems that the patient must have identified with her father's demands and restrictions at some time in childhood and built up her ego-ideal around an idealized image of him and her male teachers. Nevertheless, she did not make a masculine impression; on the contrary she looked strikingly feminine. Early in the analysis she had a dream of a plaster cast of a breast which was exquisitely beautiful and rather fragile; she thought that this breast represented herself, because she felt that she herself might easily break into bits. It might be deduced from this that her ideal-self, or her ideal-self image, was built round the fantasy of a highly idealized breast. At puberty she seemed able to free herself a little from the identification with the demands of her real father and so gained some independence. However, the disappointment with her boy friend again strengthened the relation to her internal father as a superego figure. The patient subsequently made various attempts to build up a satisfactory relationship to men but never felt certain of herself or any man she met.

In treatment, after a difficult start, she settled down well and became most cooperative. She seemed instinctively to understand what was required by the process of analysis, and while there was a strong positive transference she also attempted to bring the negative aspects into the treatment. It appeared that in trying to satisfy the expected demands of the analyst she was repeating the pattern established with her father and her teachers.

I want now to concentrate on some material which occurred about eight months after the beginning of treatment. Certain aspects of her latency oedipal conflict came clearly into the analysis, and she was angry that I did not respond to her sexual advances. She had violent revenge fantasies of separating me from my wife, incarcerating me, and reversing the child/parent relationship. She experienced some guilt but no severe depression about her aggressive impulses, and was sometimes able to express wishes to repair the fantasied damage. For example, she had a dream that her parents had quarrelled and separated, and her father had fallen ill of a broken heart because she had chosen a boy friend of whom they did not approve. When the patient visited her father in this dream, nurses and doctors stood around looking at her accusingly and she realized that she was expected to perform an operation on her father's heart. Her father had, in fact, no heart trouble, but she felt that she wanted to hurt the analyst and break his heart.

This dream illustrates certain aspects of her superego which were emerging at the time in the transference. These aspects might appear to belong to the superego of the later oedipal phase, but it can be seen that it contains elements the roots of which are known to be much earlier; the nurses and doctors, who look accusingly, represent that aspect of her superego which accuses her of causing damage to the loved father or analyst and makes demands for reparation. Klein has suggested that the beginnings of feelings of guilt and the desire to make reparation for injuring a loved object go back to the middle of the first year of infancy to the depressive position. I shall show in the following material something of the importance and history of early accusing and reproaching figures in this patient's superego formation.

Some weeks later the patient had another dream: she went shooting rabbits with a man who told her to use a stick to kill the rabbits instead of a gun. A very tame rabbit sat immobile in front of her. She did not question the advice of the man, feeling that whatever he suggested must be right; and so she took the stick and hit the rabbit hard across its head. The skin of the rabbit's head was splitting, but it was not dead. She hit it again and again until it was completely mangled, but it was still not dead and its eyes kept on looking at her reproachfully. The patient associated to the dream that her father often hit her to punish her and to keep her in her place when she became excited and provocative. She remembered having at times been furiously angry with him and frightened about the punishment, which she did not suffer at all passively. She emphasized that she could not bear to be frightened and she stressed her desire to trust somebody implicitly and to follow his lead without any need for criticism.

It seems that this dream contains two superego aspects which are closely related. First it illustrates the identification with the real father as a restricting, punishing superego figure. We might have the impression that the flirtatious excited relationship of the little girl to her father led sometimes to punishment and restriction which she eventually accepted; but more detailed analysis showed, as I shall point out later, that her identification with her real father was an attempt to deal with her unconscious persecutory fear of him by appeasement and submission.

The second superego aspect of the dream relates to the accusing eyes of the rabbit. The patient said that she could not bear its accusing eyes, and that there was nothing to do but to kill it. She had injured the rabbit too much to try to rescue it. This suggests that the injured rabbit was turning into a persecuting superego. One of the methods of dealing with persecuting superego figures is to increase aggression in order to get rid of them by killing. In early childhood, injured objects which are beyond repair are often experienced as turning into persecutors, which is an important feature of the early persecuting superego.[1]

About six to eight weeks after the rabbit dream I had to change some of the patient's sessions. Her anger about this was first analysed as a disappointment in the analyst as a father figure, but she continued to regard the change as a cruel persecution and a sign that the analyst could not be trusted, and it became clear that it had reactivated early infantile experiences. The patient had been weaned when she was about ten months old and afterwards developed severe whooping cough. During this time she rejected her mother, and her father fed her and apparently saved her life. She dramatically re-experienced much of this early situation in the transference by accusing the analyst as the mother figure that he was letting her starve to death. It seemed that the change of time meant that the analyst/mother was taking away her food, but the sessions themselves also seemed completely altered in substance; they had become bad, poisonous and persecutory. Certain superego features relating to this situation gradually emerged. Shortly after the change of time I became ill and had to stop seeing her for more than a week, which aroused acute anxiety in the patient. Much later she told me that she had been terrified as she felt that her attacks had

[1] There were no clear associations as to what the rabbit stood for, but its helplessness and trustfulness may contain a hint that it was related to early childhood. Some of the patient's associations related the splitting of the skin of the rabbit's head to feelings that her own head was often felt to be split in two, so that she could not think or make decisions. This suggested to me that there was some important splitting going on – an attempt to use the later superego aspects to split off and annihilate the early superego, an attempt which at the time of the dream was beginning to fail, as could be seen in the reproachful eyes of the rabbit and the manifest anxiety of the dream itself.

made me ill. This situation reminded her of the rabbit dream because she felt reproached and threatened by my being ill, which increased her attacks on me when I returned. She seemed unable to feel or express concern, on the contrary, she hit out mercilessly, stressing that I was quite useless and accusing me of trying to murder her. Judging from this there seems to be no doubt that the mother who weaned her was identical with the rabbit of the dream: namely, a mother who was attacked and injured and therefore became a persecuting, accusing superego figure, felt to be murderous.

During the time of my illness the patient turned to a man whom she knew slightly. She became very dependent on him, asking him to sit with her while she was trying to eat, and he at times actually spoon-fed her. In this way she repeated the turning away from the weaning mother, who was experienced as an injured, accusing, persecutory superego figure, to the saving, idealized father. There were, however, other details which became gradually clear in the transference situation. During the time following the change of the sessions and my illness the patient not only tried to injure me with words, but used the real father as a stick to beat me with, by telling me what he thought of me and what he would do to me if he knew how I was treating her. So it became clear that the patient not only turned to an idealized father figure in reality, represented by the man who helped her to eat, but projected her own aggressive feelings on to her father and so acted out fantasies of using an aggressive, sadistic father, or his penis, to destroy the analyst, as the mother figure. The throwing of the sadistic father at the mother was mainly meant as a punishment for the mother who had deserted her, but it had also some oedipal significance representing a very sadistic, mainly oral relationship between the parents.[1]

The role which the sadistic father played in her early superego remained hidden in the analysis for some time. The patient remained friendly with the young man for many months, but when later on he expressed fears of hurting her if they continued their relationship, the patient accused him of striking her a terrible blow and immediately turned away from him as she had turned away from her first boy friend. The moment a man

---

[1] Thus in the rabbit dream she is identified with both: the beating father containing her projected sadism and the beaten mother/rabbit.

expressed the slightest doubt in his love for her, her fear of his ambivalence–her deep fear of his murderous impulses–broke through and she had immediately to get rid of him. She became suicidal and felt destroyed and in bits, 'blaming the boy friend entirely for what she was experiencing. In this situation the patient was identified with the mangled rabbit/mother who had been struck a terrible blow–an identification which was aimed at warding off overwhelming persecutory guilt. The patient felt and almost hallucinated that there was a frightening revengeful mother figure waiting to attack her. She could not eat by herself unless there was a woman present to help her, i.e. to deny the existence of this frightening internal mother. The patient felt that this persecuting, punishing breast/mother would not only poison and starve her to death but would put something terrible down her throat to kill her–an anxiety which was responsible for her difficulties in swallowing. It was not difficult to deduce that this represented the sadistic penis which the persecuting mother used as a punishing weapon. It also became clear that the boy friend who was afraid of hurting her had become identified with this sadistic penis. The previous idealized relationship with the boy friend, representing the idealized saving father of early infancy, had been used to deny the existence of the early persecutory superego of a punishing mother waiting to attack the patient with a sadistic penis.

There were many later situations in the patient's life that reinforced her early persecutory superego which contained a sadistic father-attacking-the-mother, experienced as making retaliatory attacks against her. Her murderous feelings against both parents and the projection of her sadistic feelings, particularly on to the penis of the father, had been increased by primary scene experiences and the birth of her sister when she was four. In working through similar childhood situations in the transference there were repeatedly murderous, jealous attacks against the analyst followed by overwhelming anxiety caused by persecutory guilt, which was modelled on the early superego. However, the re-experiencing of these later situations gave the patient only temporary relief. The analysis of the weaning situation and the superego built round this experience which I have discussed in some detail, brought the early persecutory superego right into the analysis with convincing dynamic force. The analyst was experienced again and again as a sadistic, critical superego figure who took pleasure in destructively criticizing everything the patient was doing or saying, or who took everything out of the patient, enriching himself and leaving the patient empty and destroyed. At the height of the persecution the patient would often threaten to kill herself or would try to appease the analyst by saying: 'I agree with everything you say. I will do whatever you want me to do and admit everything you accuse me of, whatever it is.' At such times it became clear that one of the methods the patient had adopted in dealing with the persecutory superego was to surrender her ego entirely to it, an attitude which was carried over to the later superego father to whose criticism and judgement she had completely surrendered, as I have tried to illustrate in the rabbit dream.

Having established some of the connexions between the early and the later superego, I want now to examine those factors which are of dynamic importance in bringing about fundamental changes in the structure of the superego.

During the treatment of this patient I was forced to realize that the analysis of the later superego aspects, even if they were related to important parts of the early superego, brought only temporary, or no, relief. This appears to be due to the fact that the analysis of the later superego is often dynamically of secondary importance because it has mainly a defensive function against the anxieties of the early superego. If the anxieties of the early superego have broken through to the surface, the defensive function of the later superego is put out of action, and loses its force and function, as occurred with my patient, when she was left by her boy friend. As far as the early superego is concerned one often finds that it is concentrated round and related to reactions to early reality experiences, such as the weaning experiences in the case of my patient. In order to achieve a change in the early superego one has to work through the earliest ego and superego development, which means that one has to go back to the earliest relations to the mother and the breast in the transference situation. It is particularly important to understand the fixation in the earliest paranoid schizoid position (Klein, 1952) when objects are split into ideal and persecutory ones, and introjected as such into the early superego. When during analysis the fixation to this earliest position lessens, and the patient begins to move towards the depressive position as is shown in a greater capacity to experience love and hate–ambivalence–and therefore concern for the object, we encounter not only changes in the ego and the object relations but also in the superego. It seems to me that these changes in the ego and superego which begin in the depressive position are essential for normal superego development.

This patient's analysis followed a pattern which I have also experienced with other patients. The changes in the patient's superego occurred very slowly over several years and went hand in hand with gradual changes in her ego. The early relationship to the good breast/mother came increasingly into the analysis and the importance of violent oral sadistic impulses existing considerably before weaning emerged. At first her attacks on the analyst as a feeding mother always led again to fears of persecutory counter-attacks and punishment. In addition there were demands that the analyst should be an ideal breast and mother who should be inexhaustible, never frustrate, and particularly never arouse envy or hate. This ideal breast/mother also appeared as a superego figure making enormous demands on the patient to be perfect and give whatever was demanded. At this time the father appeared much less as an idealized figure, and it became clear that much of the earlier idealization of the father had been transferred from the idealized breast or mother to the father. This was very concretely expressed in a dream of the patient in which she fastened a beautiful breast neatly on to a man's jacket. As the patient's capacity to experience ambivalence increased there was a lessening of her fear of punishment, and she gained more confidence in her capacity to love and repair the damage to her loved object, indicating the emergence of a more forgiving and accepting superego. This positive change in the patient's superego seems to be typical for the superego of the depressive position.

## Conclusions

I have attempted to illustrate that the patient's adult superego contained some reparative qualities as shown in the dream of the father's damaged heart. However, a large part of her superego had retained the ruthless persecutory quality of the very early superego. She attempted to deal with some of the persecutory anxieties by uncritically surrendering to her real father as a superego figure at a later period, probably at the age of four or five. Some of the idealization of the breast and of the earlier relationship to the father was transferred and projected on to the real father with whom she identified as her ego-ideal. The real aspects of the superego father reinforced by the idealization were also used to deny and split off some of the persecutory qualities which were also projected into this relationship. This factor strengthened the later superego in its defensive function of preventing the persecutory aspects of the early superego from being reactivated.

There remains the question whether the superego development of this particular patient should be considered as a fairly typical one. I am suggesting that, while the degree of persecutory anxiety in the patient's early superego was unusually severe, the point that emerges is of general validity: that is, that there is a direct relationship between the intensity of the early persecutory superego and the patient's need to make absolute uncritical identifications with the real parents or parent substitutes as later superego figures. This factor I believe to be essential for the understanding of the later superego. Selective identification with the real objects and their qualities is an important factor of normal ego and superego development, and this is possible only if the early superego has overcome most of its persecutory quality. As the depressive position is a central factor in assisting the change from the persecutory to the more normal, ego-syntonic superego, we may say that normal superego development depends on the degree to which the depressive position has been worked through in infancy and later childhood.

# 9

# NOTES ON THE PSYCHOPATHOLOGY
# AND PSYCHO-ANALYTIC TREATMENT
# OF SCHIZOPHRENIA[1] (1963)

MY interest in the psychological approach to schizophrenia goes back more than twenty-five years. At that time I had the opportunity of interviewing a large number of schizophrenic patients in the Maudsley Hospital and I noticed that some of them regarded psychological problems as the cause of their illness. I remember a young catatonic schizophrenic girl of sixteen who explained to me that she became ill after she had discovered the facts of life. She found it unbearable to think about the details of her birth from the inside of her mother. She explained that this was the reason why she did not want to have anything to do with her mother or anybody else. She did not want to read any more because she was afraid of having to visualize again something which was similarly unbearable. In fact it seemed as if this girl had, as a result of this experience, turned away from the outer world and from all her interests which were related to it. My observations at that time had the effect of making me increasingly doubtful about the prevalent contemporary teaching, which suggested that schizophrenia should be regarded as an endogenous problem which became manifest completely uninfluenced by external circumstances. At a later time I had the opportunity of trying some psychotherapy with schizophrenics in various hospitals and was astonished that I succeeded in making good contact with some very ill schizophrenic patients and that they could be helped by simple psychotherapeutic talks. In other cases, however, I felt completely helpless, especially when I realized that, after some initial improvement, the patients became very much worse.

During my training as an analyst my second control case turned out to be a latent schizophrenic and my supervisor

[1] First published by the American Psychiatric Association (*Psychiatric Research Report* No. 17).

thought that an acute schizophrenic breakdown might occur if I continued the psycho-analytic approach. I was aware of this danger, but my interest in the analysis of schizophrenia was much too strong for me to follow this advice. I continued the analysis, though without understanding at first what was going on between the patient and myself. The material which the patient produced and the transference seemed to be very unusual and none of the analytic books helped me over it.

At this time Melanie Klein began to develop her own observations on schizoid mechanisms and object relations and published a paper on this subject (Klein, 1946). When I became convinced of the importance of Melanie Klein's work in my own analysis I found it possible to use my observations and counter-transference intuitively, and began to understand and to interpret the schizophrenic transference situation of my patient. She made slow but certain progress in her three years' analysis, which was interrupted by her marrying and joining her husband, who lived abroad. She had children and has apparently remained well. As a result of my experiences with this case, Mildred, I wrote in 1947 the paper 'Analysis of a Schizophrenic State with Depersonalization' (chap. 1 in this volume).

I will now try to give a brief picture of the difficulties which confronted me at that time and which at first left me completely helpless. I assume that many readers who have treated schizophrenic patients have probably met with similar problems.

The patient came to the analysis as if she was an automaton and communicated the impression that the uncertain relationship with me could be broken off at any moment. She often told me she had nothing to say and actually she talked very little. When she spoke, she described certain phenomena with great clarity. She felt bored and without any interest; she felt there was something like a blanket separating her from the world so that she felt dead and cut off from herself. She was afraid that her thinking might come to a standstill, and that she might drift into an unconscious state. She tried constantly to force herself to resist this tendency, but she was also afraid that if she tried to join up with herself she might force her mind completely out of joint, an anxiety which created an inhibition of all her activities. Gradually the difficulties of the patient concentrated not only on talking in the analysis but on coming to her sessions. At times she was forty to forty-five minutes late and so arrived just before the end of her session. She felt it was a hopeless fight to get up in the morning; it seemed like a fight against the Devil but there was no point in fighting this Devil because he was stronger than everybody. The patient's mother tried, as always, to help her. The patient welcomed this, but she complained that her mother's help was senseless because as soon as somebody told her what to do or asked her what she wanted to do she felt trapped and blocked. Afterwards she always became very tired and unable to do anything. I want to emphasize here that the mother of this patient was generally understanding, affectionate, and not dominating. For example, she allowed the patient to stay in bed in the morning and served her with breakfast herself.

It seemed to me at this time that I represented in the analytic transference-situation the patient's mother, and the patient expressed by her attitude the wish that I should, both in the analysis and in the outside world, be a mother who would do for her everything that she needed without her having to say or ask for anything. I interpreted the negative transference at first as her reaction against my not being this ideal mother; in other words, my being experienced as a useless and bad mother. I had often observed that the patient felt criticized and dominated by me in the same way that she had described herself as being in her relation to her mother. However, interpretations of this type appeared to make no impression. Very much later I discovered that from the beginning of the analysis a very particular transference situation had developed. On the first day of the analysis I had explained to her that she should tell me in the analysis everything she was thinking or feeling. She, however, was convinced, though without mentioning it for the first one and a half years, that I had told her that she should push everything that she was thinking and feeling aside and think of something completely different. So from the start she had formed a delusional transference to me in which I was not only experienced by her as a criticizing and dominating figure but in which she was convinced that I demanded that she should give up her own thinking and her own self in order to become somebody completely different.

I have explained that I had observed that the patient felt that having to come for treatment and to talk meant being criticized and dominated by me. It was never possible to ask her to repeat anything she was saying when she spoke indistinctly because she immediately fell into a silence which lasted until the end of the hour. The exact nature of her anxiety became clear when acute fears appeared that she might one day find herself talking in a strange voice or accent. I was then able to diagnose the patient's fear that I would force myself into her in order to dominate her so that she would lose her own thoughts and feelings and her own self. This transference anxiety, or transference psychosis, dominated her so severely that she was not only unable to show any feelings towards me but had continuously to fight against tendencies to withdraw entirely from me. Further analysis showed that the basis of this transference situation was not derived directly from the real mother but from a dominating fantasy-image whom the patient had projected on to the mother and the analyst, based on the patient's impulses to force herself omnipotently into the analyst and mother to dominate and control them. A very important cause of her lack of feelings seemed to be the necessity to get rid of her negative and positive feelings, as most of her feelings were experienced as intruding, or dominating, and consequently dangerous. As a result of the understanding and the interpretation of the problems in the transference situation real contact with the patient was established, the analysis became alive, and the patient was able to improve. Since this first successful analysis of schizophrenia I discovered in all my schizophrenic patients transference relations which were either a direct expression or a defence against the primitive object relation where the patient intruded with positive or negative parts of his personality into his objects and as a result felt treated in a similar way by his internal and external objects. These primitive object relations often lead either to the psychotic identification of the schizophrenic when he assumes a different identity or to a confusional state. Melanie Klein described these primitive object relations and the ego disturbances related to them under the collective name 'projective identification'. She stressed the splitting off and the projection of parts of the infantile self and the identification of these parts with the mother and other objects. Analysts such as Mahler, Jacobson and others have acknowledged the importance of these early object relations which lead to a fusion with the mother, but without recognizing the importance of the persecutory anxieties and the splitting processes which are part of this situation. Bion, and others besides myself, have applied the concept of projective identification to the treatment of schizophrenia and have enlarged it through a number of observations.

The study of projective identification and its relation to ego-splitting has helped us to a better understanding of certain typical schizophrenic difficulties of thought and language. For example, the splitting and projection of parts of the self leads not only to a confusion of ego and objects, but to interference with such functions of the ego as abstract thinking and the use and understanding of words, so that patients may lose the capacity to speak or may become unable to understand correctly what is being said.

I shall now examine briefly the question of the connexion between the understanding of the psychopathology and its relation to the technique of analysing schizophrenics and shall make use of Mildred's analysis again. It seemed at first that the interpretations of the positive or negative transference were quite useless; the analysis was very near breaking point, and one had to consider seriously whether analytic interpretations and the technique used so far should be continued, or whether the technique should be changed completely. Perhaps some therapists might be of the opinion that instead of interpreting that Mildred wanted an ideal relationship to me as the mother, I should have shown by action that I *was* now this ideal mother, allowing her to stay in bed, and starting to visit her at home. I shall not examine how Mildred might have reacted to such actions of the analyst, but it is important to emphasize that I myself attempt to adhere to the principle that, when my interpretations do not meet with success, my understanding and my interpretations must be at fault and need revision. Under such circumstances I do not think it useful to change my technique, but attempt to understand the analytic material and the transference better so as to reach the patient with my interpretations. With Mildred the interpretations did not help because they were only partially correct, as I had not recognized the main problem of her specific delusional negative transference. Psychotic patients, whether they are manic depressives or schizophrenics, exert on the analyst a very strong pressure to act out. It needs courage and understanding and also some certainty in one's understanding of the psychopathology to resist this pressure in order not to relinquish the analytic situation. In Mildred's analysis it was important to understand and interpret the demand for an ideal relationship as a defence against the negative transference which was a specifically paranoid one. When this hidden paranoid transference was interpreted, the relationship to the analyst became more real and a relationship between patient and analyst began to develop where besides the psychotic transference a certain non-psychotic transference appeared. This non-psychotic transference can be observed in the analysis of both acute and chronic schizophrenic patients. It is at first weak and uncertain and tends to disappear again for long periods, but it is developed and strengthened by the use of transference interpretations which have a meaning for the patient: I regard this factor as of central importance for the analysis of schizophrenia.

I have often stressed that in the analysis of schizophrenia I retain the basic principles of the classic analytic technique and compare the analysis of schizophrenia with the classical analysis of children which was developed by Melanie Klein. In the analysis of schizophrenia, as in the analysis of children, one does not insist on free association or on the patient lying on the couch. Instead one uses the words and the whole behaviour of the patient, for example his gestures and actions, as analytic material. I suggested calling the transference which develops with schizophrenics and other psychotics 'transference psychosis', and it is the task of the analyst to follow this transference psychosis in all its positive and negative details and to convey this understanding to the patient in interpretations. I observed that even in the acute states the patients are able to understand the interpretations and to respond to them, a factor which cannot only be deduced from the patient's direct confirmation, but from the change in the analytic material.

I shall now bring material from the analysis of an acute schizophrenic patient and shall attempt to show the strong positive and negative impulses related to the transference psychosis and the response to transference interpretations. In such cases the negative impulses are usually not just a direct expression of disappointment, jealousy, envy, and something similar but also usually have a paranoid character. The genital and oral transference impulses are often completely confused, and although this transference is partially derived from the later oedipal complex, certain elements of a much earlier phase of ego development, such as splitting of the ego, splitting of objects, confusion of ego and objects or projective identification, can be clearly observed. Of the family history of the patient I need only mention that Anne saw very little of her father in early infancy as he was away in the war for five years. The mother tried to continue the father's business and left the child and the older brother to a Nanny who was deeply loved and idealized by the patient. When Anne was twelve years old she had her first severe schizophrenic breakdown. She refused all food and felt persecuted by auditory and visual hallucinations. She became completely negativistic and had to be tube-fed. After about one year the patient had a remission but later she suffered further schizophrenic episodes which each time lasted about one year. I saw her in her fourth episode and after two months' analysis in the acute state she improved so much that she was able to come to my consulting-room by herself for two years. She gradually made progress but defended herself against her sexual impulses in the transference situation and acted out with a great number of men, which often caused her considerable difficulties. The danger of a new acute state was foreshadowed by a strong tendency to make herself independent of me and to deny all her problems. She was obviously terrified of bringing her sexual problems into the transference situation. I tried to prepare Anne's parents for the return of the acute condition which I expected to become manifest after the analysis had broken through the defensive state. However, when the acute state returned the parents looked upon this as a great calamity, but with some reservations they allowed me to continue the treatment in a nursing home. In the earlier (third) acute schizophrenic state the patient's sexual genital impulses had been greatly suppressed and displaced to various parts of her body. She often complained of heat or smoked a cigarette in an excited way. In contrast to this the fourth acute schizophrenic episode was characterized by sexual genital excitement and wishes which were *openly* expressed. One might therefore regard the fourth episode not so much as a relapse as an attempt to progress. As is usual in the acute phase of schizophrenia the splitting and repression diminished and her ego was temporarily overwhelmed by the strong libidinal and aggressive impulses.

In the acute state I saw the patient for one hour six times a week. In the first consultation in the clinic the patient, who was acutely excited and hallucinated, came towards me, shook my

L

hand, and said, 'I had almost forgotten you.' After this she turned away from me quickly and paced the room from one side to the other. She kept her eyes tightly shut and sometimes knocked against the chairs and other furniture; sometimes she suddenly jumped into the air. The pacing of the patient gave the impression that she was driven simultaneously by panic and despair. One felt that she did not know where she wanted to go; sometimes one felt that she wanted to run in many different directions at the same time. From time to time she exclaimed, 'Get out, get out, don't talk to me!' In between she looked in the mirror and said, 'The face is the only thing I have left. I am a cannibal, I am falling to bits, I had a haemorrhage, I am shot through the brain.' Suddenly she took a bottle which stood on the shelf and threw it out of the window as if she wanted to emphasize that she felt persecuted by me and therefore tried to throw me out. As soon as I started to talk to her she shouted at me again to stop me. I tried to show her that she was terrified of me because she believed that I had changed into somebody very dangerous. In the second consultation the patient at first continued her pacing up and down and avoided looking at me. I interpreted that she was afraid to look at me because she had turned away from me in hate and she believed now that I had become hostile and extremely dangerous. She immediately stood still, looked me full in the face and said, 'You are dead; are you going to kill me?' Then she came very close to me and said, 'I shall not turn away from you now.' She became very affectionate and put her arms around me and wanted to be kissed by me. In such a situation I would not push the patient away but control the sexual approaches by not reacting to them. After some time she put her hands round my throat and said, 'Now I will kill you.' In between she talked about her father, explaining that he was absent in the war. She asked, 'Where is my Daddy?' and stroked my face. I interpreted that she had gone right back to her childhood when her father was away in the war and she wanted him. She believed that I was her father and wanted to possess me completely. I showed her too that her love quickly changed into hate when I did not react exactly in the way she wanted. In fact her feelings changed frequently and quickly during the session. She asked me whether I came from Russia, whether I was a Nazi or a cannibal. At one moment she seemed afraid that I would kiss her and struck me hard across my face and said she would kill me. She also said, 'My mother is a man.' I interpreted that she was not sure whether I was the father or the mother and that she was also not sure whether I came as friend or enemy. She was afraid that I would eat her up in revenge, which was one of the reasons for striking me in the face. I had the impression that the patient at this time completely confused eating and sexual intercourse. To possess her father and mother sexually meant for her to eat the parents and to be eaten by them. As long as she was in the acute state I made no attempt to interpret all the material but only what was characteristic and important for the present transference situation. The patient often showed a distinct response to my interpretations. For example, when I interpreted that I had changed into somebody hostile and dangerous her anxiety lessened and in her reply, 'You are dead; will you kill me?' she not only showed her understanding of my interpretation but elaborated it further by telling me that I was persecuting because she felt I *was dead*. During the next session the patient talked about her mother as a murderess from Russia who had killed many people. She herself was also a murderer. She said she was very clever and I was stupid and empty-headed. She stressed again that her mother was a man. I said that she wanted to show me that she now was a man herself and had a penis. She responded very quickly 'Yes, I had one until I was twelve years old and then I had a haemorrhage. Harold shot me and pushed my teeth in. She immediately asked me whether I was Harold. I said she believed that Harold had taken away her penis and made her ill and she felt now that I was Harold and had taken away her penis and her mind. I also interpreted that she was envious of me and my mind and that was the reason why she wanted to enter my head and wanted to take away my penis. In this session she shouted at me several times that I was mad and prevented me from talking. It seemed to mean that she felt she had castrated me and driven me mad and was therefore afraid that I would retaliate in similar fashion. Because of the strength of her anxiety, I believe that in this situation some projective identification played an important part, namely that she feared that she had put her madness into me so that I had become a mad person. Therefore I interpreted that she knew that the thoughts which she had about Harold and me were mad ones, that she wanted to get rid of them and pushed them into me. I explained that

she was envious of my sanity which caused her to attack me
and that she was afraid that I would put her mad thoughts and
ideas back into her through my talking. That was the reason
why she felt my words as an attack and why she could not bear
my speaking. In this session the patient brought her castration
anxieties and wishes very clearly into the analysis. Madness, her
first schizophrenic illness when she was twelve years old, and
castration are very closely related for her. Harold is no real
acquaintance or relative; he is a fantasy-image of an extremely
rich and omnipotent father-figure who is generally experienced
as persecuting. Apart from the persecuting castration problem
the aggressive projection of anxiety situations and bad parts
of the ego into the analyst play an important part. Whenever
the patient projected the bad parts of herself—for example, her
illness or other unpleasant parts of her personality—into me,
her fear of my talking became very acute. The projection of the
mad or bad part of the patient plays an important part in the
analysis of most acute or chronic schizophrenic patients. It is
often accompanied by an acute negative transference caused
by the patient's fear of retaliation following the attack by
projection.

The reason for the projection relates not simply to the wish
of the patient to get rid of her illness, but also to the patient's
envy of the analyst, standing for the superior healthy adult; it
is an expression of the infantile omnipotent wish to reverse the
infant-parent position.

During the next session the patient was at first manically
excited and danced round the room. She declared she wanted
to marry me, examined my hand, saw my ring, became furious
and shouted that she hated me and my wife. Then she became
manic again and very superior and said she was now a doctor of
medicine and a man. In her manic excitement she had reversed
the situation, in an omnipotent way; however, the manic state
did not last long. She quickly became aware of her dependence
on me, was overwhelmed by fury, and attempted to destroy the
furniture in the room. At the same time she shouted that she
wanted to break up marriages. Then she talked again about me
as Harold and as a relative and about marriage. When I interpreted that she wanted to marry me as her father she replied
immediately 'obscene' and seemed disgusted. She talked about
me and my wife and said 'I want to kill you both' and then she

screamed again 'Get out, get out of here!' as on the first day of
her analysis, in the acute state.

During the next day she at first did not want to look at me.
She said, 'I don't love you, I myself am married and I love
somebody else, I am Hitler and hate the Jews.' In one moment
she said she wanted to break in my face; afterwards she tried to
tear her own dress. Later on she said, 'Kill me and rape me;
I do not want to live any more.' Here it is clear that the oedipal
situation is experienced by the patient with great intensity; it
is related to murderous fantasies which are directed against the
parents and against the analyst. In this session she was much less
persecuted and more aggressive and afterwards deeply depressed.

During the next few months many fantasies and situations
were repeated in the transference. Sometimes she complained
that I visited her during the night. These nightly hallucinations
often had a sadistic and persecuting character. She sometimes
expressed delusions of being split into a masculine and feminine
self. She called her masculine part after the musical play 'Annie
Get Your Gun'. Her omnipotent manic impulses and fantasies
were often related to this masculine self as an expression of her
independence and denial of needs. When she was in the feminine
role she often said she was full of blood and spiders and attacked
her abdomen in order to press all the bad things out. Sometimes
she tried to cut off her breasts or to damage them. She said
they were full of blood and I should suck the blood out of them.
The bad things which she experienced inside herself were,
among others, a stolen penis, blood, children, and the breasts of
her mother, which she felt she had stolen and spoilt in her
fantasies. This made it impossible for her to identify with her
good mother and to accept her own femininity. As I explained
before, the patient was unable in the chronic mute state of the
illness to bear a strong sexual transference to me and acted it
out. In the acute state it became apparent why her sexual
impulses and fantasies were so unbearable: they were accompanied by overwhelmingly strong murderous sadistic fantasies.

During the acute schizophrenic state the splitting of the ego
lessens. This leads to states of confusion but there are also
attempts to reconstruct the ego and the object relations in a
better way. In Anne the drive for integration often became clear
even during the acute state, and I was able to observe attempts
to regain her normal self and her normal thinking. The patient

sometimes asked me 'Why don't you help me to bring everything together?' or she looked questioningly at me saying 'Where has your common sense gone?' Simultaneously she talked about reflections in the mirror. Here I became by projection the mirror image of the patient, namely somebody who has lost his mind; at the same time the patient felt that she had lost the capacity to regain her own ego and her femininity. The main dynamic importance of such transference situations is the use of the analyst as the functioning integrating ego in whom the patient has not only projected her madness but whom she also suspects of containing the sane part of herself, which she attempts to regain with the help of the analyst. During the next three or four months, while still in an acute state, the patient made good progress and became much quieter and clearer. The parents were very enthusiastic and insisted, against my advice, on taking her home. This was too early, because she was not well enough, as we soon saw, to come from her house to my consulting-room. On the other hand, her parents could not bring themselves to send her back again to the nursing home. I was forced to see the patient in her own house, but this brought the progress of the analysis almost to a standstill. As a consequence of various difficulties, among which a short illness of mine played an important part, the analysis was interrupted. This shows how extremely important it is to have the complete cooperation of the parents in the analysis of a psychotic patient. Despite the interruption of the analysis, I heard that the patient has improved further and has married.

At the end of this paper I would like to say a few words about the aetiology of schizophrenia. In investigating a number of schizophrenic patients it was apparent that psychogenic trauma in infancy played an important part. Anne, apparently because of the absence of her father during the war, had been deprived of the opportunity to work through the oedipal situation with her real parents. This contributed to the fact that the oedipal fantasies remained omnipotent and unreal. The preoccupation with incest was perhaps increased through the fact that the parents were first cousins. In the case of Mildred the trauma appeared to be the birth of her brother when she was one and a half years old. In another case an early weaning situation when the patient was ten days old seemed to be an insuperable obstacle. As far as the parents of schizophrenic patients are concerned, we hear that Mildred's mother was particularly affectionate and motherly; her father however was egotistical and dominating. In the case of Anne, both parents were very neurotic and it seemed that they used the illness of their daughter to deny and split off their own problems. The mother always wanted to have Anne around when she was ill and she felt extremely guilty when she had to be sent to a nursing home during the acute episodes. Anne herself was quite aware how strongly she was able by her illness and her difficulties to influence and dominate her parents. On the other hand, it was very obvious how much she was herself influenced and dominated by them. But similar traumas and problems related to the parents of our patients are known to us from our experiences with neurotic patients and are not typical for schizophrenia. The examinations of a large number of parents and families of schizophrenic patients have shown that the parents of schizophrenics have no character traits which can be regarded as typical and the existence of a schizophrenogenic mother has been disproved by many investigators.

The analysis of schizophrenic patients again and again illustrates that disturbances and problems of earliest infancy continue, influence, and hinder later developmental phases. In discussing these disturbances I have concentrated especially on the splitting of the ego and projective identification. Even in the case of Anne, who was completely dominated by her sexual fantasies, it was possible to observe the splitting of the ego and the projection of parts of the self. In Anne's case one could also illustrate the importance of the problem of confusion which, as Melanie Klein has shown, can also be traced back to disturbances in the first year of life. The case histories of many schizophrenics emphasize that the patients had shown some signs of peculiarity from early on in life and were never able to express strong feelings. There had been a tendency to turn away from the outside world at the least provocation. However, there are other cases in which the development seemed to be comparatively normal until suddenly, for example after childbirth, a severe schizophrenia becomes manifest. I am of the opinion that psychotic parts of the personality may be split off in very earliest infancy while other parts of the self may develop apparently normally. Under certain circumstances the *split-off psychotic parts* may break through to the surface, often producing an acute psychosis, for example a schizophrenia. One has to assume that a certain predisposition to the psychosis exists from birth. In such cases the destructive instinct seems constitutionally stronger and dominates the rudimentary ego, which as a consequence develops a tendency to fragmentation and splitting. Under such circumstances the paranoid-schizoid mechanisms such as projective identification become greatly reinforced.

When we consider the question of a disturbed mother-infant relationship in the first year of life it is important to consider not only the influence of the mother on the child but the reaction of the mother to a particularly difficult schizoid infant. As Bion has often suggested, and I myself believe, some mothers of children who have a tendency to schizophrenia show a diminished tolerance towards the projections of the infant. They feel disturbed and persecuted and withdraw their feelings from the child. One has the impression that the infant not only notices the responses of the mother but actually feels responsible for it, which increases the infant's omnipotent belief that his intruding into his mother has actually changed her. This may be one of the reasons why, during the analysis, the patient's omnipotent fantasies of intrusion into the analyst play such an important part. The capacity of the analyst to bear this relation, to understand and to interpret it, makes it possible to work through and correct in the analysis the disturbed mother-infant relationship and so help the patient to find a basis for a more normal development.

# 10

# ON THE PSYCHOPATHOLOGY OF
# NARCISSISM: A CLINICAL APPROACH[1]
## (1964)

FREUD was pessimistic about the psycho-analytic approach to the narcissistic neuroses. He felt that people suffering from these diseases had no capacity for transference, or only insufficient remnants of one. He described the resistance of these patients as a stone wall which cannot be got over, and said that they turn from the physician not in hostility but in indifference. Many analysts have tried to develop methods of analysis which would deal with narcissistic patients–I am thinking of Waelder (1925), Clark (1933), and later Fromm-Reichmann (1943, 1947), Bion (1962), Rosenfeld, and others. The majority of analysts who have treated narcissistic patients have disagreed with Freud's view that there was no transference. As the transference is the main vehicle for any analytic investigation, it seems essential for the understanding of narcissism that the behaviour of the narcissist in the analytic transference situation should be minutely observed.

Franz Cohn (1940) suggested that the sharp distinction between transference neurosis and narcissistic neurosis should be disregarded. He felt that the transference in the narcissistic neurosis is of a primitive or rudimentary type–for example, there are often serious difficulties in distinguishing between subject and object–and he stresses the introjection and projection of destructive tendencies in oral and anal terms in relation to the analyst. Stone (1954) described transferences which are 'literally narcissistic', where the analyst is confused with the self or is like the self in all respects: the therapist and the patient alternately seem to be parts of each other. He stresses both the primitive destructiveness and the need to experience the analyst as an omnipotent, godlike figure, and suggests that, in the patient's

[1] Read at the 23rd International Psycho-Analytical Congress, Stockholm, July–August, 1963, and first published in the *Int. J. Psycho-Anal.*, **45**.

fantasy about the analyst's omnipotence, guilt about primitive destructive aggression plays an important part.

Many of the observations made by Cohn (1940) and Stone (1954) seem to come close to my own investigation. I notice that in their description of the narcissistic transferences the terms 'primary' and 'secondary' narcissism are not used. Instead we meet with such terms as 'omnipotence', 'confusion of the self and objects', 'introjection of objects', 'projection of aggression into objects', 'insatiable demands towards objects', and 'nullification'. The use of these terms in describing narcissistic patients seems valuable, but it appears to me important and necessary to define more clearly the nature of the relation to objects in narcissism and the particular defence mechanisms related to them. This may be a contradiction in terms, because for many analysts primary narcissism implies an objectless state. But we should remember that Freud regarded the oceanic feeling, the longing for union with God or the Universe, as a primary narcissistic experience. Federn (1929), in discussing primary narcissism, describes the baby's craving for the mother's breast, but suggests that the object is as yet not external to the ego feeling. Abraham (1924) discusses limitless narcissism as a relation to an object in which, while the object is incorporated, the individual pays no attention whatever to the interests of his object, but destroys it without the least hesitation. Balint (1960) went so far as to suggest that what Freud described as primary narcissism should be called primary object love. I myself believe that much confusion would be avoided if we were to recognize that the many clinically observable conditions which resemble Freud's description of primary narcissism are in fact primitive object relations.

In narcissistic object relations omnipotence plays a prominent part. The object, usually a part-object, the breast, may be omnipotently incorporated, which implies that it is treated as the infant's possession; or the mother or breast are used as containers into which are omnipotently projected the parts of the self which are felt to be undesirable as they cause pain or anxiety.

Identification is an important factor in narcissistic object relations. It may take place by introjection or by projection. When the object is omnipotently incorporated, the self becomes so identified with the incorporated object that all separate identity or any boundary between self and object is denied. In projective identification parts of the self omnipotently enter an object, for example the mother, to take over certain qualities which would be experienced as desirable, and therefore claim to be the object or part-object. Identification by introjection and by projection usually occur simultaneously.

In narcissistic object relations defences against any recognition of separateness between self and object play a predominant part. Awareness of separation would lead to feelings of dependence on an object and therefore to anxiety. Dependence on an object implies love for, and recognition of, the value of the object, which leads to aggression, anxiety, and pain because of the inevitable frustrations and their consequences. In addition, dependence stimulates envy, when the goodness of the object is recognized. The omnipotent narcissistic object relations therefore obviate both the aggressive feelings caused by frustration and any awareness of envy. When the infant omnipotently possesses the mother's breast, the breast cannot frustrate him or arouse his envy. Envy is particularly unbearable to the infant and increases the difficulty in admitting dependence and frustration. It seems that the strength and persistence of omnipotent narcissistic object relations are closely related to the strength of the infant's envy. Envy has omnipotent qualities; it seems that it contributes to the omnipotence of the narcissistic object relations while the envy itself may be simultaneously split off and denied. In my clinical observations of narcissistic patients the projection of undesirable qualities into the object plays an important part. The analyst is often pictured in dreams and fantasies as a lavatory or lap. This relationship implies that any disturbing feeling or sensation can immediately be evacuated into the object without any concern for it, the object being generally devalued. In severe narcissistic disturbances we can invariably see the maintenance of a rigid defence against any awareness of psychic reality, since any anxiety which is aroused by conflicts between parts of the self or between self and reality is immediately evacuated. The anxiety which is thus defended against is mainly of a paranoid nature, since narcissistic object relations date from earliest infancy when anxiety is predominantly paranoid.

Clinically, narcissistic object relations often appear to the analyst and are also experienced by the patient as very ideal and desirable object relations. For example the relation to the lavatory/mother in the analysis is frequently felt as ideal, because the patient feels relieved when everything unpleasant can be immediately discharged into the analyst during a session. When the patient claims to possess the analysis, as the feeding breast, he gives himself credit for all the analyst's satisfactory interpretations, a situation which is experienced as perfect or ideal because it increases the patient's feeling during the analytic session that he is good and important. Sometimes narcissistic patients picture themselves in a mutually satisfactory ideal relationship with the analyst where the identity of patient and analyst is not differentiated, a situation reminiscent of Freud's description of the oceanic feeling. Another instance of narcissistic idealization is the patient who feels that he is loved by everyone, or demands to be loved by everyone, because he is so lovable. All these patients seem to have in common the feeling that they contain all the goodness which would otherwise be experienced in a relationship to an object. We usually encounter simultaneously a highly idealized self image, which dominates the analytic situation, and anything interfering with this picture is rigorously defended against and omnipotently denied.

I shall now illustrate some of the problems related to severe narcissism by bringing case material from a patient who showed a marked narcissistic transference without being overtly psychotic. There is nothing in the patient's history which would seem to account for his persistent narcissistic attitude. He is the son of fairly wealthy parents, and he has two sisters. He had apparently always managed superficially to get on quite well with people, and was successful at school because of his high intelligence. When he started treatment he had just married and he had some difficulties with his wife. Apart from an occasional feeling of oneness with her he was very jealous and intensely preoccupied with her relations with other people, men and women. The analysis revealed the depth of the patient's narcissism, his lack of emotional contact with other people, and, as a result, the lack of pleasure in his life which made him envious of everybody. He particularly envied his wife who, he felt, was far more capable than he was of enjoying relations with people, including himself. When I first saw the patient he appeared slightly withdrawn from reality and from other people, and had a vaguely superior and patronizing attitude which he tried to disguise. He admitted that he occasionally felt frustrated in personal relations, with friends and his young wife, but generally he blamed them for any difficulty which arose. He was very interested in being analysed in spite of the fact that he did not feel that he really needed analysis. He pictured himself almost immediately as the perfect patient who made enormous progress, but in fact he could make very little proper use of the analysis. He constantly projected his problems into his wife or other people, including the analyst, and was quite unable to experience them as belonging to himself. He enjoyed interpreting his own dreams in detail and explaining his thoughts and feelings, but any conflict, anxiety, or depression which emerged was so quickly discharged that it could barely be experienced. He did not resent interpretations, but on the contrary took them up quickly and talked about them in his own way, feeling very self-satisfied with his knowledge since he did not feel that the analyst had made any contribution. His attitude made it extremely difficult to effect any change in his personality, so that one felt up against a stone wall in a way reminiscent of Freud's description. Behind this stone wall there seemed to be omnipotence hiding hostility and envy, completely denied by the patient and difficult to demonstrate in the analytic material. After I had shown him again and again his avoidance of any close contact with myself or with his own feelings, particularly hostility towards me, he came to a session saying that he now wanted to get closer to his problems. He then told me a dream in which he and others were travelling in a very fast train. He suddenly saw a kind of surrealistic machine land near the train and send out towards it a wide ray of very dangerous fire. Luckily the train escaped this attack by quickly moving away, but there was a feeling that the attack would be repeated. The patient felt that this machine was sent over from Russia by a man who had apparently lived in England before but felt bitter and revengeful because of some ill treatment which he believed he had received. There was a feeling in the dream that some widespread attacks were going to be made on various places in England, mainly hotels with such names as Royal, Royalty, Majestic, Palace, etc., and yet that the attacks were being directed against his parents. There also seemed to be a food shortage. Two girls were in the train with him. In another part of the dream there were a number of girls leaning against a stone wall and prostituting themselves because of the food shortage. He approached one of them and said 'Would you like a customer?' but she only laughed, and he felt disappointed, since his approach was made seriously. In his associations he thought that the Russian must be associated with himself, as he felt sympathy with him as though the Russian had a right to make these attacks. He thought he must have hated his parents to be important and therefore felt slighted by them. He thought that the Russian must have wanted to be the most important person himself and that the attacks were a result of his feeling humiliated and therefore resentful. The patient had very little emotional reaction to the dream.

The dream shows very clearly the omnipotent virulence of an extremely hostile omnipotent part of his personality which makes attacks both on the important superior parents and on a part of himself. The reason for the attacks is obviously derived from his babyhood envy of the important grown-ups because the parents, in his associations, are accused of humiliating him and making him feel small. It is also clear in the dream that the Russian has a paranoid grudge, which is an admission of his own paranoid attitude which is consciously denied. The train moving quickly to avoid any contact with the destructive rays is related to his train of thought and his own self containing the two breasts (girls). In fact he prides himself on being able to move extremely quickly and cleverly, and so in his thoughts being able to avoid any contact with his destructive self. The dream implies that making contact with the analyst as an important parental figure arouses dangerous, envious, paranoid impulses. It is interesting in the dream, that the envious paranoid Russian is placed in the distance, while the destructiveness emanating from him influences the patient's train of thought, his contacts and relations to his parents and women. The dream shows clearly how in narcissistic relationships envy is split off and kept away from self-awareness, and at the same time the patient's destructiveness keeps his object relations devalued and so enables him to by-pass his difficulties. An interesting feature in the dream is the food shortage which makes the girls into prostitutes. This implies that the importance of the breast is denied, and women are devalued into prostitutes, who, lacking food or breasts cannot feed themselves and therefore have to come to the patient to get money for food: this would also indicate a projection of the dependence into the prostitutes.

As the patient had started the session by saying that he had made up his mind to get on with the analysis, in other words wanted to come closer to me, it is clear that the dream reveals not only his attitude to women but to the analyst also. He deals with his fear of being rejected by me by approaching me–in a superior way turning me into a prostitute. It is interesting that the prostitutes lean against a stone wall, which would confirm that the stone wall of the narcissistic transference has to be linked with narcissistic object relations, which are emerging in the analysis.

Following this dream the patient's aggressive superiority towards the analyst was more openly admitted in dreams and associations, but his desire to possess the analysis and feel that it was his own creation was only admitted openly after the following dream. The patient was shopping, and was offered a special kind of salt packed in self-made containers. It was much cheaper than ordinary salt, only ninepence for four pounds. He asked the storekeeper whether it was as good as ordinary salt. In spite of the storekeeper's assurance that it was perfectly all right, the patient himself did not believe it. On leaving the shop it took him about two hours to get home, and he felt guilty because he was afraid that his wife would be waiting anxiously for him. The patient remarked that he had had to buy salt the day before because they had run out of it. He felt sure that the salt must have something to do with the analysis, as four pounds reminded him of coming four times a week to his sessions. He stressed that the salt was so much cheaper because obviously the people had made it up themselves. I could show the patient in this dream that ostensibly he comes to me to have analysis, but he maintains that what he gets from me is his own self-made version of the analysis which he pretends to himself is as good as the ordinary analysis. He obviously tries in the dream to get reassurance from the shopkeeper/analyst that this is right and normal, but he admits that he does not really believe this himself. Staying out late implies a projection into his wife of his feelings of dependence and the anxiety about having to wait. The dream illustrates that the patient has not as yet admitted to himself his dependence on me; it is denied and projected, and this continuously leads to acting out. I would like to add here the general meaning of the self-made version of the analysis, which is clearly represented in this dream, because it plays a very important part in the analysis of many narcissistic patients. While ostensibly the narcissistic patient maintains that he has a superior and sometimes more creative breast in his possession, which gives him better analysis and food than the mother-analyst could ever produce, careful analysis reveals that this highly valued posses-sion of the patient represents his own faeces which have always been highly idealized, a fact carefully concealed by the patient. The unmasking of the situation, while it may temporarily lead to the patient's feeling severely deflated, is essential if real relations to external and internal objects are ever to be established.

In a later dream the patient illustrates how he entirely reverses the relationship to the analyst by omnipotent projective identifi-cations. In the dream the patient was a doctor holding a surgery. He had a cake, and four women were coming to see him. He suspected that these women were only pretending that they were ill in order to get attention. There was some trouble on the roof of the house and he was starting to repair it. A noise was heard of something falling down, or of hammering, and at the first sound the women quickly withdrew, afraid that something might fall on them. In his associations the patient described the women as fat and greedy. The dream shows in an undisguised way that the patient has put himself in the role of the analyst who not only possesses the cake—the breast—but also does the reparative work. His own greedy attitude of simply wanting to get food from the analysis without really admitting that he is ill, and withdrawing from me quickly whenever I make an inter-pretation which might touch him, is projected on to the four women who, as often before, represent the analysis or the analyst (cf. the four pounds of salt). We notice that in the dream the patient has become more appreciative of the analyst and the reparative work of the analysis, and feels critical of his own greedy demands on the analyst and of his constant withdrawals whenever he hears an interpretation which he feels is good. However, he evacuates entirely his unsatisfactory attitude into the analyst, who in the dream is changed into the patient's unsatisfactory self, while he takes over the role of the analyst whom he admires.

I shall now go on to discuss some of the more practical con-siderations in the analysis of narcissistic patients. A powerful resistance in their analysis is derived from their superior omni-potent attitude, which denies any need for dependence and the anxieties related to it. This behaviour is often extremely repetitive, and there are many alternative versions which are used by the narcissistic patient. The intelligent narcissist often uses his intellectual insight to agree verbally with the analyst and recapitulates in his own words what has been analysed in previous sessions. This behaviour not only blocks any contact and progress, but is an example of the narcissistic object relation I have been describing. The patient uses the analytic interpretations but deprives them quickly of life and meaning, so that only meaningless words are left. These words are then felt to be the patient's own possession, which he idealizes and which gives him a sense of superiority. An alternative method is shown by patients who never really accept the analyst's interpretations, but constantly develop theories, which they regard as superior versions of analysis.

In the first case the patient steals the interpretations representing the breast from the analyst/mother, turning them into faeces; he then idealizes them and feeds them back to the analyst. In the second case the patient's own theories are produced as if there were idealized faeces, which are presented as food superior to the breast, which the analyst/mother provides. The main source of this resistance and behaviour comes from the narcissistic patient's denial of envy, which is only forced into the open when he has to recognize the analyst's superiority as a feeding mother. The patient whose dreams I have discussed here gradually admitted that he had to keep vague and uncertain that it was I who actually gave him the analysis, because any real clarity about my role led to unbearable feelings of his being small, hungry, and humiliated, which he deeply resented even when I was available. Occasionally resentment broke through, and the patient felt that I had all the answers and gave him only some. Why should he listen to me or depend on me if what I gave him was not complete? This resentment was derived from envious feelings against the analyst/mother who, possessing the breast, only feeds the child, instead of handing over the breast to him completely. At first such a break-through was only fleeting and the patient guarded against such feelings by quickly putting himself into a superior position to me by thinking of something at which he excelled. There was a powerful resistance also from his ideal self-image which he was slowly able to describe in the following way: 'I want to feel good and have a perfect relation to you. Why should I admit anything bad which would

M

spoil the good picture I have of myself, which I feel you must admire too?'

The rigid preservation of the ideal self-image blocks any progress in the analysis of narcissistic patients, because it is felt to be endangered by any insight and contact with psychic reality. The ideal self-image of the narcissistic patient may be thought of as a highly pathological structure based on the patient's omnipotence and denial of reality.

Only very slowly was the patient able to admit that the keeping up of the ideal self-image meant an elimination of all my interpretations which might endanger the perfect image of himself. He began to notice that he constantly lost contact with everything which had been discussed during the sessions. This was painful to him, but the pain was again quickly eliminated, despite the fact, that it meant expulsion of the good experience with the analyst, which had led to the painful insight. This attitude is very characteristic of the narcissistic patient, and not only pain but insight is expelled again and again. For example, when my patient's need to be dependent came more to the surface, he at first projected the dependence into his wife and acted it out with her by creating a situation where she was depressed and in need. He then explained to her the reasons why she was depressed, and became angry when she did not immediately understand his interpretations and behave properly. However, he gradually became aware that this expulsion of his dependence, and thus insight, constantly created more difficulties and frustrations in his life. We discovered that whenever the patient acknowledged any real understanding about himself and tried not to project his feelings, he became anxious and depressed. At that moment he became confused and he heard himself saying, 'This is dangerous', in response to which he again expelled the anxiety, depression, and insight. I then showed him that what was endangered in such a situation was not his sane or good self but his omnipotent mad self. This struck him very forcibly, and he said it felt to him like driving in his car and coming up against a red light. This of course was a danger signal to stop, but he felt that his danger signal made him feel that he wanted merely to accelerate to get through the red light without stopping, in other words to get through the danger of being confronted with sanity and reality and back into his idealized omnipotent position.

*Clinical Prognosis.* The clinical result of the analysis of a narcissistic patient depends on the degree to which he is gradually able to acknowledge the relationship to the analyst, representing the mother in the feeding situation. This implies an overcoming of some of the problems I have been describing and therefore a recognition of separation and frustration and a working through of what Melanie Klein has called the depressive position. We have also to take into account that some narcissistic patients have often a less narcissistic, a more normal object-directed part of the personality, and improvement has to be measured in terms of the integration of the narcissistic parts of the personality with this. To bring about an improvement, the omnipotent narcissism of the patient and all the aspects related to it have to be laid bare in detail during the analytic process and to be integrated with the more normally concerned part of the patient. It is this part of the analysis which seems to be so unbearable. Splitting results again and again when either the normal or the omnipotent parts of the self are denied. Often the attempt at integration fails because mechanisms related to the omnipotent narcissistic self suddenly take over control of the normal self in an attempt to divert or expel the painful recognition. However, there are patients who gradually succeed in their struggles against narcissistic omnipotence, and this should encourage us as analysts to continue our research into the clinical and theoretical problems of narcissism.

# 11

# THE PSYCHOPATHOLOGY OF
# HYPOCHONDRIASIS (1964)

KNOWLEDGE about a disease called 'Hypochondriasis' dates from the time of Hippocrates, and ever since then it appears to have been a common illness, judging from the literature throughout the ages. At the time of Boswell, who himself suffered from it, hypochondriasis in England was so common as to be called the 'English Malady'. There is a large psychiatric literature on the question as to whether hypochondriasis ever existed as a separate disease entity. Bleuler thought that all patients suffering from chronic hypochondriasis were schizophrenics. Raeke, Westphal, Sommer, Wolfsohn and later Schilder were all in favour of regarding severe chronic hypochondriasis as a 'psychotic disease entity'. Bleuler defined hypochondriasis as a condition consisting in 'continuous attention to one's own state of health, with a tendency to ascribe disease to oneself from insignificant signs and even without such'. The severity of hypochondriasis varies a great deal and it may be valuable to differentiate the disease entity 'hypochondriasis', which is a very chronic psychosis, generally believed to be of bad prognosis, from 'hypochrondriacal states', which are more temporary: they may be psychotic or neurotic in origin. Hypochondriacal states are found in the neuroses and psychoses, as in hysteria and obsessional neurosis; in depressive and neurasthenic conditions; in schizophrenia; and also in the initial states of organic psychosis. They are common in adolescence and in middle age. Temporary hypochondriacal anxieties, for example, may arise when early infantile psychotic, particularly paranoid, anxieties are stimulated and have to be worked over again by the individual. This would explain why hypochondriacal anxieties frequently arise in phases of readjustment, for example at puberty or in middle age. The meaning of these hypochondriacal phases would be similar to the function which Melanie Klein attributes to the infantile neurosis, which she connects with the working over again of early psychotic anxieties.

Chronic hypochondriasis seems to me to be a symptom of a quite different nature. Many external and internal factors contribute to its psychopathology, which I shall discuss in some detail in this chapter. It is interesting to note that whilst hypochondriacal anxieties appear to be a frequent symptom in psycho-analytic patients in analysis, there is relatively little psycho-analytic literature on the subject.

### Review of the Psycho-Analytic Literature on Hypochondriasis

Freud discussed hypochondriacal anxieties as early as 1896. He drew attention to the relationship between the obsessional neurosis and hypochondriacal anxiety, and suggested that the obsessional self-reproaches could transform themselves into hypochondriacal anxiety.

In 1911 he wrote: 'I shall not consider any theory of paranoia trustworthy unless it also covers the *hypochondriacal* symptoms by which that disorder is almost invariably accompanied. It seems to me that hypochondria stands in the same relation to paranoia as anxiety neurosis does to hysteria.' (Freud, 1911, p. 56, n. 3).

In 1914 he said: 'I am inclined to class hypochondria with neurasthenia and anxiety-neurosis as a third "actual" neurosis' (1914b, p. 83). He compared the damming up of ego libido and object libido, and suggested that hypochondriacal anxiety emanating from the ego libido is the counterpart of neurotic anxiety, which he connects with object libido. He explains in some detail that in both neurosis and psychosis (paraphrenia) there is an internal working over of the libido, whether ego-libido or libido attached to real or imaginary objects in the mind. The hypochondriasis of paraphrenia arises, in Freud's opinion, through failure of working over libido in the mental apparatus. In my view, what *cannot* be worked over in the mental apparatus, in hypochondriasis, is not merely libido, but a mixture of libidinal and aggressive impulses and objects which can be specifically defined as a confusional state – a point I shall discuss later.

It seems that as Freud thought of hypochondriasis as an actual neurosis more related to physiology than psychology, he did not believe that the hypochondriacal anxieties had an unconscious

content. Freud made no contribution to the problem of hypochondriasis after 1914. In 1926 he developed his new theory of
the ego as the sole seat of anxiety. Even then he did not completely discard the theory of actual neurosis. His concept of
actual neurosis has been criticized by many writers and it may
well be that it has inhibited rather than stimulated research on
the problem of hypochondriasis.

Ferenczi in 1914 connected hypochondriasis with anal erotism.

Schilder contributed more than any other psycho-analyst to
the problem of hypochondriasis. He drew attention to the similarity of the psychopathology of hypochondriasis and depersonalization, and also stressed that hypochondriacal sensations are
common to neurasthenia as well as to depersonalization. He
thought that the hypochondriacally affected organ is often
genitalized and sometimes symbolizes genitals.

Schilder said there must be a similar mechanism at work in
conversion hysteria, neurasthenia and hypochondriasis. 'Doubtless the conversion is very closely related to projection.' 'In
comparison with our innermost feelings and strivings the body
is outward. When conversion takes place, what has been a
psychic problem is now a disease of the body, which belongs
partly to the outward world, although not so far outward as
other objects.' Schilder concluded that hypochondriasis and
neurasthenic symptoms must have an unconscious meaning
since the conversion implies the getting rid of tormenting conflicts. He described the attempts of the hypochondriac to get
rid of the disturbing part of the body by expelling it. This
attempt at projection, however, fails. He wondered why there
is this projection on to the body and said that in his opinion the
'psychic experience of the body is not as central as the vital and
libidinous problems of the individual which form the centre of
ego and personality'.

He stressed the fixation of the hypochondriac in the narcissistic
phase. He also emphasized a fixation to an early stage of development of the postural model of the body (body schema) which he
believed is not only influenced by bodily sensations, but by
psychological development, for example, by oral sadistic and
sado-masochistic impulses in the infant.

Schilder also drew attention to the importance of compulsive
self-observation, both in hypochondriasis and depersonalization.
He said that to scrutinize hypochondriacally an organ means to

externalize it to a greater or lesser extent. He described a case of hypochondriacal neurasthenia. During the analysis the patient had at first a very strong negative transference. At one period of the treatment the patient projected all his mental and physical sufferings on to the analyst. Schilder called this process 'narcissistic projection'. At a later date, the patient succeeded in identifying himself with the analyst as a healthy person. Schilder did not connect this interesting clinical experience with his theory that the hypochondriac attempts, but fails, to project.

One may criticize Schilder for not attempting to coordinate his many theories and observations about hypochondriasis. However, by acknowledging the importance of the unconscious mental content of hypochondriacal sensations, he showed the way to a deeper analytical understanding of this disease.

Melanie Klein has further opened up our understanding of hypochondriasis by her contributions to the meaning of narcissism. She emphasized that even in narcissistic states, which include hypochondriasis, libidinal and aggressive impulses remain attached to good and bad objects within the ego. She drew attention to the relationship of the conversion symptoms in hysteria and hypochondriasis: 'Experience has shown me that those anxieties which underlie hypochondriasis are also at the root of hysterical conversion symptoms. The fundamental factor common to both is the fear relating to persecution within the body (attacks by internalized persecuting objects, or to harm done to internal objects by the subject's sadism, such as attacks by dangerous excrements), all of which is felt as physical damage inflicted on the ego.' She emphasized that the processes underlying the transformation of persecutory anxieties into physical symptoms have further to be elucidated.

Klein illustrated her theories in several clinical contributions. She showed that during the analysis the hypochondriacal anxieties altered from a paranoid content to a depressive one before they could finally be given up. In an earlier paper she developed the theory that in certain circumstances the mechanism of projection may be put out of action. The ego would then be at the mercy of persecution from within, from which there would be no escape: 'A fear of this kind is probably one of the deepest sources of hypochondria.'

I suggest that this early theory of Klein's is based on the subjective experience of the hypochondriac, who constantly attempts to expel his hypochondriacally disturbed organs and who, at the same time, complains that he is unable to do so. I have tried to show in an earlier paper on hypochondriasis (1958) that the inability of the hypochondriac to use the mechanism of projection is only apparent.

Melanie Klein has always drawn attention to the very close relationship of physical sensations and unconscious fantasies. In her view, for example, sensations due to hunger may be attributed by the young infant to an internal bad mother or breast and experiences of a similar kind contribute to the concreteness with which the infant experiences his internal fantasies. This would imply that the young infant often experiences mental anxieties within his body. She also stressed that the development of hypochondriacal anxieties may be stimulated by external factors, such as parental anxiety about the child's health and body.

Heimann (1952) discussed the libidinal interest of the patient in his hypochondriacal symptoms and its relation to self-observation. She described a type of narcissism, where the internal object represented by the body organ is preferred to external objects. The internal object is also hated because it is felt to be injured. Repressed hostility towards the environment is converted into sensations of the organ. Munro, in 1948, described how her patient felt that he had had not only bad, deprived parents, but retaliating and persecuting ones. They existed inside him, perpetually frustrated and frustrating. Munro stressed that while oral sadistic impulses dominated the picture, there was concurrently genital excitement. The patient had masturbated compulsively as a child.

Thorner (1955) said that in hypochondriasis the persecuting inner objects are expelled from the core of the ego into the body. In his opinion this implies an ego split which follows the body-mind boundary. Anna Freud (1952) drew attention to hypochondriacal anxieties in orphan children. She thought the children themselves identify with the lost mother, while the body represents the child. She wondered whether hypochondriacal psychotic phases in the adult are related to regression to this early stage of mother-child relationship.

Fenichel described hypochondriasis as an organ neurosis whose physiological factor was still unknown. He also thought that the hypochondriacally affected organ represents not only the endangered penis but simultaneously the object which, along with its ambivalent cathexis, is introjected from the external world into the subject's body. Simmel has stressed the unconscious equation of the hypochondriacally affected organ and the introjected object. Szasz (1957) has developed a theory that the ego takes the body of the self as an object. Anxieties connected with the body, like hypochondriacal anxieties, are experienced by the ego as related to a fear of losing the body, or parts of the body. In Szasz's theory of hypochondriasis, introjection of objects plays no part. He explains, however, the phenomenon of phantom limbs and phantom pains in terms of internalized objects seen as phantoms.

I will now try to relate these views to my own clinical observations and theories.

## The Role of Introjection and Projection

Most contributors emphasize the importance of introjection in hypochondriasis, a view with which I am in full agreement. Schilder speaks of projection into the body and Thorner has something similar in mind. But the importance of the mechanism of projection into external objects in hypochondriasis has, so far, been overlooked. In my view, the hypochondriacal patient constantly projects parts of his mental and sometimes physical self as well as internal objects into external objects, but it is characteristic of the disease that the external object, after the projection, is immediately re-introjected by the ego and split off into the body and body organs. In many cases frequent re-projections and re-introjections take place. This process can, however, only be observed by careful analysis.

## Sadistic and Masochistic Impulses in Hypochondriasis

A number of writers have mentioned the role of sadistic and sado-masochistic impulses in hypochondriasis. In my view, sadistic impulses and fantasies from oral and urethral sources play a predominant part in hypochondriasis, but my experiences with several severe hypochondriacal patients have shown me that it is oral sadism of an omnipotent nature which seems to be the central factor. It is in particular the omnipotent, spoiling quality of oral envy and its relationship to anal projection which exerts its destructive power over both external and internal objects and the body.

## Self-observation in Hypochondriasis

The importance of self-observation has been stressed by Schilder and Heimann. I found that sadistic scoptophilia, which is derived from oral sadism, is an important factor in the hypochondriac's self-observation. Self-observation also plays a role in the splitting process emerging as a mental watchfulness keeping the unbearable impulses and anxieties out of the mental sphere. It also often has a compulsive character, and it is used in the unsuccessful attempt of the hypochondriac to differentiate between good and bad objects and parts of the self within the body, where they exist in a state of constant confusion.

## The Role of Castration Anxiety in Hypochondriasis

Some writers have stressed the importance of castration anxiety, or displacement of genital impulses into the body or body organs. I have found that hypochondriacal patients are often preoccupied with sexual fantasies, which means that they are constantly sexually over-excited. Sometimes castration anxieties are easily recognizable even on very superficial analysis. On deeper analysis it appears that the hypochondriac's genital organization is very precarious, and his sexuality is of a sadistic nature. In addition, genital, anal, and oral impulses are often quite confused. This may be due to an early development of genital sensations, as occurs in children who are unable to find satisfaction at the breast, owing to excessive oral envy, as Melanie Klein has described. In other cases there seems to be a direct link between oral persecutory anxieties and genital anxieties, a factor opening the way to regression. This may account for the observation that hypochondriacal anxieties are often concentrated first on the penis. In some cases hypochondriacal anxieties related to the penis, combined with impotence, may act as a defence against severe hypochondriacal anxieties affecting the whole body or many parts of it. These cases are particularly resistant to treatment unless it is possible to mobilize the early confusional anxieties against which the genital symptoms are a defence.

## The Role of Early Infantile Mechanisms and Anxieties in Hypochondriasis

It has been stressed by many authors that the hypochondriac is fixated in the narcissistic phase. However, the full meaning of this observation has not been sufficiently investigated. I regard certain early infantile confusional anxieties, combined with splitting processes, as an important factor opening the way to the later development of hypochondriacal and psychosomatic diseases.

As Melanie Klein has shown, the confusional state appears to be caused mainly by a failure of the normal splitting or differentiation between good and bad objects and good and bad parts of the self, as a result of which depressive and persecutory anxieties often become confused (Klein, 1957, p. 68).

I suggest that the confusional state is so difficult for the ego to bear because the good part of the self and the good objects, on which the stability of the ego depends, are constantly in danger of being overwhelmed by the bad self and the bad objects with which they are confused. This also means that the depressive anxiety which stimulates the reparative drive cannot be worked through in the mind. Even if there is concern for objects, and therefore desire for reparation, no reparation can take place because the normal split between good and bad objects is necessary in order to allow the depressive anxieties to be worked through successfully.

It is my view that as a result of this failure of normal splitting and differentiation between good and bad objects, *abnormal splitting processes* or *mechanisms* develop in attempt to get rid of the confusional anxieties.

In hypochondriasis and the psychosomatic diseases, the confusional anxieties are split off into the body, a process which probably starts in early infancy, but becomes reinforced during later development. Further splitting processes go on simultaneously. Excessive oral-sadistic, omnipotent impulses, particularly envy, also seem unbearable to the early ego, which gives rise to splitting. In hypochondriasis the oral sadism and its later derivatives are partly split off, and the part which is split off seems to be projected by the ego into external objects and quickly introjected into the body and body organs.

I want to mention here that it is characteristic of the

hypochondriacal state that the mental anxiety content is largely retained after the projection of the anxieties, or sometimes delusions, on to the body or organs of the body. In psychosomatic diseases, the anxiety content is often lacking. One can conclude from this that the split between the mental and physical spheres is not as complete in hypochondriasis as in psychosomatic diseases.

## Hypochondriacal States as Defence

Hypochondriacal delusions and sensations are common in all phases of psychotic illness, particularly in schizophrenia. This type of hypochondriasis may be considered as a by-product of the regression to an early infantile state. Chronic hypochondriasis, however, which is a psychosis of a non-deteriorating kind, cannot be regarded simply as a regressive state. It often has a defensive function against an acute schizophrenic or paranoid condition.

## The Role of External Factors in Hypochondriasis

Hypochondriacal anxieties in children and adults may appear to be caused by a mother who is too anxious about the health of her child. But severe hypochondriasis is never produced by this factor alone. Anna Freud has mentioned hypochondriasis in orphan children, which would mean that hypochondriasis has its origin sometimes in neglect and lack of maternal care. I found in the history of several hypochondriacal patients that they shared their mother's bed in early childhood, or even latency. This factor seemed not only to increase the patient's genital over-stimulation, but profoundly stirred up the patient's persecutory anxieties in relation to the penis. In this way the tendency to regression and the predisposition to hypochondriasis is considerably increased.

CASE STUDY

I shall now discuss details of the analysis of a patient suffering from severe hypochondriasis. The patient was twenty-one when he started analysis with me. He complained of severe pressure in his chest which made him feel as if he might fall to pieces. He was also concerned about various hypochondriacal sensations in his arms, legs, head, heart and stomach. He believed that he was suffering from a heart and stomach disease. He had always been slightly hypochondriacal. However, a severe hypochondriasis developed after a sexual daydream without manual masturbation, which left him with some irritation in his penis. He thought he was dangerously ill, suffering from some undefined sexual disease. He believed that he was in a very bad physical state, but he found it even more unbearable that his family seemed to be concerned about his condition. The analysis later on revealed that he could not bear the concerned look of his parents, because he was convinced they regarded him as 'crippled', which meant to him 'castrated'. Much later in the analysis he admitted that he was afraid that his parents would regard him as mad.

FAMILY HISTORY

The patient was born in Europe. He had one brother, three years older. He cannot remember very much of his early childhood until the age of six, when his father suddenly lost all his money and the whole family had to go to relatives in another European country, where they lived very poorly in one room. Shortly after this it was decided by the parents that the mother should share her bed with the patient, and the father with the elder brother. This arrangement apparently continued until the patient was nearly twelve years old, when he rebelled against it after hearing people remark that it seemed unsuitable for such a big boy to sleep with his mother. When the patient was sixteen, the family left Europe to escape from Nazi persecution.

After this the fortunes of the family improved, particularly owing to the business success of the older brother, on whom the father greatly relied.

The analysis can be divided into three periods. During the first period, which comprises roughly four and a half years, the patient became aware of various problems which gradually improved, but his hypochondriasis, particularly the pressure in his chest, remained most resistant to treatment.

First he began to realize his extremely envious and jealous rivalry with his brother. He also became aware of the intense oedipal relationship which was reinforced by the lengthy period during which he had been sleeping with his mother. It became apparent that the loss of his father's money and position was attributed by the patient to his own omnipotent fantasies. At this period severe castration anxieties seemed to be in the foreground, and the patient was frequently preoccupied with homosexual fantasies. Dreams appeared in which one woman attacked another one in a very sadistic manner. When he became aware of his own envious rivalry with women, some of his sexual difficulties, particularly the impotence which the analysis had revealed, cleared up. He developed a number of fairly satisfactory relations with girls but he never acknowledged that he was better.

The patient had always been afraid of marriage. At the age of twenty-four he met a very attractive girl to whom he became engaged, but at that moment very severe anxieties set in. He was afraid of being trapped and completely destroyed in the process. There followed fifteen months of severe indecision and anxiety, with constant hypochondriacal complaints, before he made up his mind to marry. He was still convinced, on his wedding day, that he would collapse physically, but nevertheless he went through with it.

A few weeks before the marriage, he had a dream that he was walking with his fiancée towards his room. Suddenly a door opened and a mulatto appeared, who was a gangster who had tried to rob his room. The patient challenged him and put his hands into the gangster's pockets, without being able to discover anything stolen. The mulatto had a smile on his face. There were two people standing near by. The patient shouted for help, but they did not make any move to help and the mulatto escaped. The patient realized that he would now feel afraid of him, and in physical danger for the rest of his life, since the mulatto would never forgive him for having challenged him, and would sooner or later take his revenge.

In his associations to the dream the patient first talked of a film about Nero, which had frightened him; he also mentioned that he had told his fiancée that he was ill and having treatment. He was terrified of her reaction to this revelation. He was particularly afraid that she would feel sorry for him and that this would reawaken in him the unbearable anxiety which he had felt when he first became ill and could not stand the sympathy of his family. I interpreted that the mulatto represented the patient's sadistic, omnipotent Nero-self, which his proposed marriage was forcing to come more into the open. This omnipotent self meant madness to him, which he felt he and I had not done anything to stop. The escape of the gangster seemed a pictorial representation of the mechanism of splitting. It seemed that the omnipotent, sadistic, mad self was not only forced into the open, but became more split off, which was represented in the dream by the gangster's escape. The patient seemed afraid that as he now knew more about his sadism and madness, he would be in constant fear of being suddenly overwhelmed by it.

As his hypochondriacal anxieties increased very considerably during the next three years, it became clear that the gangster representing his sadism had escaped into the patient's body. The representation of the sadistic self as a mulatto suggests that the patient's omnipotent, sadistic impulses were derived from anal impulses. The deeper oral source of his omnipotent, sadistic self was revealed much later on in the analysis.

The three years following the mulatto dream, which almost coincided with the patient's marriage, may be considered as the second period of analysis. The patient's hypochondriacal symptoms, particularly the pressure in the chest, but also various sensations in the head, heart and other parts of the body, increased considerably. At times the patient almost completely lost interest in outside life, being obsessionally preoccupied with his illness. At first, the marriage seemed to be more successful than the patient had hoped. However, a few months later, the patient's mother became seriously ill with cancer of the throat and died. Before her death, the patient recovered some of his concern and affection for her, and did everything he could to help her. When she died, however, he felt intensely responsible for killing her. His guilt feelings continued for many months; he was preoccupied with her death and seemed constantly identified with her, and had fantasies of her feeling very lonely, sexually frustrated, shut up and bored in her grave. He had many hypochondriacal symptoms at that time, but they were not prominent. As the months went on, the patient felt worse and worse. He got no satisfaction from his wife or work. The constant state of dissatisfaction and boredom increased his hypochrondiacal anxieties in his chest and his fear of falling to pieces. He also felt some tension and pressure in his head. Gradually during the analysis he linked this physical feeling in his head with a mental one and described it as 'concern in his head'. He felt persecuted by this concern and sometimes explained that it seemed to run after him wherever he

went. He wanted to get rid of it because he did not know what
to do with it, and he also felt that it was quite unbearable. While
constantly trying to expel the concern, he was also afraid to lose
it, because he often thought that if he succeeded in getting rid of
it, he would no longer be able to love or care. This concern or
tension seemed, in the analysis, to represent mainly the patient's
mother, who seemed anxious and concerned about him, but was
also felt to be damaged and therefore demanding and accusing.
He wanted the tension in his head to be cured, which implied
that he wanted to have his mother restored, but he could never
decide whether the concern was a good or bad thing, because he
could never make up his mind whether the damaged mother was
really a good mother or a revengefully persecuting one, and so
felt at a loss about what to do with his concern.

Earlier on in this chapter I described the difficulties of working
through the confusional state–the confusion between persecutory
and depressive anxieties in the mental apparatus–as an important factor in producing hypochondriacal anxieties. During this
period of analysis the relation between the confusional state and
the patient's obsessional anxiety became increasingly clear. He
constantly brooded over what might be important, worried
whether he had neglected anything or had made a mistake. It
became apparent that he was never sure that he could recognize
and value anything that was really important, because anything
important was immediately devalued and therefore neglected.
This inability to differentiate between good and bad objects, due
to the envious devaluation of the good object, is an important
feature of the confusional state. The obsessional doubts which
were continued as obsessional self-observation of the body, were
unsuccessful attempts to deal with the confusion.

The patient had never talked much at any period of his
analysis, but during this period he became particularly silent.
Often he lay on the couch, breathing heavily, for fifteen minutes
without saying anything. Sometimes he said that he was bored
and unable to get any satisfaction in life and that he was worried
about the constant pressure in his chest. I made many interpretations about the meaning of the patient's behaviour. For
example, I interpreted the constant heavy breathing in the sessions as a projection of his physical and mental disturbances into
me, but he never gave any conscious acknowledgement that I
was correct. Generally he reacted to my interpretations with

complete silence, which lasted until the end of the hour. This behaviour was very repetitive and went on for many months.

About this time, he had two dreams which considerably helped to overcome the almost complete hold-up in the analysis. In the first, he was in my consulting-room. I, the analyst, seemed to be depressed and frantic about his lack of progress. In my despair I took some fluid and rubbed it into his head. After this, I looked into his eyes with an ophthalmoscope. Apparently I saw that some change had taken place inside him because I looked more satisfied. He watched me all the time during this procedure, and as soon as he saw that I felt better, the pressure in his chest disappeared. He was again silent after telling me this dream, which in its manifest content seemed to confirm many of my previous interpretations, and at the same time gave a vivid illustration of what had often been acted out by behaviour in the sessions.

I interpreted first the patient's silence not so much as an attack on me, but as an expression of his complete passivity as a result of the massive projection of his anxieties into me. It seemed that I had not only to look and find out for myself what was going on in him, but all his concern and anxiety about his lack of progress had been projected into me. The details of this dream were only understood after several weeks' work, and in the meantime the patient reported another dream. In this dream he was walking in the street with a friend of his called Sidney. He wanted to visit somebody known to both of them, in a hospital. He asked Sidney the way but, to his horror and amazement, Sidney remained completely silent; he would in no way assist him to visit the person who was ill. Sidney's behaviour in the dream corresponded closely to that of my patient during his analytic sessions.

I interpreted to the patient that Sidney stood for a part of himself, the part which horrified and amazed him because the Sidney part of him refused to give me, the analyst, any help in finding access to the physical sensations which disturbed him so much. When I asked him for associations as to the reason for Sidney's behaviour in the dream, the patient volunteered to describe the unpleasant characteristics of Sidney who, he thought, was extremely envious of him and would not give him any business information which would be useful to him, in spite of the patient's generosity towards him. I was now able to interpret that the patient's uncooperative behaviour in the analysis was due to the envy he felt of me and my work. I related this to the ophthalmo-cope dream and showed him that he felt he was depressing me and making me frantic by his envious, frustrating behaviour. I also interpreted that he was envious of my physical and mental health, and this stimulated the projection of his problems into me: he wanted to have my health and give me his illness. I also showed him that the pressure in his chest was directly related to how he unconsciously thought that I, the analyst, would be feeling as the result of his frustrating attacks and projections. In fact, he had internalized me as a frustrated, depressed object containing his problems. The manifest dream went so far as to say that if I, the analyst, was satisfied, no longer frustrated, he, the patient, would be well.

I have previously pointed out that the hypochondriacal patient constantly projects his self and his internal problems into the analyst, and that this is followed by immediate re-introjection. The dream seems to illustrate clearly the patient's projection into the analyst, and his re-introjection in the form of a hypochon-driacal sensation. The analyst's satisfaction in the dream implied that no further damaging, frustrating attacks by projection have taken place and therefore the analyst could now be introjected as an undamaged, good object, which meant to the patient that he himself could feel well and be well.

This dream gave the first indication that the patient realized that he could be cured of one of his most intractable hypochon-driacal symptoms – the pressure in his chest. Gradually, after the working through of this dream in the analysis, the patient's behaviour changed. He talked much more in the analysis, and he also became more responsive; for example he acknowledged my interpretations as correct when he thought so, which he had never done before. For the first time he admitted that he wanted to make an effort to get better, but at this apparently favourable moment a new anxiety developed. The patient feared that he had been waiting too long, that he had missed his chance, which meant to him that he felt he had gone too far and could not undo the damage he had done. These anxieties did not centre so much around his fear of losing me as an external object, as being concentrated almost exclusively on his stomach as an internal object. He was convinced that his stomach had been destroyed beyond repair, mainly by neglect, and it now became the centre of his continuous hypochondriacal self-observation and preoccupation.

One is justified here in speaking of a new phase in the treatment, which I will call the third period, because his hypochondriacal anxieties about the stomach assumed a distinctly depressive character, while the anxieties connected with his chest had been a mixture of persecution and depression. The patient was convinced that he was developing an ulcer of the stomach, but he could not make up his mind to be examined by a physician, who, he feared, might confirm his own diagnosis, or find out something worse, such as cancer. But mainly he was afraid that the analysis might be devalued by turning to another doctor. An X-ray examination revealed that there were signs of some gastritis. The patient felt little reassured by this and the severe hypochondriacal anxieties about his stomach went on for almost a year. The relationship to the physician who treated him for the gastritis seemed to be very similar to the one he had about me in the dream where I looked into his eyes. Whenever the patient decided that the doctor looked anxious he became acutely anxious and his stomach symptoms greatly increased.

Apart from the anxieties about his stomach, the patient's main complaint was his boredom. While previously the boredom was mainly related to his work and the sexual relationship with his wife, it extended now to food. He complained that everything tasted the same and gave him no satisfaction, and so he had no appetite. He became aware that the moment he put some food into his mouth it became devalued and therefore boring, so he quickly swallowed it, almost without chewing, and put the next bit into his mouth. This bit was devalued again, and so it went on. This form of eating appeared to be the main cause of the patient's physical irritation of his stomach, the gastritis.

During this time it seemed that the analysis had also turned into food. He complained of the analysis being boring, and of his always getting the same interpretations. He seemed eager to have interpretations, but they were devalued almost the moment they were given to him. This transference situation seemed to be a repetition of the patient's feeding experience, which had been outwardly normal—his mother told him that he had been a good baby and had been breast-fed for over nine months. He had obviously been unable to enjoy the feeding because constant envious devaluation of the breast had prevented real oral satisfaction.

The patient gradually became more conscious of his fear of

what the analysis might reveal. One day he had a fantasy of my looking at him with X-ray eyes. He was angry that I might be finding something out about him and was aware that he wanted to keep associations back from me. He said it was enough that *I* was earning my fee, why should *I* have the satisfaction of enjoying my work and getting him well? The sadistic, envious part of him, which had appeared so often in dreams, seemed to come more into the open.

About this time he had a holiday with his wife, to which he had been looking forward for a long time. However, during the holiday he treated her badly, frustrating her in every way. He spoilt the holiday for both of them, but instead of feeling sorry for himself he became aware of how much he loved her and how afraid he was of losing her. This was an entirely new but frightening experience to him. About this time he became concerned about a boy of his acquaintance who had developed schizophrenia. The patient was identified with him and developed severe anxieties at night. He was terrified that people were breaking into his flat and he was afraid of going mad. His fear of madness, which had always existed since his breakdown, came fully into the open. It was caused by the fear of being overwhelmed by his sadistic, envious impulses, identified with his schizophrenic part, which seemed now to be breaking into his self and overwhelming him, just as he had feared in the mulatto dream.

He told me that he was looking at the Stock Exchange quotations of certain shares every day. The shares did not belong to him, but to other people. He explained that he was waiting for them to go down, to shrink away into nothing. He did not want anybody to gain anything. At the same time he developed an intense fear himself of shrinking into nothing and becoming dried up. Whenever he met friends who told him that he looked thin, he became panicky, fearing that the shrinking process had started. At this time his hypochondriacal fears seemed clearly to have some delusional character. When he felt in a panic about his body shrinking, he had to eat something quickly, or he wanted to come to analysis to get something from me. He hoped that thus the shrinking process could be stopped.

About this time the patient had a dream that he was looking at the breasts of a young, attractive woman through a keyhole. Suddenly the breasts changed and became ugly and withered. The woman came out of the room and ran after him, apparently to have sexual relations with him. He was frightened and tried to fight her off, but she touched his penis. He woke up with an emission and felt utterly exhausted.

In his associations, he related the woman to his mother, whom he often looked at when she undressed in the bedroom. Other associations were with previous dreams where women had appeared looking like breasts; and references to the analyst being more silent than usual. He also reminded me of his fear of spontaneous emissions which had started at the beginning of his illness when he had first developed hypochondriacal anxieties and sensations about his penis, before they had spread to other parts of his body. The dream revealed that the shrinking attack on the breast was caused by the patient's sadistic scoptophilia. Scoptophilia and oral impulses are, of course, closely related, as Fenichel and others have shown. The dream also revealed that it was the attacked and withered breast-mother, represented in the analysis as the silenced analyst, who made a withering, exhausting attack on his penis, which seemed identified with his whole body, as the body symptoms on waking indicated.

I am suggesting that the dream illustrates that the hypochondriasis, while starting with castration anxiety and hypochondriacal anxieties about the penis, had its origin in the patient's oral anxieties and fantasies.

The patient now became much more dependent on the analysis. I was often possible during an analytic hour to help him to understand his fears and give him some relief. He developed at this time a suspicion that while I contained the cure he wanted, I might sadistically withhold it from him.

One day he offered me a ridiculously large sum of money if I would give him his health in one interview, so that he would no longer have to come to me. It became clear that he had much more openly regressed to an early oral level, which had been foreshadowed by the increasing anxiety about his stomach. His sensations and fear of shrinking implied that he had internalized and was identified with a breast, which he felt he had caused to shrink and to disappear into nothing. He felt there was still hope that a good breast existed in the outside world, but he feared that the analyst, representing the mother as the possessor of the good breast, would deliberately, sadistically withhold it from him and tantalize him in this way. This fear was strikingly reminiscent of his own previous tantalizing withholding of material in the transference. So I tried to show the patient that now, where he was admitting how much he needed me and how important I was to him, he was afraid that I would be mean and envious of him and keep my knowledge to myself to prevent him from getting better. In other words, his persecutory fantasies in relation to oral envy came more into the open.

Other fears appeared at that time: he felt that all the anxieties in his body would join together, persecute and destroy him. The reason for this was related to a lessening of the splitting processes. It had become apparent that his various hypochondriacal anxieties were connected with split-off parts of objects and self, which were beginning to come more together. This attempt at integration was associated with a greater anxiety about falling to pieces and being overwhelmed by greed and aggression which were experienced as persecution from within.

I was reminded here of my experiences with schizophrenic patients, where I had often found that, at times when splitting was lessening, an acute confusional attack threatened to come to the surface. In fact, at this time the patient was acutely afraid of a schizophrenic breakdown. However, no hospitalization or even interruption of his work was necessary. After this phase of the treatment, the patient was much improved, though still needing analysis. His hypochondriasis had changed more into neurotic anxieties, which were less severe and of a more temporary nature. He was also able, for the first time, to undertake long business trips abroad, and he was able to build up an important international business organization.

I want here briefly to remark on the patient's regression to the oral level in the analysis, and the distinct improvement following the analysis of this process. I think it was most important that not all of the self was involved in the regression, because by that time the confusion of good and bad objects and good and bad parts of the self had been sufficiently sorted out by the analysis to enable a part of the self and the ego to identify with the analyst as a good object. Strengthened by this identification, the ego was able to bear the release of the split-off, sadistic oral envy. As a result of the lessening of splitting, the anxiety and the confusion temporarily increased, but simultaneously the ego was further strengthened through the release of libidinal feelings, which are invariably bound up with the split-off aggression. This made it possible for the patient to experience his wish for dependence on the analyst and so to gain relief and some satisfaction in the analysis and in the interpretations. As a consequence, the patient was able to introject the analyst as a good object more securely on the oral level, which decreased his oral fixation. The resultant lessening of persecutory anxiety, which had particularly interfered with his genital development, diminished his castration anxiety and he felt more secure in his manliness and his achievements. All this resulted in a considerable improvement in the patient's hypochondriasis. The patient stopped treatment in July 1960 and reports that he has remained well since then.

I want now briefly to recapitulate: I am suggesting that early infantile splitting processes related both to confusional anxieties and oral sadistic envy constitute one of the fixation points of hypochondriacal states. The ego seems unable to work through the confusional state in the mental apparatus. It constantly projects the confusional state, including the internal objects and parts of the self, such as oral sadism, into external objects which are immediately re-introjected into the body and body organs. These early processes constantly influence the later sexual genital development. A characteristic of the chronic hypochondriac is his inability to gain proper oral gratification, which extends also to the genital sphere. The constant anxiety created by the patient's genital frustration increases the tendency to regression and mobilizes the early oral confusional anxieties. As a defence against this danger, the hypochondriacal state becomes manifest. In addition, I believe that severe chronic hypochondriasis is often a defence against a schizophrenic or paranoid condition.

# 12

# AN INVESTIGATION INTO THE NEED OF NEUROTIC AND PSYCHOTIC PATIENTS TO ACT OUT DURING ANALYSIS (1964)

IN investigating the need of patients to act out during analysis, I have come to understand that some acting out occurs in every analysis, and that one might well be justified in saying that partial acting out is not only inevitable but is in fact an essential part of an effective analysis. It is only when this partial acting out increases and becomes excessive, that both the analysis and the patient are endangered.

As far back as 1914 Freud discussed the question of acting out. In explaining the process of analysis he says: 'We may say that the patient does not *remember* anything of what he has forgotten and repressed but *acts* it out' (Freud, 1914a). Freud then relates the acting to the repetition compulsion and continues: 'As long as the patient is in the treatment he cannot escape from this compulsion to repeat; at last one understands that it is his way of remembering.' Later on he says: 'We soon perceive that the transference is itself only a piece of repetition and that the repetition is a transference of the forgotten past not only on to the doctor, but also on to all the other aspects of the current situation. We must be prepared to find, therefore, that the patient abandons himself to the compulsion to repeat, which now replaces the impulsion to remember, not only in his personal attitude to his doctor but also in every other activity and relationship which may occupy his life at the time.'

In this formulation Freud emphasizes that acting out is intimately bound up with the transference which inevitably penetrates into all aspects of the patient's life. He also states clearly that we have to recognize the reactivation of past experiences, which means acting out, as the method by which the patient remembers.

I fully accept Freud's views so far that this reactivation or acting out is a necessary part of any analysis and I propose to call this 'partial acting out' to differentiate it from excessive or total acting out, which Freud discusses in the second part of the same paper. Here Freud states that acting out is related to the strength of the patient's resistances and one gathers that his technique at that time of analysing resistances and dealing thus with the way in which the transference penetrated into the patient's current life outside was not yet an adequate therapeutic instrument. To prevent excessive acting out Freud on the one hand exerted constant pressure on the patient to remember instead of acting out and on the other actually prohibited the patient from undertaking important new activities while he was under analysis. It is clear that the concept of the transference penetrating into the current situation puts serious responsibilities upon the analyst, who is inevitably helping to reactivate the repetition of past situations in the transference.

There are many analysts who use Freud and Ferenczi's later advice about prohibitions to reduce the danger of acting out, but most of the analysts who have written on the subject, such as Fenichel and Greenacre, agree that prohibitions do not prevent excessive acting out. If we regard some acting out as an important and necessary part of any analysis, we must face the fact that the prohibition of certain activities in the beginning and during analysis must necessarily interfere with the course of the analysis. After all, we want to reactivate past situations, not to suppress them from the start. The answer to the problem, irrespective of whether we are dealing with partial or total acting out, seems to lie in a different direction, namely a better understanding of the transference as a reactivation of the earliest object relations, including the earliest anxieties and mechanisms on which the development of the ego depends. This makes it necessary to evolve a technique which will not only discover resistances and trace the defences of the mature ego, but which will enable us to follow details of what is being transferred from the past by studying the inter-relationships between the analytic situation and the patient's everyday life. I am here following closely Melanie Klein's views and technique as stated in her paper on the 'Origins of the Transference' (1952): 'My conception of the transference as rooted in the earliest stages of development and in deeper layers of the unconscious is much wider and entails a technique by which the unconscious elements of the transference are deduced from the whole material presented; for instance, reports of patients about their everyday lives, relations and activities, not only give insight into the function of the ego, but also reveal, if we explore their unconscious content, the defences against the anxieties stirred up in the transference situation. For the patient is bound to deal with conflicts and anxieties re-experienced towards the analyst by the same methods as he used in the past. That is to say, he turns away from the analyst as he attempted to turn away from his primal objects; he tries to split the relation to him, keeping him either as a good or as a bad figure; he deflects some of the feelings and attitudes experienced towards the analyst on to other people in his current life, and this is part of "acting out".'

Like Freud, Melanie Klein emphasizes the reactivation of the past experiences in the analysis and their penetration into everyday life. She adds, however, the reason why she believes that the reactivation of early experiences in analysis must necessarily lead to a need to act out in everyday life, namely that in the analysis the patient repeats the way he originally turned away from his primal object.

I would develop this view still further. I suggest that it depends on the extent of the hostility with which the patient turned away from his very earliest object, namely the mother's breast, whether the patient is capable of cooperating in the analysis with only partial acting out or whether he is constantly driven to act out excessively.

If there has been little hostility in the patient's turning away from the breast, we shall encounter in the analysis only partial acting out, provided that the transference is fully understood and interpreted,[1] or even if early oral phases of infantile development are being re-experienced in the transference.

On the other hand, the patient's need of excessive acting out is in my opinion always related to an excessively aggressive turning away from the earliest object. In order to arrive at a possible therapeutic solution of our problem we have now to examine some of the factors which may be responsible for the way in which the infant turns away from this early object. Following

---

[1] I wish to make clear that I have to delimit the area of discussion and that I am concentrating only on the need of the *patient* to act out. Excessive acting out can also be produced artificially by a faulty psycho-analytic technique or by an analyst who projects his own problems into the patient and so forces him to act out. Both Fenichel and Greenacre have stated that it is often the counter-transference of an ill-adjusted analyst that drives patients to excessive acting out.

Melanie Klein's observations of early infantile development, I suggest that the infant always experiences love and hate towards the breast, from the beginning of life. The first three months, approximately, of the infant's life are characterized by splitting the relationship to the breast into a good and bad one, and also by schizoid defence mechanisms which are used by the infant to deal with his anxieties, which at this earliest phase of development are of a paranoid type. The extent of the paranoid anxiety relates to the strength of the infant's hostile feelings experienced during this early phase and this hostility depends again both on external and on internal inborn factors.

If the hostility and so the paranoid anxiety in this early phase is not excessive, the split between the loved and the hated object is never very rigid; the infant soon begins to realize that his love and hate are directed towards one and the same object. This enables him to experience guilt and depression and the anxieties then centre round the fear of losing a loved object. This increases his capacity to feel love and to introject a good object more securely which again strengthens his ego and makes it possible for him to bear frustration without entirely losing his love. This phase of development has been called by Melanie Klein the 'depressive position'. If the infant is able to deal with frustration on the depressive level, it follows that, in the inevitable frustrations of childhood, he has the ability to turn away from the primary to a secondary object without excessive hate towards the primary object, so that the latter is no longer experienced as entirely bad. So that even when, for example, he is full of hostility towards the analyst for one reason or another, and therefore acting out by turning to the outside world to find good objects, such a patient retains some good relationship with the analyst and consequently some insight and cooperation in the analysis. Under such circumstances the negative transference can be worked through without disastrous acting out.

If, however, in infancy excessive hostility, and consequently excessive paranoid anxiety, is experienced towards the primary object, fixation to the object in the paranoid schizoid phase takes place. The stronger the fixation and the deeper the split between a bad and a highly idealized object the greater the difficulty of later working through the depressive position, on which depends the individual's capacity to cope with frustrations without entirely losing the good object. This also means that the attitude to objects characteristic for the early paranoid phase, that of split-ting of the object into good and bad ones, is not sufficiently modified and when the infant turns away from primary to the secondary objects he does so with intense hostility, leaving the primary object entirely bad and persecuting and turning to secondary objects as entirely good, or rather idealized. It follows that no good relationship to the primary object can be retained in turning away. As in this process the primary object, the breast, is also introjected in this persecutory form, any introjection of a loved object cannot be retained; and in spite of a need for more and more good and ideal relations to objects, the primary perse-cutory anxiety soon re-asserts itself and even the secondary objects soon turn bad.

It is the patient who is strongly fixated in the paranoid schizoid position and has turned away from his primary object with in-tense hostility who tends to act out excessively. In this he is con-stantly repeating his early relations to objects. He deals with frustrations by splitting the analyst into a good and a bad object, and he constantly acts out in an extremely repetitive way by either projecting the ideally good or the bad figure of the analyst on to an external object. In either case fundamentally he is turn-ing away from the analyst as a real object in a completely hostile manner. This cannot lead to insight, because some acknowledge-ment of a relationship with the analyst in which good and bad feelings can be tolerated simultaneously is necessary for any real insight to develop. If this patient finds new objects and develops new interests, it soon turns out that hostile feelings and rejection of the analyst are the motive forces driving him to these actions, or are *felt* to be responsible for them. This makes it difficult for the patient to persist in and have any confidence in the activities in his outside life. They may soon be given up, and the patient then relapses, leading to what appears as a strong negative thera-peutic reaction; or he has constantly to find new objects or activi-ties, a search which is also an element in manic behaviour. This may be one explanation of the fact that we so often find excessive acting out in manic patients.

If we now try to draw conclusions from our investigation, the direction which our therapy must follow becomes clearer. If par-tial acting out is looked upon as a cooperative and necessary pro-cess, the therapy has to attempt to help the patient who tends to act out *in toto* to develop into a patient who acts out partially.

This means that we have to analyse in the transference the patient's fixation on the paranoid level of development and the defences which prevent him from working through his depressive feelings; in other words, the analyst has to try to mobilize the patient's capacity for experiencing love, depression and guilt. If this analysis is successful, love and hate becomes less split up and both can be increasingly experienced towards the analyst as one object. This brings insight to the patient about the hostility contained within the excessive acting out. Depression will then emerge in the transference situation and the whole problem of acting out will diminish. The final result depends on the capacity of the patient to introject the analyst securely as a good object and to transfer and project the good feelings into external activities and on to secondary objects with a minimum of hostility to the analyst, who stands for the primary objects. This kind of acting out, in which new activities and interests may develop, is of course the necessary basis for any successful analysis, and without this no analysis can ever be successfully ended.

There is, however, a danger that the analysis of a patient acting out excessively may follow another course. He may suddenly attempt to give up most of his ego activities and his relations to objects in everyday life, and show regressive behaviour in the analysis, acting like a small dependent child; for example he may constantly ask for advice, reassurance, extra sessions and other tokens of love from the analyst, thus not only acting out himself but also trying to induce the analyst into acting out towards him.

This regression may at times be unavoidable. But the danger of a deep regression, sometimes even into a psychosis, is increased if the analyst is taken unawares, or if, though realizing the problem, he does not adequately interpret the reasons for this need to regress, or if he encourages it by being unable to resist the pressure from the patient tempting him constantly to act out with him.

The risk of such a regression is greater at a time when the analysis has succeeded in mobilizing positive transference feelings and the patient has become aware that all his object relations and activities including his adult sexuality are based on a completely hostile turning away from the primary object which the analyst represents. He then begins to feel intense guilt about all activities outside the analysis, because they represent a hostile independence of the analyst. These guilt feelings are very difficult to bear, because they contain not only depressive but strongly paranoid elements. If the depressive anxieties in the superego predominate, the need to make reparation can assert itself and the excessive acting out gives way to normal cooperation in analysis by partial acting out. If, however, the paranoid anxieties in the superego gain the upper hand, the attempt at reparation fails and the patient is driven back to the earliest fixation to the mother on the paranoid schizoid level. This is the moment when we have to deal with the regression in the transference and the patient starts to act out excessively with the analyst. The meaning of this behaviour needs to be seen from two closely related angles. First, in so far as the analyst in the regression represents the patient's primary object accusing the patient of having aggressively turned away to secondary objects and other activities, and so of having built up his life at the primary object's expense, the patient unconsciously feels that the best way of placating the analyst now is to give up all the activities of his life, and to act like a baby. This is a common cause of the type of acting out that is characterized primarily by infantile behaviour. Secondly, this acting out in the regression must be seen as a desperate attempt to induce the analyst to act out towards the patient with overt friendly behaviour, so as to deal in some way with another aspect of the persecution that he expects from the analyst standing for the primary object: the patient now anticipates that all the hostility that he has expressed towards the analyst in his excessive acting out will actually lead to retaliation by the analyst with similar hostile activities. He therefore tries with every means at his disposal to get friendly acting out from the analyst to obscure and counteract these fears.

In dealing with this acting out in the analysis it is first of all important for the analyst to be able to maintain the analytic situation and to resist the intense pressure of the patient driving him to act out. This in my experience is only possible if the analyst realizes that the overwhelming demands for a good relationship cover up the patient's intense persecutory fear—a fear which is based on, and corresponds to, his own hostile activities when turning away from his primary object. If the analysis of the patient's persecutory fears gradually succeeds in mobilizing the patient's depressive anxieties and need to make reparation, the acting out by means of regression diminishes.

I will now briefly give some clinical material from a patient who after excessive acting out was heading for a total regression in analysis. There had been a constant real danger of her stopping analysis, to reside permanently in a mental hospital or to commit suicide. The patient was suffering from a severe depression and eating difficulties. She had previously acted out excessively her aggressive turning away from mother to father at weaning time by aggressively turning away from the analyst to an idealized male figure in her current life. The analysis enabled her to avoid a total acting out at this time, when she was threatening to give up the treatment altogether. When later she became aware that all her intellectual activities and her interest in men were related to her contempt and total hostility towards her mother, whom I at the time represented, she felt that she had to return to a good relationship to me, as the mother, instead of abusing and ridiculing me constantly as she had been doing for some time. She tried to cooperate again and after some weeks she said she had no other friends apart from myself, demanded constant reassurance and love from me, and also demonstrated that every day she was less able to look after herself. In one session she behaved like a small child, who could do nothing, not even walk or think. She said that now I had to do everything for her, and had to take her to a nursing home because she felt she would be unable to talk and feed herself and would otherwise die. She then ceased to respond to anything that I was interpreting and lay motionless. This situation seemed quite alarming until I interpreted to her that she could not talk or think or move because she felt that everything she was doing was wrong and so she had to stop it. She replied almost immediately that that was the only thing she was thinking about all day long: 'Everything I am doing is wrong. I cannot go on. I must stop it.'

I then elaborated to her that she was feeling like this because not only her friendship with other people but all her activities—walking, talking, eating, and even thinking—seemed to her a hostile act against myself, and that was why she had to stop them. She almost immediately became able to think and to cooperate better in the sessions. This situation had of course to be worked through many times, but the analysis was able to prevent total regression. One of the main difficulties in this analysis has been the patient's constant pressure to drive me to acting out. She was so desperately in need of seeing me behaving towards her in a friendly way, because she was so afraid of my cruelty; a particular anxiety was that I would wish to drive her back to being dependent on me in order to show myself as having the superiority over her of the mother over her baby, and then to abandon her, as she in the earlier phase of the analysis had been attempting to do to me. The difficulty of this analysis was that while the patient was constantly looking for a loving and kind mother in external life, her internal mother was felt by her to be extremely cruel, corresponding to her own hostile turning away from her in infancy, and therefore no external figure whom she discovered could be trusted.

Many patients fixated on the paranoid schizoid level show a great number of additional problems, which make treatment difficult. The early splitting processes interfere with the capacity for verbal thinking and sublimation, as well as other aspects of ego development.[1] Consequently in the patient who acts out excessively, one may anticipate varying degrees of ego disturbance and ego weakness, interference in the capacity for verbal thought and inhibition in sublimation. These problems in themselves increase the patient's tendency to deal with difficulties by action rather than by thought. Greenacre (1950) has pointed out that the patient who acts out has suffered 'more or less emotional disturbances in the early months of infancy with increased orality, diminished tolerance of frustration and a heightened narcissism'. Greenacre also found disturbances of verbal thinking, which, however, she connects with difficulties in the second year.

There are, of course, patients whose illness is characterized by acting out in everyday life. Fenichel has described some of them as impulse neuroses or 'acting out characters' and included among them delinquents, perverts, and others. I have observed that most acute and chronic psychotic patients are continuously acting out in life. Patients who suffer from an acting out character or whose illness drives them to act out continuously in life will also act out excessively during analytic treatment. Their acting out will have all the elements considered here, but will also contain other factors, specific to their illness. I cannot discuss all the problems related to these diseases but will concentrate on the acting out of chronic schizophrenic patients during their analysis. From our investigation so far we would expect to find, in the schizophrenic, extreme tendencies to act out during analysis,

[1] I refer here to the work of Dr Segal and Dr Bion on these problems.

both because of the degree of his fixation in the paranoid-schizoid position and the intense hostility with which he has turned away from his primary objects. In addition to the factors mentioned so far, there is a problem in chronic schizophrenia which, in my opinion, greatly increases the schizophrenic's need to act out. This problem is the acute confusional state against which the latent and chronic schizophrenic patient has constantly to defend himself. If the analysis is making progress and the emotions related to the confusional state appear in the transference, the patient uses excessive acting out as a defence against this situation.

I will first discuss the psychopathology of the confusional state in some detail. In my paper on 'Confusional States in Chronic Schizophrenia' (chap. 3), I suggested that when the schizophrenic patient is making progress in his analysis and splitting processes lessen, a state of confusion is likely to occur. I described how when love and hate come nearer together and aggressive impulses predominate, the patient does not experience guilt and anxiety, and as a result better integration, but it appears that his love and hate and his good and bad objects become confused. I thought that the schizophrenic's state of confusion must be based on states of confusion in earliest infancy, when good and bad objects could not be kept apart. I suggested that splitting processes became reinforced or new ones developed as a defence against the confusional state.

In later papers on schizophrenia, I concentrated more on the importance of confusion of self and object caused by projective identification as one of the features of the confusional state.

Melanie Klein, in her book *Envy and Gratitude*, has greatly clarified the problem of confusion and confusional states. She states, for example, that excessive envy, a corollary of the destructive impulses, interferes with the building up of a good object so that the normal split between the good and bad breast cannot be sufficiently achieved. The result is that later differentiation between good and bad is disturbed in various ways, the reason for which she describes in detail. For example, she suggests that excessive envy both interferes with the capacity of the infant for complete satisfaction, even if external circumstances are satisfactory, and also increases the intensity and the duration of the sadistic attacks on the breast, thus making it difficult for the infant to regain the lost good breast. Klein feels that it is the basic failure to split the good from the bad object which is responsible for states of confusion in early infancy and later on. From this description one can draw the further conclusion that the acuteness and duration of states of confusion must relate to the strength of inborn envy and it is of course extreme states of confusion which we are faced with in the acute schizophrenic. (I want to emphasize here that I am not ignoring external factors. We know that schizophrenics frequently have a history of some feeding difficulties or other traumas in early infancy, but often the external difficulties are slight and the severity of the illness is quite out of proportion to the external factors.)

The latent and chronic schizophrenic has built up elaborate splitting processes as a defence against the confusional state, and these often make it difficult for him to feel much emotion. If he comes closer to experiencing any emotion of love, he is immediately threatened with a confusional state. This may be the reason why schizophrenics so often break down when they come into close contact with a love object.

I will now present material illustrating the acting out of a chronic schizophrenic patient defending herself against an acute confusional state which made its appearance when the acting out lessened. Anne had been treated by me analytically for a short time during an acute schizophrenic attack and she continued coming to me regularly for analysis during a mute phase which lasted for two years. During the analysis in the acute phase, I had realized Anne's great fear of any sexual impulses. The analysis in the mute phase confirmed her sexual inhibition and only very gradually did she admit to me her intense sexual preoccupation and fantasies. She started to read with great interest, and selected books which she found sexually stimulating. After a year's analysis she confessed that she spent hours rocking herself, which was a kind of masturbation. She then described dreams and associations which clearly showed that her positive feelings for me in the transference were becoming stronger and were also more conscious. At this point she began acting out excessively with many men whom she got to know mainly at a club, where there was opportunity for dancing. Each time she went to this club she managed to pick up some man, usually a foreigner. She often hinted to me that the man she was looking for was an ideal figure, a man she could marry. In fact these men were far from ideal and occasionally she was in danger of being raped by one of them. She only once went to bed with a man and then without having complete sexual relations with him. Generally she only allowed some physical contact, kissing and touching her breasts. She generally met these men twice, after which they failed to telephone, or did not turn up at a meeting place. Only very occasionally did she stop the relationship on her own account. When it was clear that the relationship had come to an end, she returned to the club after a few days to pick up a new acquaintance. This behaviour lasted about ten months.

She spent most of the time during the sessions telling me about the men she met or was going to meet. Before she had been going to the club, there had been some acknowledgement of interpretations of her strongly positive feelings towards me. Now she reacted more and more with boredom or contempt, or great anger, to interpretations of the positive transference. She insisted frequently that there was no need to come for treatment because she was all right, or that there was no point in coming since she did not listen to what I was saying. It was clear to me that by her acting out she was insisting on keeping me in a devalued role, because she was afraid of being overwhelmed by envy and jealousy if she allowed me to become more important to her. It was equally clear that she avoided coming in contact in real life with a man who could be a love object to her, mainly because she did not feel capable of loving anyone. Her choice of very sexual and often crude and sadistic men was very over-determined. First of all, with them she could deny her own incapacity to love and it was also easy to project on to them her own murderously sadistic sexuality through which she was afraid of destroying any love object who aroused her envy.

There was also a sadistic desire to hurt her parents by acting almost like a prostitute, together with a need for punishment and humiliation on account of guilt. Some of my interpretations gradually made some impression on her. She became dissatisfied with herself and with the many men she got to know at the club and increasingly concerned and depressed about her inability to love. I was aware then that she was moving closer to me, but also closer to the confusional state, because she started to sleep very badly. About this time she became interested in a coloured student with whom she had interesting talks and who did not attempt to seduce her. A relationship without any physical contact had not been possible for her before, because it made her feel too bored. At this point the analysis had to be interrupted by my holiday. Her relationship with this man continued for about three weeks, but she then developed a delusion of being married to him. Gradually she became confused, and was taken by a colleague to a nursing home, where I continued the treatment on my return. In the confusional state, the delusion about being married to her friend disappeared, but she now declared that H., an uncle of hers, was the one she loved and was married to. She always added that he had shot her through the head and driven her mad. After a few weeks of analysis in the acute phase, she admitted that she was madly in love with me, that I was the only person she wanted to marry. Sometimes she expressed murderous fantasies about the women whom I was married to in her fantasies, but it was mainly myself whom she tried to kill by strangling after coming close to me in a very seductive manner. She told me long stories about her parents being dead and about herself having been adopted, or about having been thrown out by her family. At other times she said she did not want her family, she had found another one and got herself mixed up with it. The most striking factor was not the turning away from her family to a multitude of objects, all of whom she projected on to me in rapid succession, but the confused way she talked about most people. For example, she said how good her mother was to her, and how she had given her presents and a piano; she was a murderess, a butcher. She said her father was a rich man, who had taken her abroad for holidays to make her better; he was a boxer who only talked about war, and who had said that she was mad and that she would get worse and worse until she died. She talked about me in a similar way. She said I had saved her life, and driven her mad. I had a beautiful voice, to which she liked to listen, and I was a murderer. Another time she said: 'How did you manage to be so handsome and tall? I'll break your face in. You are mad, why have you stolen my face bones.' This was often followed by stealing objects from me and trying to destroy them or by attempting to get her arm inside my coat. Sometimes she looked at my tie with admiration and touched it, then suddenly pulled it so hard that I had to control her. She stroked my hands; a short time afterwards she proceeded to scratch them as hard as she could.

The most striking feature about the confusional state seemed to be that the uncle, the parents and myself were simultaneously experienced as love objects and persecutors. Her wish to kill me out of jealousy and frustration, because I would not marry her, was much on the surface, but more detailed observation showed that the attacks on me were mostly an expression of envy. It was her envy of everything I possessed which made her feel she wanted to rob me, attack me or put herself into me. The forcing of herself into me and other people, which she called 'stealing lives', very much increased her feelings of confusion and loss of identity. Her behaviour, which she called 'mad love' was characterized by the simultaneous experience of attraction and envy, which made any pleasure in her relationship to me impossible for a considerable time.

From my description of the acute confusional state it will have become clear that the patient could not keep her love objects separate from the persecutory objects. She also experienced love and extreme envy simultaneously, making her feel that her love was madness. When her interest in me became stronger, her envy increased and she devalued me and transferred her interest to the men in the club.

She obtained some sexual satisfaction from the club but from the point of view of the transference situation one important purpose was achieved: her interest in me, which had become overwhelmingly strong, sexualized, and dangerous, had been split off by the acting out and projected on to the men in the club. Her choice of the many unsatisfactory men was a further attempt to diminish the strength of her feelings for me by dispersing them and splitting them up. She herself and her supposed love objects became, through this dispersal, more and more devalued.

When the patient became aware, to some extent, that she was responsible for the unsatisfactory situation in her outside life and that she was avoiding any possibility of meeting a man whom she could love, she became depressed and tried more successfully to find a love object away from me. When she succeeded she broke down. There was of course an element of acting out in this love relationship because she wanted to use it to turn away from me completely. But the analysis of the acute condition showed that this was not the main reason for her breakdown. When the splitting lessened, her interest in the one person became stronger, this increased her envy to an extreme degree, so that the mad love, the confusional state, broke through.

When I saw her for the first time in her acute state, she

mumbled to herself interspersed among the most wildly confused thoughts: 'Will I always go mad if I fall in love and let myself go?' If we tried to formulate an answer to this question we might say: only if a schizophrenic patient becomes gradually able to achieve a normal split between a good and bad object will she be able to achieve a love relationship and the confusional states will not repeat themselves.

## Conclusions

From this and other clinical material I came to the conclusion that the excessive acting out of the schizophrenic starts as a defence against the confusional state and is an attempt to keep love and envy separate. There is an attempt to achieve splitting between a good and bad object, but this ends in failure. What we see expressed in the acting out is a series of abnormal splitting processes in which the love object is devalued, split up, and projected into many devalued objects. The resultant confusion and uncertainty about the goodness or badness of the object is relatively unimportant since the objects are so numerous.

I will now briefly compare the excessive acting out of the non-schizophrenic patient which I described in the first part of my paper with the excessive acting out of the schizophrenic.

Both types of patient are strongly fixated in the paranoid schizoid position and have experienced intense hostility both from internal and external sources. But there are important differences. In the first group of patients, who may be neurotic or manic depressive, the splitting between the good and bad object has been achieved. This splitting is often excessive and a deep gap exists between a highly idealized and an extremely bad object, which is exploited by the acting out, when the primary object is generally completely devalued and the secondary ones idealized. In the schizophrenic group of patients, where excessive envy plays a decisive part, the split between the good and bad object has never been achieved. Consequently the aggressive turning away from the primary object, which is also devalued, does not lead to an idealization of the secondary ones, but to a succession of objects, which are never experienced as wholly good or bad.

## Summary

In this paper I have suggested that some acting out is an inevitable part of any analysis, because in the transference the patient repeats the way he has turned away from his infantile object relations, in particular from the primary relation to his mother's breast. Whether the patient acts out partially or excessively depends on the degree of the hostility with which he has turned away from this object. The patient who has rejected the primary object with excessive hostility, and therefore acts out excessively, is also strongly fixated to his primary object at the earliest level of development—the paranoid schizoid position; and has a predominantly persecutory superego. These factors would explain why patients who act out excessively show a strong tendency to regress to this early fixation when they begin to experience guilt about their excessive acting out in analysis, affecting all their activities in everyday life.

Patients who have turned away from their primary object with little hostility act out only partially in analysis and show themselves capable of object relations, which Melanie Klein has described as characteristic for the depressive position. This shows the direction of the therapeutic task in dealing with excessive acting out. We have to understand and analyse the fixation of the patient to the paranoid schizoid position and the paranoid anxieties related to his hostile turning away from the primary object, and also the defences which prevent the normal working through of the depressive position. If we succeed in mobilizing depressive anxiety, guilt, and reparation in our patient, he becomes more cooperative and the excessive acting out ceases.

In the latent or chronic schizophrenic patient the acting out takes a different course, because in his excessive acting out he turns away from a state of confusion where good and bad objects cannot be differentiated. This makes the acting out a particularly difficult task to deal with because it is the progress in the analysis which threatens the patient with the appearance of an acute confusional state and so often leads to temporary hospitalization or even stoppage of the analysis.

The psychopathology of the acute confusional state has been greatly clarified through the discovery of the role which excessive envy plays in preventing normal splitting between good and bad objects. This has opened the way to a better understanding and analysis of the schizophrenic's basic anxieties and his defences against them, of which excessive acting out is an important one.

# 13

# THE PSYCHOPATHOLOGY OF DRUG
# ADDICTION AND ALCOHOLISM
## (A Critical Review of the Psycho-Analytic Literature)
## (1964)

ALCOHOLISM and drug addiction have always presented a difficult psychiatric and social problem. Psycho-analysts, along with many others, have from early on been interested in the treatment of these disorders, and have attempted to investigate and understand their underlying psychopathology. A large psycho-analytic literature has developed and many analysts have made several contributions to the subject over the years. This paper aims to give a picture of the psycho-analytic literature on alcoholism and drug addiction and to correlate the psycho-analytic findings. An attempt will be made to see whether, on the basis of the ideas on which there is a consensus of opinion among the authors of this literature, one can speak of *the* psycho-analytic theory of drug addiction or alcoholism.

Freud never wrote a detailed essay on alcoholism or drug addiction, but there are many isolated remarks or suggestions in his writings which throw some light on the psychopathology of addiction. In 1897 in a letter to Fliess (Freud, 1950) he suggests that masturbation is the primary addiction and that the other addictions, such as alcohol, morphine, tobacco, etc., only enter into life as substitutes or replacements for it. In another letter to Fliess he discusses the relation of dipsomania to repressed sexuality and thinks that in this condition there is a substitution of one impulse for an associated sexual one. In the *Three Essays on Sexuality* (1905) he says that there is in some children 'a constitutional intensification of the erotogenic significance of the labial region. If that significance persists, these same children when they are grown up . . . will have a powerful motive for drinking and smoking.' In *Jokes and Their Relation to the Unconscious* (1904) he writes: 'A cheerful mood, whether it is produced endogenously or toxically, reduces the inhibiting forces, criticism among them, and makes accessible once again sources of pleasure which were under the weight of suppression. Under the influence of alcohol the grown man once more becomes a child who finds pleasure in having the course of his thoughts freely at his disposal without paying regard to the compulsion of logic.' In his 'Contributions to the Psychology of Love' (1910) Freud contrasted the relation of the lover to the sexual object with that of the wine drinker to wine. Whereas the lover may pursue an endless series of substitute objects, none of which ever gives full satisfaction, the drinker is more or less bound to his favourite drink and the repeated gratification does not affect the recurrence of his strong desire. The great lovers of alcohol describe their attitude to wine as the most perfect harmony, a model of a happy marriage. In 1911 he refers to the part played by alcohol in alcoholic delusions of jealousy and suggests that drink removes inhibitions and undoes the work of sublimation. As the result of this, homosexual libido is freed and the drinker suspects the woman he is jealous of in relationship to all the men whom he himself is tempted to love. In 1917 he compares toxic hallucinations, such as alcoholic delusions, with the wishful psychosis of 'amentia' (Freud, 1917a). He believes that alcoholic delirium arises when alcohol is withdrawn, which implies that it is a reaction to the loss of alcohol which is experienced as unbearable. In 'Mourning and Melancholia' (1917b) he expresses the view that alcoholic intoxication, in so far as it consists in a state of elation, belongs to the manic group of mental conditions. In mania there is a relaxation in the expenditure of energy on repression. In alcoholism the freeing of impulses from repression is made possible by the toxin. In 1928 in a paper on 'Humour', Freud (1927) again refers to intoxication. He compares humour with elation and suggests that it signifies the triumph not only of the ego but also of the pleasure principle. He writes '(The) rejection of the claims of reality and the putting through of the pleasure principle bring humour near to the regressive or reactionary processes which engage our attention so extensively in psychopathology. Its fending off of the possibility of suffering places it among the great series of methods which the human mind has constructed in order to evade the compulsion to suffer—a series which begins with neurosis and culminates in madness and which includes intoxication, self-absorption and ecstasy.' From these quotations of Freud's views it is clear that he realized that the root of addiction goes back to the oral phase of development, but he also saw that there was a connexion between addiction and infantile masturbation. He also makes it clear that he believes that the drinker often regards alcohol as an ideal object, which would explain why the drinker becomes so deeply attached to alcohol–representing this object. By connecting the psychopathology of mania and humour with alcoholism and intoxication Freud laid the foundation for a deeper understanding of the addictions.

Abraham (1908a) discusses the psychological relations between sexuality and alcoholism. He suggests that alcohol, by removing inhibitions, increases sexual activity, not only of a normal but of a perverse type, such as incest, homosexuality, scoptophilia and exhibitionism. He stresses that perversions like sadism and masochism come to the fore, so that many brutal crimes are perpetrated in states of alcoholic intoxication. In discussing drinking as an escape he says that the drinker makes use of alcohol as a means of obtaining pleasure without trouble. He gives up women and turns to alcohol. He then projects his feelings of guilt on to his wife and accuses her of being unfaithful. Abraham regards diminished potency as the main cause of the drinker's jealousy. In his paper 'The First Pregenital Stage of the Libido' Abraham (1916) stresses the importance of oral craving in all addictions. He observed patients who suffered from compulsive and excessive eating and noticed that if their desires were not satisfied these patients underwent torture similar to that of 'morphinists and a good many dipsomaniacs'. In the same paper Abraham discusses the addiction to taking medicines and says that the depressed or excited neurotic is often favourably influenced, though only for a time, merely by swallowing medicines, even when they have no sedative action. It is interesting to note that Abraham stressed only the oral factors in the addictions without relating them to the manic depressive states.

Ferenczi (1911a), contributing to the psychopathology of alcoholism, describes a case of alcoholic paranoia with delusions of jealousy. He believes that there was an insoluble conflict between the patient's conscious heterosexual and his unconscious homosexual desires, but suggests that alcohol played here only the part of an agent destroying sublimations. In a footnote to the same paper he says that in the great majority of cases alcoholism is not the cause of neurosis, but the result of it. Both individual

and social alcoholism can be cured only by the help of psycho-
analysis, which discloses the cause of the flight into narcosis and
neutralizes it. He points out that when alcohol is withdrawn there
remains at the disposal of the psyche numerous other paths to the
'flight into disease'. In his discussion of cases at a later date
(1916–1917; 1919a) he again mainly refers to unconscious homosexuality as the chief problem underlying alcoholism.

Juliusburger makes several contributions to the psychology of
alcoholism: he stresses (1912) the importance of unconscious
homosexual impulses in dipsomania, combined with a tendency
to auto-erotism and masturbation; he regards (1913) unconscious
homosexuality as only one of the factors in alcoholism; he discusses the sadistic tendencies in alcoholics which are often
noticeable in those suffering from delusions of jealousy; and he
believes that the desire for intoxication is related to a wish to lose
individual consciousness completely, stressing the tendency to
suicide.

Pierce Clark (1919) stresses the importance of deep regressions
in alcoholism, such as primary identifications with the mother
combined with intense self-love (narcissism). He is particularly
impressed by the relation between depression and alcoholism. In
several of his cases there were irregular but also definitely
periodical depressive episodes. He describes a woman patient in
whose case the drinking was precipitated by feelings of loneliness,
depression and inadequacy. It seemed that the alcoholic habit
was formed to overcome unpleasant situations and to help the
patient to forget. Another patient, however, a dipsomaniac, became increasingly depressed and suicidal during the later stages
of the drinking bout. At times he assumed paranoidal attitudes
towards women, with whom he was intimate. Clark agreed with
other observers that in some cases homosexual, in others sado-
masochistic or exhibitionistic traits, were more on the surface.

Kielholz made many contributions to the psychopathology of
alcoholism and the alcoholic psychosis (delirium tremens). He
regards alcoholism as a narcissistic neurosis related to the manic-
depressive psychosis. There is an obvious regression to narcissism,
which shows itself in the vanity, egoism and the increased self-
esteem of the alcoholic. He discusses the relation of excessive
drinking to feasting and the psychology of festivals, and compares
the alcoholic's spree with manic elation. Alcoholic intoxication
is followed by alcoholic melancholia. He thinks that the split be-

tween the ego ideal and the ego is deep and unbearable both in the pure melancholias as well as in the alcoholic melancholias. As a result of this split, the death instinct turns against the ego, often leading to suicide. In the manic state of the alcoholic spree the death instinct is turned outwards and the sadism is openly expressed and acted out. Kielholz agrees with other authors about the frequency of perversions among alcoholic addicts. In discussing the delirious hallucinatory experiences of the alcoholic, he says that, contrary to existing opinion, he found in analysis deeply rooted infantile experiences. In a case of delirium tremens he discovered strong scoptophilia, and homosexual and persecutory anxieties which could be related to primary scene experiences and fantasies. In discussing the treatment of alcoholism he suggests that it is important to control the drinking and advised complete abstinence on the lines of Freud's advice in the treatment of phobias. In stressing the importance of narcissism Kielholz is in agreement with Clark. In relating the alcoholic's spree to manic elation he follows Freud's view. Kielholz, even more than Clark, emphasizes the importance of depression in alcoholism.

Rádo made a number of important contributions to the problem of drug addiction. In 1926 he stresses the predisposition to addiction and suggests that 'some manifestation of oral erotism is always present in a marked form even in those cases of drug mania, in which the drug is not taken by mouth at all'. He believes that the 'alimentary orgasm' which is first experienced by the infant at the breast is revived in drug addiction, and sexual excitation belonging to fantasies of the oedipal situation is discharged not by means of onanism but through the alimentary orgasm. He suggests that in chronic drug addiction the 'whole mental personality represents an auto-erotic pleasure apparatus. The ego is completely subjugated and devastated by the libido of the id.' Or, so to say, 'converted back into the id'. 'The outside world is ignored and the conscience disintegrated.' He says that on the one hand it is due to the destructive instinct, that the higher mental organizations and differentiations have been overthrown; on the other hand, the aggressive tendencies attach themselves to the superego of the drug addict, so that the unconscious tension of the conscience is actually intensified and this involves a strong need for punishment, which results in a vicious circle.

Rádo thinks that an important function of drugs is to supply a shield against stimulation from within, which becomes necessary when through excessive stimulation the pain barrier has been broken through. He also observes that drugs produce feelings of tension and at the same time they relieve existing tensions, the final result being the conversion of painful into pleasurable tension. The stimulant clears a way for the hampered intentions of the id; at the same time it appeases the inhibiting influences, which are mainly the tensions produced by the conscience. The second effect of the intoxicant is the production of states of well-being which vary greatly in intensity and quality. Rádo stresses the erotic nature of this state and feels that in drug addiction the intoxication has become a sexual aim. The whole peripheral sexual apparatus is left on one side, a state which he calls 'meta-erotism'. Sooner or later failure to achieve pharmacotoxic orgasm occurs from physiological and psychological reasons. Terrible anxiety states, torturing excitement, and frightful visions appear, which are related to a powerful reaction of the conscience. Rádo made many observations on the role of the conscience in drug addiction, which seem in contradiction to his statement in the same paper that in the aetiology of morbid cravings no specific role can be ascribed to the unconscious tension of conscience and the sense of guilt. Rádo compares the deteriorated state of the drug addict with certain features in the final stages of schizophrenia, but he is more emphatic in elaborating the similarity of mania and melancholia to the state of intoxication and the state of depression which follows it. In 1933 Rádo stresses and elaborates the importance of the narcissistic disposition of the drug addict, and suggests that when people have remained fundamentally narcissistic they react to frustration with 'tense depression'. He believes that the basis of drug addiction is an initial 'tense depression' – marked by painful tension and at the same time a high degree of intolerance of pain. This sensitizes the patient to the pharmacogenic pleasure-effect, so that marked relief is found in the use of a drug. He continues the theme of the earlier paper by emphasizing that drugs effect their function by allaying or preventing pain and by producing euphoria and stimulation and thus serve the pleasure principle. The resulting elation is a necessary basis for the development of a 'pharmacothymia'. In the pharmacogenic elation the ego regains its original narcissistic state, which is related to magic wish-fulfilment and omnipotence. It gets rid of depression, increased anxiety, and a bad conscience. But elation is transitory, depression follows and consequently a renewal of the need for elation – a cyclical process. He makes quite clear that pharmacothymia is a narcissistic disorder, which produces a disruption, by artificial means, of the natural ego organization. The drugs cause a valueless inflation of narcissism and prevent awareness that self-destruction is progressing, because elation has reactivated the patient's narcissistic belief in his invulnerability and immortality. He believes that a lethal dose of the drug is not taken to commit suicide, but to dispel the depression for ever. Rádo stresses the masochism in drug addiction, which in his opinion plays an important part in the psychotic episodes. The terrible hallucinations and deliria, in which the patient believes that he is persecuted or threatened, particularly by the danger of castration or sexual attacks, are fantasies which satisfy masochistic wishes. The narcissistic pleasure ego desires pleasure without pain and for that reason latent masochistic wishes are projected and turned into terror fantasies. Rádo does not believe that the drug addict uses the withdrawal-treatment for masochistic satisfaction but to rehabilitate the depreciated value of the poison. He is of the opinion that the homosexuality of the drug addict develops under the influence of masochism. He is impressed by the frequency of perversions in drug addiction such as fetishism or sadism. In 1953 he confirmed his earlier theory of the importance of the extensive puncturing of the pain barrier in the aetiology of both depression and drug addiction. He introduces his theory of the spurious pleasure in elation which inflates the ego or 'action self'. He describes that the euphoric effect of the drugs is produced in two steps: they introduce pleasure beyond the mere relief from pain and then cause the patient to become intoxicated with spurious pleasure. He confirms the close relation of narcotic intoxication and the spurious pleasure of mania. In 1958 Rádo stresses the omnipotence of the drug addict, who–sensitized by his depression–sees in the narcotic pleasure effect the fulfilment of his longing for miraculous help and responds to it with a sense of personal triumph. He now divides drug addiction into three groups: the psycho-neurotic or manic-depressive group, the schizophrenic, and the psychopathic group. In discussing the treatment of drug addiction, he advises that first the drug should be withdrawn, preferably in a specially equipped hospital, with psychotherapeutic support to prevent the potential dangers of violence and suicide. He does not refer to psycho-analytic treatment of the drug addict in this paper, but points out that generally speaking the prognosis of drug addiction is unfavourable.

Rádo follows Kielholz, Juliusburger, and Clark in stressing the importance of narcissism and depression in the addictions. In emphasizing the manic aspects he follows Freud, Abraham, and Kielholz. He introduces the concept of the alimentary orgasm and suggests that the drug supplies a shield against pain – which seems an obvious observation. Rádo, however, is the first analyst to draw attention to the important fact that the drugs are used as a permanent defence against pain. He seems more aware than other writers of the deteriorating nature of the addictions, which he relates to the uncontrolled release of destructive instincts.

Simmel made a number of contributions to the psychopathology and treatment of drug addiction and alcoholism from 1928 to 1949. In 1928, when discussing drug addiction, he suggests that addicts suffer from narcissistic neuroses (manic-depressive illness), which they ward off by using mechanisms of the obsessional neurosis. He believes that the drug-effect concentrates on the superego. He says: 'the victim of addiction is a melancholic who makes his guardian superego drunk with the poison with which he murders the object in the ego. To the outward observer, however, he is in a state of mania so long as he is indulging in the poison. For a superego paralysed by a toxin ceases to make any demands: it is no longer able to mediate in the interests of self-preservation.' Simmel is also aware of the importance of sadism in drug addiction and he feels that because of the murderous impulses and the need for self-punishment the treatment of the drug addict is fraught with danger, particularly of suicide. In 1930 Simmel stresses the importance of pathological narcissism and cyclothymia in the pre-morbid personality of the drug addict. When the drug addiction develops the patient becomes more and more the narcissistic child and the infantile pleasure principle breaks through into consciousness. In discussing severe drug addiction he describes a regression to the sucking phase where the patient (particularly during the withdrawal-treatment) represents a being who is no longer able to use his mental apparatus to deal with stimuli. In its place the body responds to tension and stimuli auto-erotically, which may explain the colics, vomiting and coldness from which the drug addict suffers during withdrawal-treatment. Simmel is impressed by the addict's oral fantasies of wishing to eat up and be eaten up by other people, which he relates in the last resort to the patient's desire to lose his ego boundary like the infant in the mother's womb. He also stresses the relationship of sleep and drug addiction. Sleep is a fulfilment of every infantile sexual aim, feeding at the breast or masturbation. Sleep is to be regarded as a repetition of the situation inside the mother, but sleep and the pre-natal state also symbolically represent death. The drug addict who desires sleep and death has come under the power of the death instinct, driven by the domination of the omnipotent pleasure principle. There is, however, also a tendency to divert the 'introverted hate' to the outside again, to poison somebody else instead of one's own self, a situation which is acted out by seducing others to make them addicts.

Simmel attempts in this paper to clarify the relation of drug addiction to physical illness, obsessional neurosis, manic-depressive states and perversion. He connects, for example, drug addiction to obsessional ceremonial and masturbation, and suggests that the desire for drugging is often only a new edition of the conflict of masturbation in the same way as the obsessional neurosis. Drug addictions often start as psycho-neurosis under the domination of the obsessional neurotic mechanism, but change under the experience of intoxication into a narcissistic neurosis of the manic-depressive type. Simmel observes that in physical illness, depression and drug addiction the aggressive, destructive instincts are turned against the ego.

In physical illness the pain related to the bodily organ corresponds to the internal object of melancholia against which the aggression is directed. This explains, in Simmel's view, why the relief of the physical pain by means of the drug may link the drug effects to the melancholic mechanisms. The drug addiction also acts as a defence against melancholia: it may then be regarded as an 'artificial mania'. However, the progressive pharmacotoxic mania, in contradiction to spontaneous mania, does not help the patient to find his way back to objects. Originally the drug protects the ego in its conflict between the id, reality, and the sense of guilt, but in the course of the addiction the drug usurps the place of all the objects against which aggression was once directed. Simmel compares the withdrawal-treatment to the

P

depressive phase of the manic-depressive illness, and suggests that the drug addict increases his dosage not in spite of, but because of, the expected torture of withdrawal, a situation which serves his need for punishment by a severe superego. Simmel is also of the opinion that drug addiction is closely related to perversions and may also act as a defence against criminality. He is aware of the symbolic meaning of drugs and suggests that during analysis it becomes apparent that drugs are often identified with urine and faeces and related to a compulsion to drink something disgusting. Often the bottle or syringe represents the phallus, but in the deepest symbolic layer the phallus stands for the maternal breast which the drug addict longs to unite with. Simmel believes that the mother of drug addicts is often seductive and spoiling as a feeding mother, herself deriving auto-erotic pleasure from the feeding. This mother becomes the early superego of the drug addict, easily seduced and seducing, which explains in his opinion why the superego of the fully developed drug addict is easily corrupted by the id.

Concentrating on alcoholism, Simmel (1949) discusses its effect on the ego and the superego, and confirms the importance of the aggressive instincts in alcoholism, which he believes to be closely related to the manic-depressive illness. He feels it is essential in alcoholism to establish whether the disintegration of the ego is the cause or result of the alcoholic's chronic consumption of liquor. It depends on the extent of the morbidity of the ego whether alcohol helps the patient to find an artificial adaptation to external reality or whether his ego is doomed to disintegrate progressively and to lose its superego guidance in the clash between infantile instinctual cravings and the demands of reality. If the ego regresses beyond the phallic, the anal and the oral stage to its earliest pre-ego stage, which Simmel terms the gastro-intestinal stage, the alcoholic becomes an addict. Then the structure and dynamics of alcoholism are not different from any other drug addiction. Through this regression more and more activities of the alcoholic are de-genitalized and the painful experiences accompanying infantile masturbation are then transformed into pleasurable feelings. Through this regressive process more and more diffusion takes place, love is replaced by hate, and in this way the process of identification reverts to the tendency for the alcoholic actually to devour his objects. The drink itself becomes interchangeable with the hated object, fundamentally the mother. Simmel suggests that alcoholism implies chronic murder and chronic suicide, but he feels that the homicidal impulses are more prominent in alcoholic addiction than in other addictions like morphinism, where the patient is driven more by suicidal impulses. He confirms his earlier suggestion that all addictions, and especially alcoholic addictions, are protections against depression. The feelings of guilt and despair which torment the alcoholic after he had become sober may be partially caused by the alcohol but are much more related to the clinical depression which follows the alcoholic mania. He regards it as significant progress in the analysis of alcoholics when the manic reaction following the consumption of alcohol begins to fail and is replaced by feelings of misery, depression and guilt.

Simmel follows Kielholz, Juliusburger, Clark, and Rádo in stressing the relation of the addiction to depression. He also emphasizes, however, the manic character of the addiction, a view he shares with Freud, Abraham, Kielholz, and Rádo. Both Simmel and Rádo attempt to clarify the dissolution of the superego and the gradual ascendency of the destructive instincts in the addictions. Simmel stresses the desire for oneness with an object, the wish to eat and to be eaten, observations which have subsequently been taken up by Lewin. He has made many detailed observations on changes in the character structure of addicts. As Simmel had a sanatorium (nursing home) in Tegel for many years, one may assume that he had many more alcoholics or drug addicts under observation and treatment than most analysts, but he gives no clue as to how many patients he has actually treated and with what result.

In 1932 Glover (1932a) made his most detailed contribution on drug addiction. He attempts to throw light on the development of the psycho-analytical approach to drug addiction and alcoholism by critically examining the work of other analysts from the historical point of view. He emphasizes, for example, that the relation of drug addiction to libidinal aetiology and to regression to orality and homosexuality could not be maintained. Too little attention had been paid to the progression of instincts, to the view that the psychopathological states are exaggerations of normal states in the mastery of anxiety. He demands that one should examine the impulsion forward to overcome 'the discomforts of an unconscious paranoid organization'. In other words, he wonders how far an obsessional state or an addiction implies a

defence against an 'underlying paranoid layer'. He believes that
fresh progress had been made by paying more attention to the
reactions produced by the aggressive group of impulses; for
example, by relating the unconscious homosexuality to the problem of sadism. In view of Freud's emphasis (from 1917 onwards)
on the importance of aggression in ego-development he feels that
it is remarkable that these teachings have not been fully reflected
in aetiological formulations concerning paranoia. He compares
in some detail Melanie Klein's work with that of Abraham, Van
Ophuijsen, Kielholz, Feigenbaum, Fenichel, and others. He feels
that early sadism and the early Oedipus complex, which Klein
studied, play an important role in the delusions of poisoning and
the drug addictions. He says: 'I cannot find any adequate explanation of drug addiction which does not assume an active
oedipal situation at a stage when object relations are little
more than the psychic reflection of organ relations.' He draws
attention to Schmideberg's suggestion that in drug addictions
there are mechanisms at work whereby dangerous introjected
objects can be transmuted into good substances and where
good substances can be used to neutralize or expel malignant
ones. Glover has studied the relation between drug addiction,
psychotic states, obsessional neurosis and neurotic character
peculiarities. He feels that in drug addiction one can detect more
clearly than in well-defined neuroses or psychotic states the
existence of a series of nuclear oedipal situations. These earliest
nuclear formations are arranged in cluster formation rather than
simply in consecutive series. Glover is aware that acceptance of
an early polymorphous ego organization involves some recasting
of the existing rather rigid descriptive views of narcissism. A good
deal of what has hitherto been considered as belonging to a narcissistic organization would have to be relegated to a system of
object relations. He feels that the term 'oral fixation' is much too
vague. In discussing the possibility of establishing a specific
mechanism for drug addiction he suggests that this specific reaction represents a transition between the more primitive psychotic
phase and the later psychoneurotic phase of development. He
believes that different types of drug addictions represent varia-
tions in the amount of original erotogenic sources of libido
(and consequently different fusions of sadism). In Glover's experience the main fantasy of drug addicts represents a condensa-
tion of two primary systems, one in which the child attacks and

later restores organs in the mother's body, and one in which the mother attacks and later restores organs in the child's body. These fantasies also represent masturbation systems. Glover in his conclusions stresses particularly the defensive function of drug addiction. He says its defensive function is to control sadistic attacks, which though less violent than those associated with paranoia are more severe than the sadistic attacks met with in obsessional formations. He also emphasizes that drug addiction acts as a protection against psychotic reaction in states of regression. In one of his cases a paranoidal system appeared after the withdrawal of the drug. In another case there was no notable paranoid reaction after the deprivation, but the melancholic element was extremely conspicuous. However, even in the most acute stages the melancholic mechanisms are not pure. Glover is particularly interested in whether the addict chooses a noxious or harmless substance. He believes that in the choice of a noxious habit the element of sadism is decisive. The drug would be a substance (part-object) with sadistic properties which can exist both in the outer world and within the body, but which exercises its sadistic powers only when inside. 'The situation would represent a transition between the menacing externalized sadism of the paranoid system and the actual internalized sadism of a melancholic system.' In the great majority of 'benign addictions' the restorative and life-giving properties of the substance are clearly manifest. The benign substances are more related to erotogenic interests, the exploitation of later and more predominantly genital libidinal development as a reassurance against early masochistic phases. Glover also stresses that the addict exploits the action of the drug in terms of an infantile system of thinking.

The significance of addiction can be described as follows. By 'cutting off' the body (sensory perceptions) the drug appears to have obliterated instinctual tension or frustration: it can also kill, punish or indulge not only psychic 'objects' in the body but the body as 'self'. By 'cutting off' the external world the drug can obliterate not only actual instinctual stimuli from without but stimuli due to projected instinct. By the same obliteration it can kill or punish external objects with or without projected characteristics: it can also rescue them by keeping them at a distance. This 'double action' accounts for the extreme sense of compulsion associated with addiction. It is specially marked in cases where both 'self' and 'introjected objects' are felt to be bad and dangerous and the only chance of preserving a good self lies in isolating it in the external world in the form of a good object (1932a, p. 326).

Glover explains that his 'main aim in this paper (1932a) is to draw attention to the significance of drug-addiction as representing a compromise between projective and introjective processes', and he therefore avoids using the term 'superego'. In 1939 Glover says that '(most) drug addictions bear (close) resemblances to manic-depressive disorder. They are *diphasic* in nature, the phase of painful abstinence corresponding to the depressive phase of cyclothymia. . . . Actually an addiction occurring in a depressive type may be a substitute for and a safeguard against suicide.' On the other hand, Glover continues, the amount of projection used by some addicts suggests a close affinity with paranoid states, a connexion which is also suggested clinically by the frequent appearance of persecutory ideas and delusions of jealousy in certain cases of alcoholism.

For practical purposes three main types of addiction can be distinguished. The mildest forms are those due to reinforced unconscious homosexuality. Next come addictions with a cyclothymic organization. Cases of this type are inclined to favour frequent self-imposed abstinences. By way of contrast the third or paranoid type of addiction is more chronic and shows only occasional spontaneous remissions. Differential diagnosis is not difficult.

Glover stresses more than Rádo and Simmel the importance of early aggressive impulses. While he seems to agree with Rádo, Simmel, Kielholz, and Clark that manic-depressive states and addictions are related, he has made an important original contribution in emphasizing the relation between the addictions and paranoia. In examining the paranoid cases of addiction Glover is clearly not just considering latent homosexuality but early paranoid anxieties dating from the first year of life.

Glover gives the impression in his earlier paper (1932a) that most addicts belong to the paranoid group. Later (1939) he changes his mind, emphasizing that most addictions resemble the manic-depressive disorder.

Knight has contributed several papers on the dynamics and treatment of alcoholism. He stresses that alcoholic addiction is a symptom rather than a disease. In many cases psychotic trends, particularly paranoid and schizoid features, are to be discovered. During the period of excessive drinking the patient temporarily goes into a psychotic state and there is often a regressive acting

out of unconscious libidinal and sadistic drives. Knight is, however, also of the opinion that alcoholism represents an attempt to
find some solution to, or cure of, the emotional conflict. He has
made an attempt to define the character of the alcoholic and he
has also described what he considers a typical family constellation in alcoholic patients. The mother seems generally to be over-
indulgent and over protective. She tries to appease the infant by
satisfying him constantly, so that the child's eventual weaning
can only mean his betrayal by the mother, who led him to expect
indulgence, and the child tries by every means to recapture this
lost experience. Throughout his life he will try to obtain passive
indulgences from people and will develop characteristically oral
ways of pacifying himself when his wishes are frustrated. Because
his wishes are so great they are bound to be often frustrated. He
reacts to this with rage, which is usually felt as a seething discomfort and a resentful turmoil within. All psychological distress
resulting from feelings of inferiority, from the patient's passivity,
from frustration and rage, and from guilt or spitefulness is
assuaged by the pacifier 'alcohol'.

The father of the alcoholic is almost invariably cold and un-
affectionate, rather dominating towards his family and incon-
sistently severe and indulgent towards his son. There is generally
repressed resentment and rage against this powerful father-figure
and the drinking often represents part of an unresolved adolescent revolt against the father. Knight emphasizes that by drinking the patient's deeply disturbed self-esteem is restored. He
relates the desire to drink to the old infantile craving for the
breast, but this craving is reinforced by the patient's defiance of
society, his parents, and by his masculine protest. After the
drinking he is depressed, intensely remorseful and disgusted with
himself. He is also terrified by the dangerously destructive behaviour in which he has indulged. But his sublime confidence in
the magic of the alcohol remains in spite of the hangover. The
patient feels betrayed by the alcohol, but still remains attracted
to it in the same way as he felt betrayed by his mother but nevertheless craved for her indulgences. In discussing the technique of
treatment Knight emphasizes that the so-called orthodox technique of analysis cannot be maintained with alcoholics, because
they cannot stand the detached attitude of the analyst; and the
more severe the case, the less able is the patient to cope with this.
He compares the alcoholic and the schizophrenic, both of whom,

in his opinion, are at all times hypersensitive to any evidence of rejection on the part of the analyst. Therefore the analyst must be much more active and must not adopt any attitude of criticism or condemnation of drinking or any debauches which may occur during the analysis. He suggests that it is helpful in getting the analysis going to have quite a number of friendly analytic interviews with the patient sitting up. During these occasions one can establish initial rapport, bring much important material out into the open and into the patient's awareness by skilful questioning and then gradually manœuvre the patient on to the couch in order to proceed with analysis. As the alcoholic's need for indulgence and affection is so great some of his needs must be met rather than merely analysed and interpreted. Knight has treated his alcoholic patients in a sanatorium and he feels that for patients with chronic drug or alcohol addiction institutional supervision is imperative. The sanatorium must offer the patient a new reality which not only isolates him from his previous neurotic life situation but also provides scientifically controlled management of his readjustment in the institution. Such control must aid the psycho-analytic treatment by being directed against the pleasure principle in such a way as to drive the patient to the analysis of his behaviour as the only solution. During the treatment in hospital one is impressed by the splitting of the transference. There is often a spurious form of positive transference in which the analyst is thought of as a saviour but the rest of the institution is considered worthless and beneath contempt. All the split-off bits of the negative transference must be brought into the analysis and interpreted for the analysis to make some headway. In the institutional analysis the analyst may use information supplied by the nurses, when the interpretations about his spurious love are continually denied by the patient. Knight's observations differ greatly from the work of the analysts quoted so far. He stresses the pathological early and later environment of the alcoholic and makes suggestions as to the necessity for modification of analytic treatment in cases of alcoholism. He seems to agree with Simmel as to the many technical difficulties arising in the treatment of drug addicts and alcoholics.

A number of analysts have investigated the relation of drug addiction and alcoholism to food addiction; I would mention particularly Wulff, Robbins, Benedek, and Fenichel. Wulff

(1932) describes a disease entity which is marked by compulsive greedy eating, somnolence, dull depression, disgust in relation to one's own body and a tendency to periodicity. He differentiates this 'food addiction' from melancholia and suggests that while in melancholia there is a sadistic destructive incorporation, in the food addiction syndrome there is simply an erotic introjection which takes the place of the genital relationship. In the four cases he describes the author does not find early eating disturbances— the addiction having started only at puberty. He does, however, stress the strong constitutional oral erotism in the families of these patients and believes that there is a regression to the stage of incomplete object-love with partial incorporation of the object. He thinks that the castration complex plays a central part because the objects craved for, particularly sweets, bread, and meat, stand unconsciously for the devoured penis. He regards it as striking that the patients, who, in their depressions, are disgusted with their own body, have, during their good periods, a similar feeling of disgust towards all food, which extends to the functions of eating itself. During the periods of food craving they particularly like dirty food, remnants of food off strange plates or even uneatable rubbish. He believes that all this disgusting and dirty craving represents the symbolic representation of the desired penis. In discussing the craving for sleep, Wulff suggests that the patients were overcome by the compulsion to sleep after eating. After a restless tormenting deep sleep they woke in a very depressed mood feeling tired and beaten up. Sometimes they masturbated in their sleep. In one of the patients, after food, instead of sleep, there was a sinking into daydreams of a sexual, sometimes oral-erotic, or other perverse content. It is surprising that Wulff does not believe that there is an ambivalent relation to the introjected penis, for instance penis envy. In fact he sees the incorporation of the penis purely as libidinal relation to the penis.

Benedek (1936) described an addiction to alcohol which was essentially a struggle against polyphagy. When her patient had taken alcohol all her inhibitions vanished and she ate enormous quantities of food. She could consume the most impossible things without her stomach rebelling. After taking a large quantity of food she invariably felt remorse. When the patient ate, she thought that her figure altered and increased in size and that her breasts became larger. She then wanted to destroy her body and tear off her breasts. The alcoholic addiction seemed to follow these anxieties and impulses. The author believes that in this case there was a psychotic paranoid hatred of women, which was related to the patient's violent hatred of her own body and the rejection of her femininity. She thinks that the driving force behind the urge was the annihilation of femininity or the need to ward off repressed homosexual impulses. If the patient had been able to incorporate the desired object, the breast, it would have furthered the development of her femininity. But this identification had to be repudiated and in the symbolic action of destroying the food she destroyed the mother and the mother's breast, and equally she destroyed her own feminine body and breasts by the refusal of food. While Benedek stresses that the full ambivalence appropriate to the oral stage was left out of the transference, she seems to believe in her theoretical description that the libidinal homosexual attachment to the mother was primary and that the destruction of the internalized breast was simply a defence against the libidinal attachment to the mother. She describes another case of addiction to food with an identical symptomatology. This patient was dominated by the idea that she had controlled her desire to eat because she must not want to eat in order not to have the body of a woman. Benedek stresses that the dominant idea should be regarded as a monosymptomatic psychosis. The dominant idea has a superego character which makes it intelligible that the patient's attempt to master her tensions first takes shape in the symptom of depression. The superego automatically heightens the underlying oral instinctual tension and this leads to the addiction to food or alcohol. She regards the addiction as a sign that the tension cannot be mastered intrapsychically and is being dealt with by external means, the addiction. Benedek does not give the early infantile history of her patients and it is not quite clear in this paper how much she believes that the early disturbance in the infant's relations to the mother and the breast are responsible for the disease she describes. One has the impression that the central problem is regarded as that of homosexuality.

Robbins (1935) reports a case where, in contrast to Benedek and Wulff, early nutritional disturbances could be connected with the later development of alcoholism. In the transference experience the patient's very early relationship to his mother's breast was repeated. He had been an aggressive infant, had suckled greedily at the breast, but had been forcefully weaned after a short time. Following the withdrawal of the breast he had pyloric spasm with violent regurgitation and was in severe danger for many months. As a result of this the breast was felt to be poisonous, the whole world bitter and hostile. The liberation of murderous impulses activated by the profound deprivation were first directed towards the mother, then towards all those who fed him with projection on to them of his own aggressive impulses. They all became dangerous and any expression of love in the form of food offered from outside was violently rejected as poisonous, and relief was sought by a regression to the first few satisfactory days of life. In this way a compensatory, internal and highly satisfactory fantastic relationship to the mother was built up. He needed no nutrition from the outside; he contained it all within himself, a fantasy which was reinforced by the alcohol. Robbins regards alcoholism not so much as an illness in itself but as a spontaneous attempt at cure, and he emphasizes that the consumption of alcohol should not be disturbed until the underlying neurosis or psychosis has been thoroughly explored with the acquisition of insight.

Robbins regards the early infantile oral problems as the main cause of the alcoholism, and he has given very detailed analytic case material as evidence of his findings. This makes it a particularly lively and important contribution. We should remember that Freud, Abraham, Rádo, Simmel and Benedek have mentioned the importance of oral factors in the addictions and in alcoholism.

Bergler in 1944 stresses the importance of early oral factors in alcoholic addiction. He believed that alcoholics have experienced weaning from the mother as 'malice'. For this reason these patients want to take revenge for their oral disappointment by attempts to concoct habitually situations in which they are refused and disappointed. This enables them to plead self-defence when they attack their self-constructed imaginary enemies with the sharpest aggression. They finally revel in self-pity, enjoying psychic masochistic pleasure. Bergler feels that drinking can be regarded as a self-cure and reparation. By drinking they may make good the mother's refusal, they feel independent of her and in this way triumph over her. He stresses that it is particularly the internal mother who is harmed by the drinking. It is interesting how closely Bergler follows Robbins's observations about the importance of the weaning situation in alcoholism and he also suggests that drinking should be regarded as an attempt at reparation or self-cure.

Fenichel (1945c) discussed both the addiction to drugs and addictions without drugs. He defines addicts as persons who have a disposition to react to the effects of alcohol, morphine or other drugs in such a way that they try to use these effects simultaneously to satisfy an archaic longing which is sexual, a desire for security, and a desire for the maintenance of self-esteem. He feels that drug addicts are fixated to a passive narcissistic aim and that they are solely interested in getting their gratification, never in satisfying their partners. In other words, objects are nothing to them but deliverers of supplies. These patients are intolerant of tension, and after feeling elated, pain and frustration become all the more unbearable, inducing an increased use of the drug. Under the influence of the drug, erotic and narcissistic satisfactions visibly coincide again and there is an extraordinary increase in self-esteem. In certain addictions, particularly alcoholic addiction, Fenichel stresses the disappearance of the superego through the alcohol. He agrees with other writers that the periodicity of certain drinking disorders is related to the periodicity of the manic-depressive states. He discusses addictions without drugs, and suggests that 'in food addicts, no displacement has transformed the original object (food)'. 'Later stages of development may have added other unconscious meanings to the pathologically craved food', but 'in severe cases the field of eating remains the only interest connecting the person with reality'. He emphasizes that there is a characteristic relationship between food cravings, food phobias and certain types of anorexia. In discussing the therapy of addiction Fenichel suggests that the best time to begin an analysis is obviously during or immediately after withdrawal, but it is not to be expected that the patient will remain abstinent throughout analysis. If he has an opportunity he will probably use the drug again whenever the resistance in his analysis predominates. This is the reason why addicts are to be analysed in an institution rather than as ambulatory patients. He also stresses the tendency of the addict to act out during analysis. Fenichel follows Rádo, Simmel and Glover in observing the relationship between drug addictions and the manic-depressive states. In stressing the disappearance of the superego in alcoholism he follows Simmel. He agrees with Juliusburger, Clark,

Kielholz, Rádo, Simmel, and Bergler in emphasizing the nar-cissism of the addict.

Weijl made several contributions to the psycho-analytic treat-ment of alcoholic addiction. In 1945 he stresses the importance of the pleasure principle for understanding alcoholic addiction. The alcohol is particularly used in order to diminish the tension and pain created by the activity of the superego. It makes the individual less sensitive to the criticism of the external world, the original source from which the superego was derived. By the use of alcohol the superego loses its influence on the ego which can be boundlessly magnified and becomes intoxicated with its own per-fection and self-sufficiency. At this point the well-known artificial manic phase of drunkenness is reached. The overcoming of guilt feelings means a reduction in the existing unpleasure, but the fact that the alcoholic behaves improperly and does forbidden things increases again his guilt feelings. In this way a vicious circle is created which leads to repeated recourse to alcohol. Weijl stresses the importance of alcohol in certain actions and ritual customs and suggests that the alcohol has a two-fold sym-bolic meaning, representing the father as well as the mother. Alcohol represents a symbol of the desired milk, and therefore becomes a substitute for the mother, camouflaging the uncon-sciously-desired milk. The author particularly emphasizes the re-lation of alcoholism to the totem meal, which he regards as the primal sin of killing the father by eating. He believes that the excessive use of alcohol represents a fantastic primitive way of solving the Oedipus conflict (the killing of the father and the union with the mother). Weijl suggests that the state of intoxica-tion is manic and is followed by depression in which the alcoholic coma suggests an imitation of death; death being the punishment for the primal sin. He stresses that alcoholic addiction has to be regarded as an artificial manic-depressive psychosis on a dimi-nished scale. He thinks that alcohol addiction is a fantastic satis-faction of the wish for eternal life, because after partial suicide by means of alcohol there is a revival and an ever-repeated sug-gestion of death and re-birth. In the treatment of alcoholism the author stresses that total abstinence is absolutely necessary for any alcoholic, as the alcohol attacks the superego and opens the way for the liberation of the id. For this reason the alcoholic must stay in an institution, particularly at the beginning of the treat-ment. He regards it as an essential part of the psycho-analytic treatment that the inferiority feelings of the alcoholic should be neutralized and that his ego should be built up, but he does not specifically discuss how this is achieved.

Weijl joins the majority of authors in stressing the relationship of alcoholism to the manic-depressive psychosis. He also follows Simmel, Fenichel, and others in emphasizing the attack of the alcohol on the superego.

Meerloo has studied the problem of drug addiction from many different angles, and has also treated several drug addicts by psycho-analysis. He feels that it is difficult to establish sharp demarcations between physical and psychological drug habit formations. But certain abstinence symptoms he believes are psychogenic in origin: for example, abstinence symptoms, such as heavy pains in the muscles and abdomen, could be related to periods of destructive rage after oral frustrations by the mother. He also found fantasies of being swallowed up by the bottle, and of being sucked in by the mother, which were related to this feeling of physical misery. He feels that diverse regressions such as catalepsy, mania, psychopathic behaviour, hallucinosis, epileptic seizures or delirium tremens should be regarded as psychosomatic syndromes, but our knowledge of the dynamics of drug addictions is in his opinion not sufficiently refined to expose the underlying psychological mechanisms.

Meerloo attempts to differentiate between the psychology of the alcoholic and that of the morphinist and other drug addicts. He comes to the conclusion that the majority of alcoholics are manic-depressive oral types while most drug addicts are of a schizoid type living in a magic infantile world. He suggests that there are three mental mechanisms which are common to all types of addiction, a craving for ecstatic experience, an unconscious drive towards self-destruction, and an unconscious, unresolved need for oral dependency. Meerloo agrees with Lewin in his suggestion that in his narcotic stupor the drug addict experiences union with the breast. In this way the drug addict may be compared with the manic patient, though the addict differs from the manic-depressive in that he needs the alcohol or drug in order to overcome his anti-cannibalistic defences. Only then is he able to regress to this passive, oral, nirvanic state. To a greater extent than for the manic patient the bottle or drug symbolizes not only the infantile gratification but also the devouring goddess who in devouring them brings the children to an eternal nirvana. He stresses that the ecstasy of the intoxicated person and the drug addict is a pseudo-elation: he relives an old unhappiness which is a repeated fight against the introjected mother. In a state of ecstasy both regressive and progressive forces come into play. Ecstasy extends the ego and silences the hostile voice of conscience, but it also induces the oceanic sensations of merging with the universe which in the final analysis is antithetical to self-preservation. Suicidal and masochistic tendencies play a strong role in all addictions. The patient, for example, wishes to make a hideous spectacle of himself so that he may accuse some-one else (usually a parental figure) and he secretly enjoys mas-querading as an innocent victim. As far as treatment is concerned the author stresses that abstention from alcohol and drugs may take place spontaneously or in the course of psycho-analytic treatment. The author first tries psychotherapy outside the clinic, but if this fails he has the addict 'reconditioned' in the clinic, though by another physician. In the analytic situation the absten-tion symptoms tend to become very severe, since they are fortified by the patient's resistance to analysis. They are used as reproaches and attacks on the analyst. He has observed the de-velopment of hallucinatory symptoms typical of delirium tre-mens. Following these experiences and the alleviation of these fears the patient often stops drinking heavily. Psycho-analytic treatment of alcoholics and drug addicts is not only difficult be-cause of the pharmacological involvement and counteracting social influences, but also because of the very early infantile roots of the neurosis and the great difficulty in reaching them by analysis, since addiction is such an easy way to act out. He emphasizes that many patients try to bribe the analyst with pas-sive and temporary abstinent behaviour, waiting only for one mistake, a display of firmness, or disturbing interpretations by the analyst to escape back into alcoholic or narcotic patterns. The author describes the treatment of an opium addict who changed from opium to alcohol and to barbiturates and cocaine but in the last year of treatment remained completely free from drugs.

Meerloo agreed then with the majority of authors that most alcoholics belong to the manic-depressive group, but he adds the view that drug addicts are more of a schizoid type. He agrees with most authors in the importance of oral factors. In discuss-ing aggression he emphasizes the self-destructive rather than the destructive components. He follows Simmel, Fenichel and Weijl and others in stressing the silencing of the superego during narcotic ecstasy. In discussing the longing of the drug addict for narcissistic oneness with the object Meerloo agrees with Rádo, Simmel, Weijl, Fenichel, Bergler and others.

## Conclusions

From the discussion of these contributions it emerges that there is agreement among the majority of authors on the importance in both the drug addictions and alcoholism of oral factors, narcissism, mania, depression, destructive or self-destructive impulses and perversions, such as homosexuality or sado-masochism.

In discussing the orality of addicts some contributors talk in a more general way of constitutional intensity of orality (Freud), revival of the alimentary orgasm (Rádo), or regression to the sucking phase (Simmel); while others are more specific in emphasizing the importance of the weaning trauma: Robbins describes how early weaning can change the frustrating external breast into a poisonous one leading to a defensive building up of a highly idealized internal mother or breast, which contributes to illusions of self-sufficiency. Bergler suggests that weaning has been experienced by the alcoholic as malice and a revenge pattern is constructed around this belief.

When describing narcissism some writers talk of a narcissistic disposition (Rádo), a regression to narcissism (Kielholz), primary identification (Pierce Clark), oceanic sensations of merging with the universe (Meerloo), or fixation to a passive narcissistic aim (Fenichel), while some authors, such as Simmel, stress the pathological narcissism 'where more and more defusion takes place enabling the death instinct to become more powerful and where the addict withdraws into a pre-natal state symbolizing death'.

In discussing the relationship of the addictions or alcoholism to depression and mania the majority of authors stress the importance of the manic-depressive psychosis, namely, Kielholz, Rádo, Simmel, Fenichel, Weijl, and Meerloo (in alcoholism). Some authors are more emphatic about the relationship of the addictions to mania (Freud) or to manic defences such as the desire to escape (Abraham and Ferenczi) or stress simply the depressive or suicidal impulses (Pierce Clark).

The views of the authors when describing destructive or self-destructive impulses present some difficulty because they refer to sadism and masochism (Abraham, Juliusburger, and Pierce Clarke) simply as an alternative to the terms 'aggressive' or 'self-destructive' impulses. Kielholz prefers to speak of the death instinct directed against the ego, often leading to suicide in cases of alcoholic melancholia, while in the alcoholic manic spree the death instinct is turned outwards and sadism is openly expressed and acted out. Some authors make quite clear that they regard the predominance of the destructive impulses or aggression as of major importance in understanding the addictions (Rádo, Simmel and Glover).

The majority of authors mention some perversion such as homosexuality, masochism or sado-masochism as appearing frequently in drug addicts and alcoholics, some stating specifically however that such perversions are only to be seen as part of the general picture. Thus Juliusburger stresses that homosexuality is only one of the factors in alcoholism. Glover believes that only very mild cases are due to unconscious homosexuality while Rádo emphasizes the fact that the homosexuality of the addict is only of secondary importance, developing under the influence of severe masochism.

Paranoid delusions, persecutory anxieties and paranoia have also been mentioned by at least seven contributors, but it is clear that most of the authors differ as to the aetiology of the paranoia they have in mind. Glover talks of a very early infantile paranoid phase as the main source of the drug addict's difficulties, while Kielholz traces the persecutory anxieties of his case of delirium tremens to primary scene experiences and fantasies.

Some authors are convinced that alcoholism and the drug addictions have a particularly destructive effect in so far as they influence the conscience or superego. Simmel, Fenichel, Weijl, Meerloo, and others believe that the addictions paralyse the superego and in some way eliminate its influence. Rádo, however, makes two apparently contradictory statements, that the conscience disintegrates, and that the aggressive tendencies attach themselves to the superego, increasing its severity and so producing a vicious circle. There would, however, be no contradiction if one assumes that with the disintegration of the more mature conscience the more archaic destructive persecutory superego makes its appearance.

Some authors believe that the alcohol or drug represents the

Q

good or bad object. Freud and Robbins describe the alcohol as an ideal object. Simmel regards the bottle or syringe as being, at the deepest layer, the maternal breast with which the addict longs to unite. He does, however, also speak of the drug as an image combining all the bad objects in the alcoholic's life. Glover makes the most detailed contribution to this problem by stating that drugs frequently represent part objects: in the case of the malignant addictions the bad sadistic object; in the benign addictions a good, life-giving one. Glover also draws attention to the inter-relationship between systems of good or bad external and internal objects, and the use of drugs to attack good or bad objects, and he links this with the mechanisms of introjection and projection. It is clear that Glover believes that the choice of a dangerous (malignant) drug relates to the existence of malignant bad and dangerous part objects.

## Discussion of Treatment and Management

Only a few of the authors mentioned in the review (Knight, Fenichel, Simmel, Kielholz, Weijl, and Meerloo) have discussed the technical difficulties which arise in the treatment of both alcoholics and drug addicts. They are generally in agreement that supervision in an institution is essential in order to control and manage the patient and his treatment. Kielholz and Weijl particularly stress the importance of complete abstinence. Meerloo first tries psychotherapeutic treatment outside the clinic. If this fails he has the patient admitted to an institution and the drug withdrawn there by another physician; he then apparently continues the treatment in the institution. Knight, who emphasizes the importance of institutional treatment, stresses the need to modify the analytic approach, believing that the alcoholic cannot tolerate ordinary analytical passivity. He discusses the importance of analysing the typical split in the transference, between the spuriously idealized analyst and some other member of the staff with whom the negative transference is acted out.

# BIBLIOGRAPHY

(Items marked with an asterisk are referred to only in chapters 7 and 13 on Drug Addiction)

ABRAHAM, K. (1908a). 'The Psycho-Sexual Differences between Hysteria and Dementia Praecox.' In: *Selected Papers of Karl Abraham*. (London: Hogarth, 1927.)

*(1908b). 'The Psychological Relations between Sexuality and Alcoholism.' *ibid.*

*(1916). 'The First Pregenital Stage of the Libido.' *ibid.*

(1924). 'A Short Study of the Development of the Libido, Viewed in the Light of Mental Disorders.' *ibid.*

ACKERMAN, N. W. (1938). 'Paranoid State with Delusions of Injury by "Black Magic".' *Bull. Menninger Clin.*, **2**.

*ALEXANDER, F. (1929). *The Psychoanalysis of the Total Personality*. (New York: Nerv. ment. Dis. Co.)

(1951). 'Schizophrenic Psychoses. Critical Considerations of the Psychoanalytic Treatment.' *Arch. Neurol. Psychiat.*, **26**.

ALEXANDER, F. and MENNINGER, W. (1936). 'The Relation of Persecutory Delusions to the Functioning of the Gastro-Intestinal Tract.' *J. nerv. ment. Dis.*, **84**.

ALTMAN, L. L. (1957). 'On the Oral Nature of Acting Out.' *J. Amer. Psychoanal. Assoc.*, **5**.

BAK, R. C. (1939). 'Über die dynamisch-structurellen Bedingungen des primären Beziehungswahns.' *Z. f. Neurol. u. Psychiat.*, **166**.

(1943). 'Dissolution of the Ego, Mannerism, and Delusion of Grandeur.' *J. nerv. ment. Dis.*, **98**.

(1946). 'Masochism in Paranoia.' *Psychoanal. Quart.*, **15**.

BALINT, M. (1960). 'Primary Narcissism and Primary Love.' *Psychoanal. Quart.*, **29**.

BARBARA, D. A. (1944). 'Positive Transference in Schizophrenia.' *Psychiat. Quart.*, **18**.

BARKAS, M. R. (1925). 'Treatment of Psychotic Patients in Institutions in the Light of Psycho-Analysis.' *J. Neurol. Psychopathol.*, **5**.

BENDER, L. (1934). 'The Anal Component in Persecutory Delusions.' *Psychoanal. Rev.*, **21**.

BENEDEK, T. (1933). 'Mental Processes in Thyrotoxic States.' *Psychoanal. Quart.*, **3**.

(1934). 'Some Factors Determining Fixation at the "Deutero-Phallic" Phase.' *Int. J. Psycho-Anal.*, **15**.

*(1936). 'Dominant Ideas and their Relation to Morbid Cravings.' *Int. J. Psycho-Anal.*, **17**.

BERES, D. (1958). 'Vicissitudes of Superego Functions and Superego Precursors in Childhood.' *Psychoanal. Study Child*, **13**.

BERGLEF, E. (1955). 'Eight Prerequisites for the Psychoanalytic Treatment of Homosexuality.' *Psychoanal. Rev.*, **31**.

BERGLER, E. and EIDELBERG, L. (1933). 'Der Mammakomplex des Mannes.' *Int. Z. Psychoanal.*, **19**.

(1935). 'Der Mechanismus der Depersonalisation.' *Int. Z. Psychoanal.*, **21**.

BERKELEY-HILL, O. (1921). 'The Anal Complex and its Relation to Delusions of Persecution.' (Abstract). *Int. J. Psycho-Anal.*, **4**.

(1922). 'A Case of Paranoid Dissociation.' *Psychoanal. Rev.*, **9**.

BIBRING, E. (1928). 'Klinische Beiträge zur Paranoiafrage. I. Zur Psychologie der Todesideen bei paranoider Schizophrenia.' *Int. Z. Psychoanal.*, **14**.

(1929). '. . . II. Ein Fall von Organprojektion.' *Int. Z. Psychoanal.*, **15**.

BIBRING, G. (1940). 'Über eine orale Komponente bei männlicher Inversion.' *Int. Z. Psychoanal.*, **25**.

*BIGELOW, NEWTON, J. T. with LEHRMAN, R. and PALMER, J. (1939). 'Personality in Alcoholic Disorder: Acute Hallucinosis and Delirium Tremens.' *Psychiat. Quart.*, **13**.

BION, W. R. (1954). 'Notes on the Theory of Schizophrenia.' *Int. J. Psycho-Anal.*, **35**.

(1956). 'Development of Schizophrenic Thought.' *Int. J. Psycho-Anal.*, **37**.

(1957). 'The Differentiation of the Psychotic from the Non-Psychotic Personality.' *Int. J. Psycho-Anal.*, **38**.

(1958). 'On Hallucination.' *Int. J. Psycho-Anal.*, **39**.

(1959). 'Attacks on Linking.' *Int. J. Psycho-Anal.*, **40**.

✳ (1962). *Learning from Experience.* (London: Heinemann Medical.)

BIRD, BRIAN (1957). 'A Specific Peculiarity of Acting Out.' *J. Amer. Psychoanal. Assoc.*, **5**.

*BIRSTEIN, J. (1913). 'Ein psychologischer Beitrag zur Frage des Alkoholismus.' *Zentralbl. f. Psychoanal. u. Psychother.*, **3**. Abstr. in *Psychoanal. Rev.*, **2**.

BJERRE, P. C. (1911). 'Zur Radikalbehandlung der chronischen Paranoia.' *Jahrb. f. Psychoanal.*, **3**.

*BLEULER, E. (1911). 'Alkohol und Neurosen.' *Jahrb. f. Psychoanal.*, **3**. Abstr. in *Psychoanal. Rev.*, **8**.

(1916). *Textbook of Psychiatry.* (London: Allen & Unwin, 1923; New York: Macmillan, 1924; etc.)

BOLLMEIER, L. N. (1938). 'The Paranoid Mechanism in Overt Male Homosexuality.' *Psychoanal. Quart.*, **7**.

BOSWELL, J. (1777). *The Hypochondriack.* (Stanford Calif. Univ. Press, 1928.)

BRILL, A. A. (1911). 'Psychological Mechanisms of Paranoia.' *New York Med. J.*, **94**.

*(1919). 'Alcohol and the Individual.' *New York Med. J.*, **109**.

*BROMBERG, W. and SCHILDER, P. (1933). 'Psychological Considerations in Alcoholic Hallucinations–Castration and Dismembering Motives.' *Int. J. Psycho-Anal.*, **14**.

BRUNSWICK, R. MACK (1928a). 'Supplement to Freud's *History of an Infantile Neurosis.' Int. J. Psycho-Anal.,* **9**.

(1928b). 'The Analysis of a Case of Paranoia.' *J. nerv. ment. Dis.,* **70**.

(1930). 'Entgegnung auf Harniks kritische Bemerkungen.' *Int. Z. Psychoanal.,* **16**.

BYCHOWSKI, G. (1930). 'A Case of Oral Delusions of Persecution.' *Int. J. Psycho-Anal.* **11**.

(1933). 'Activität und Realität.' *Int. Z. Psychoanal.,* **19**.

(1945). 'The Ego of Homosexuals.' *Int. J. Psycho-Anal.,* **26**.

*(1952). 'Pharmacothymia.' In: *Psychotherapy of Psychosis* (New York: Grune & Stratton.)

*CARVER, A. E. (1931). 'The Psychology of the Alcoholist.' *Brit. J. med. Psychol.,* **11**.

*CHASSELL, J. O. (1938). 'Family Constellation in the Etiology of Essential Alcoholism.' *Psychiatry,* **1**.

CHEYNE, G. (1733). *The English Malady.* (London.)

*CLARK, L. PIERCE (1919). 'A Psychological Study of some Alcoholics.' *Psycho-anal. Rev.,* **6**.

(1933). 'Treatment of Narcissistic Neuroses and Psychoses.' *Psychoanal. Rev.,* **20**.

*CORIAT, I. (1917). 'Some Statistical Results of the Psychoanalytic Treatment of the Psychoneuroses.' *Psychoanal. Rev.,* **4**.

*CROWLEY, RALPH M. (1939). 'Psychoanalytic Literature on Drug Addiction and Alcoholism.' *Psychoanal. Rev.,* **26**.

*DANIELS, G. (1933). 'Turning Points in the Analysis of a Case of Alcoholism.' *Psychoanal. Quart.,* **2**.

DARLINGTON, H. (1939). 'The Meaning of Headhunting. The Analysis of a Savage Practice and its Relationship to Paranoia.' *Psychoanal. Rev.,* **26**.

DEUTSCH, H. (1921). 'Zur Psychologie des Misstrauens.' *Imago,* **7**.

(1933). 'On the Psychology of Manic Depressive States, especially Chronic Hypomania.' In: *Psycho-Analysis of the Neuroses.* (London: Hogarth, 1964.)

(1942). 'Some Forms of Emotional Disturbances and their Relationship to Schizophrenia.' *ibid.*

*EDDISON, H. W. (1934). 'The Love Object in Mania.' *Int. J. Psycho-Anal.,* **15**.

EISLER, M. J. (1929). 'Über wahnhafte Selbstanklagen.' *Int. Z. Psychoanal.,* **15**.

EISSLER, K. (1951). 'Remarks on the Psycho-Analysis of Schizophrenia.' *Int. J. Psycho-Anal.,* **32**.

FEDERN, P. (1928). 'Narcissism in the Structure of the Ego.' In: *Ego Psychology and the Psychoses.* (London: Imago, 1953.)

(1929). 'The Ego as Subject and Object in Narcissism.' *ibid.*

(1943). 'Psychoanalysis of Psychoses.' *ibid.*

*(1953). 'Manic-Depressive Psychosis.' *ibid.*

FEIGENBAUM, D. (1930). 'Analysis of a Case of Paranoia Persecutoria. Structure and Cure.' *Psychoanal. Rev.,* **17**.

(1936). 'On Projection.' *Psychoanal. Quart.,* **5**.

(1937). 'Depersonalization as a Defense Mechanism.' *Psychoanal. Quart.*, **6**.

*FENICHEL, O. (1933). 'Neuroses related to Perversion.' In: *Outline of Psychoanalysis.* (New York: Norton, 1934.)

(1945a). 'Neurotic Acting Out.' In: The *Collected Papers of Otto Fenichel,* 2nd series. (London: Routledge, 1955.)

(1945b). 'Organ Neuroses: Hypochondriasis.' In: *Psychoanalytic Theory of Neurosis.* (New York: Norton.)

*(1945c). 'Perversions and Impulse Neuroses: Drug Addiction.' *ibid.*

FERENCZI, S. (1911a). 'On the Part Played by Homosexuality in the Pathogenesis of Paranoia.' In: *First Contributions to Psycho-Analysis.* (London: Hogarth, 1952.)

*(1911b). 'Alkohol und Neurosen. Antwort auf die Kritik von Herrn Prof. Dr E. Bleuler.' *Jahrb. f. Psychoanal.*, **3**.

(1911c). 'Stimulation of the Anal-Erotogenic Zone as a Precipitating Factor in Paranoia. Contribution to the Subject of Homosexuality and Paranoia.' In: *Final Contributions to Psycho-Analysis.* (London: Hogarth, 1955.)

(1914). 'Some Clinical Observations of Paranoia and Paraphrenia.' In: *First Contributions to Psycho-Analysis.* (London: Hogarth, 1952.)

*(1916-17). 'The Psychic Consequences of a "Castration" in Childhood.' In: *Further Contributions to Psycho-Analysis.* (London: Hogarth, 1926.)

*(1919a). 'An Attempted Explanation of some Hysterical Stigmata.' *ibid.*

(1919b). 'Technical Difficulties in an Analysis of Hysteria.' *ibid.*

FRAIBERG, S. (1952). 'A Critical Neurosis in a 2½-Year-Old Girl.' *Psychoanal. Study Child*, **7**.

FREUD, A. (1951). 'Negativism and Emotional Surrender.' Read at the 17th International Psycho. Analytical Congress, Amsterdam.

(1952). 'The Role of Bodily Illness in the Mental Life of Children.' *Psychoanal. Study Child*, **7**.

FREUD, S. (1896). 'The Nature and Mechanism of Obsessional Neurosis.' *S.E.* **3**.

*(1905a). *Jokes and their Relation to the Unconscious. S.E.* **8**.

(1905b). *Three Essays on the Theory of Sexuality. S.E.* **7**.

*(1910). 'A Special Type of Choice of Object made by Men (Contributions to the Psychology of Love I).' *S.E.* **11**.

(1911). 'Psycho-Analytic Notes on an Autobiographical Account of a Case of Paranoia (Dementia Paranoides).' *S.E.* **12**.

(1914a). 'Remembering, Repeating and Working Through.' *S.E.* **12**.

(1914b). 'On Narcissism: an Introduction.' *S.E.* 14.

(1915). 'A Case of Paranoia Running Counter to the Psycho-Analytic Theory of the Disease.' *S.E.* 14.

(1916-17). *Introductory Lectures on Psycho-Analysis. S.E.* **15-16**.

(1917a). 'A Metapsychological Supplement to the Theory of Dreams.' *S.E.* 14.

(1917b). 'Mourning and Melancholia.' *S.E.* 14.

(1918). 'From the History of an Infantile Neurosis.' *S.E.* **17**.

(1921). *Group Psychology and the Analysis of the Ego. S.E.* **18.**

(1922). 'Some Neurotic Mechanisms in Jealousy, Paranoia and Homosexuality.' *S.E.* **18.**

(1924). 'Neurosis and Psychosis.' *S.E.* **19.**

(1926). *Inhibitions, Symptoms and Anxiety. S.E.* **20.**

(1927). 'Humour.' *S.E.* **21.**

(1931). 'Female Sexuality.' *S.E.* **21.**

(1933). *New Introductory Lectures on Psycho-Analysis. S.E.* **22.**

(1950). *The Origins of Psycho-Analysis.* (London: Imago.)

FROMM-REICHMANN, F. (1943). 'Psychoanalytic Psychotherapy with Psychotics.' In: *Psychoanalysis and Psychotherapy. Selected Papers* ed. Bullard (Chicago: Univ. of Chicago Press, 1959.)

(1947). 'Problems of Therapeutic Management in a Psychoanalytic Hospital.' *ibid.*

(1949). 'Notes on the Development of Treatment of Schizophrenics by Psychoanalytic Psychotherapy.' *ibid.*

GARDNER, G. D. (1931). 'Evidences of Homosexuality in One Hundred and Twenty Unanalysed Cases with Paranoid Content.' *Psychoanal. Rev.*, **18.**

GARMA, A. (1932). 'Die Realität und das Es in der Schizophrenie.' *Int. Z. Psychoanal.*, **18.**

GILLESPIE, R. D. (1929). *Hypochondria.* (London: Kegan Paul.)

*GLOVER, E. (1931a). 'The Prevention and Treatment of Drug Addiction.' *Proc. Roy. Soc. Med.*, **24.**

(1931b). 'The Thereapeutic Effect of Inexact Interpretation. A Contribution to the Theory of Suggestion.' *Int. J. Psycho-Anal.*, **12.**

*(1932a). 'On the Aetiology of Drug-Addiction.' *Int. J. Psycho-Anal.*, **13.**

*(1932b). 'Common Problems in Psychoanalysis and Anthropology: Drug Ritual and Addiction.' *Brit. J. med. Psychol.*, **12.**

*(1939). *Psychoanalysis.* (London: Bale.)

GREBELSKAJA, S. (1912). 'Psychologische Analyse eines Paranoiden.' *Jahrb. f. Psychoanal.*, **4.**

GREENACRE, P. (1950). 'General Problems of Acting Out.' In: *Trauma, Growth and Personality.* (New York: Norton; London: Hogarth, 1953.)

*GROSS, ALFRED (1935). 'The Psychic Effects of Toxic and Toxoid Substances.' *Int. J. Psycho-Anal.*, **16.**

HÁRNIK, J. (1930). 'Kritisches über Mack Brunswicks Nachtrag zu Freuds *Geschichte einer Infantilen Neurose.*' *Int. Z. Psychoanal.*, **16.**

*HARTMANN, H. (1925). 'Kocainismus und Homosexualität.' *Zeit. f. Neur. u. Psychiat.*, **95.**

HASSALL, J. C. (1915). 'The Role of the Sexual Complex in Dementia Praecox.' *Psychoanal. Rev.*, **2.**

HAYWARD, M. L. (1949). 'Direct Interpretation in the Treatment of a Case of Schizophrenia.' *Psychiatric Quart.*, **23.**

HEIMANN, P. (1950). 'On Counter-Transference.' *Int. J. Psycho-Anal.*, **31.**

(1952). 'Preliminary Notes on Some Defence Mechanisms in Paranoid States.' *Int. J. Psycho-Anal.*, **33.**

*HIGGINS, John W. (1953). 'Psychodynamics in the Excessive Drinking of Alcohol.' *Arch. Neur. Psychiat.*, **69.**

# 248      BIBLIOGRAPHY

\*HILLER, E. (1922). 'Some Remarks on Tobacco.' *Int. J. Psycho-Anal.*, 31.

HITSCHMANN, E. (1912). 'Swedenborg's Paranoia.' In: *Yearbook of Psychoanal.* ed. Lorand. Vol. 6. (New York: Int. Univ. Press, 1950.)

   (1913). 'Paranoia, Homosexualität und Analerotik.' *Int. Z. Psychoanal.*, 1.

\*HOCH, P. and ZUBIN, J. (1958). *Problems of Addiction and Habituation.* (New York; Grune & Stratton.)

HOLSTIJN, A. J. WESTERMAN (1933). 'Oral Erotism in Paraphrenia: Facts and Theories.' *Int. J. Psycho-Anal.*, 15.

\*JELLIFFE, S. E. (1917). 'The Mentality of the Alcoholic.' *New York. med. J.*, 105.

  \*(1919). 'Alcohol in Some of its Social Compensatory Aspects.' *New York. med. J.*, 109.

\*JULIUSBURGER, OTTO (1912). 'Beitrag zur Psychologie der sogenannten Dipsomanie.' *Zentralbl. f. Psychoanal.*, 2, pp. 551–7. Abstr. in *Psychoanal. Rev.*, 1.

  \*(1913). 'Zur Psychologie des Alkoholismus.' *Zentralbl. f. Psychoanal.*, 3.

  \*(1916). 'Alkoholismus und Sexualität.' *Z. f. Sexualwissenschaft*, 2.

KANZER, M. (1957a). 'Acting Out and its Relation to the Impulse Disorders.' *J. Amer. Psychoanal. Assoc.*, 5.

  (1957b). 'Acting Out, Sublimation and Reality Testing.' *J. Amer. Psychoanal. Assoc.*, 5.

KATAN, M. (1939). 'A Contribution to the Understanding of Schizophrenic Speech.' *Int. J. Psycho-Anal.*, 20.

KAUFMAN, M. RALPH (1932). 'Some Clinical Data on Ideas of Reference.' *Psychoanal. Quart.*, 1.

  (1939). 'Religious Delusions in Schizophrenia.' *Int. J. Psycho-Anal.*, 20.

KEMPF, E. (1920). *Psychopathology.* (St. Louis: Mosby, 1920–21; London: Kimpton, 1921.)

\*KIELHOLZ, A. (1924). 'Einige Betrachtungen zur psychoanalytischen Auffassung des Alkoholismus.' Abstr. *Int. Z. Psychoanal.*, 10.

  \*(1925). 'Trunksucht und Psychoanalyse.' *Schweiz. Arch. f. Neur. u. Psychiat.*, 16.

  \*(1926). 'Analyseversuch bei Delirium tremens.' *Int. Z. Psychoanal.*, 12.

  \*(1931). 'Giftmord und Vergiftungswahn.' *Int. Z. Psychoanal.*, 17.

KIMURA, R. (1933). ('Psychoanalytical Investigation concerning Delusion. Formation in Paranoia.') Author's abstr. *Int. Z. Psychoanal.*, 19.

KLEIN, M. (1930). 'The Importance of Symbol-Formation in the Development of the Ego.' In: *Contributions to Psycho-Analysis, 1921–45.* (London: Hogarth, 1948.)

  (1932). *The Psycho-Analysis of Children.* (London: Hogarth.)

  (1933). 'The Early Development of Conscience in the Child.' *ibid.*

  (1935). 'A Contribution to the Psychogenesis of Manic-Depressive States.' *ibid.*

  (1940). 'Mourning and its Relation to Manic Depressive States.' *ibid.*

  (1946). 'Notes on some Schizoid Mechanisms.' In: *Developments in Psycho-Analysis* ed. Riviére. (London: Hogarth, 1952.)

(1948). 'A Contribution to the Theory of Anxiety and Guilt.' *Int. J. Psycho-Anal.*, **31**.

(1952). 'The Origins of Transference.' *Int. J. Psychol-Anal.*, **33**.

(1957). *Envy and Gratitude.* (London: Tavistock; New York: Basic Books.)

*KNIGHT, R. P. (1937a). 'Psychoanalysis of Hospitalized Patients.' *Bull. Menninger Clin.*, **1**.

*(1937b). 'The Dynamics and Treatment of Chronic Alcoholic Addiction.' *Bull. Menninger Clin.*, **1**.

*(1937c). 'The Psychodynamics of Chronic Alcoholism.' *J. nerv. ment. Dis.*, **86**, pp. 538–48.

*(1938). 'The Psychoanalytic Treatment in a Sanatorium of Chronic Addiction to Alcohol.' *J. Amer. Med. Assoc.*, **111**.

(1939). 'Psychotherapy in Acute Paranoid Schizophrenia with Successful Outcome.' *Bull. Menninger Clin.*, **3**.

(1940). 'The Relationship of Latent Homosexuality to the Mechanism of Paranoid Delusions.' *Bull. Menninger Clin.*, **4**.

(1946). 'The Psychotherapy of an Adolescent Schizophrenic with Mutism.' *Psychiatry*, **9**.

*KNIGHT, R. G. and PROUT, C. T. (1951). 'A Study of Results in Hospital Treatment of Drug Addiction.' *Amer. J. Psychiat.*, **108**.

LAFORGUE, R. (1936). 'A Contribution to the Study of Schizophrenia.' *Int. J. Psycho-Anal.*, **17**.

LANDAUER, K. (1914). 'Spontanheilung einer Katatonie.' *Int. Z. Psychoanal.*, **2**.

*LEVY, L. (1924). 'The Psychology of the Effect Produced by Morphia.' *Int. J. Psycho-Anal.*, **6**.

*LINDEMANN, E. and CLARKE, L. D. (1952). 'Modifications in Ego Structure and Personality Reactions under the Influence and Effects of Drugs.' *Amer. J. Psychiat.*, **108**.

*LOLLI, G. (1952). 'Alcoholism 1941–1951: "A Survey of Activities in Research", "Education Therapy", "The Treatment of Alcoholic Addiction".' *Quart. J. Stud. Alcohol.*, **13**.

LONDON, L. S. (1931). 'Mechanism in Paranoia.' *Psychoanal. Rev.*, **18**.

*LORAND, S. (1945). 'Survey of Psychoanalytic Literature on Problems of Alcohol.' *Yearbook of Psychoanal.* ed. Lorand. Vol. 1. (New York: Int. Univ. Press.)

MAEDER, A. (1910). 'Psychologische Untersuchungen an Dementia Praecox-Kranken.' *Jahrb. f. Psychoanal.*, **2**.

MAYER-GROSS, W. (1935). 'On Depersonalization.' *Brit. J. med. Psychol.*, **15**.

*MARX, NORBERT (1923). 'Beiträge zur Psychologie der Kokainomanie.' *Z. Neur. Psychiat.*, **80**.

*MEERLOO, JOOST A. M. (1952). 'Artificial Ecstasy.' *J. nerv. ment. Dis.*, **115**.

MORICHAUX-BEAUCHANT, R. (1912). 'Homosexualität und Paranoia.' *Zentralbl. f. Psychoanal.*, **2**.

MUNRO, LOIS (1948). 'Analysis of a Cartoon in a Case of Hypochondriasis.' *Int. J. Psycho-Anal.*, **29**.

NUNBERG, H. (1920). 'On the Catatonic Attack.' In: *The Practice and Theory of Psychoanalysis.* (New York: Nerv. ment. Dis. Co., 1948.)

—— (1921). 'The Course of the Libidinal Conflict in a Case of Schizophrenia.' *ibid.*

—— (1924). 'States of Depersonalization in the Light of Libido Theory.' *ibid.*

—— (1936). 'Homosexuality, Magic and Aggression.' *ibid.*

O'MALLEY, M. (1923). 'Transference and Some of its Problems in Psychoses.' *Psychoanal. Rev.,* **10.**

OPHUIJSEN, J. H. W. van (1920). 'On the Origin of the Feeling of Persecution.' *Int. J. Psycho-Anal.,* **1.**

OPPENHEIM, HANS (1912). 'Zur Frage der Genese des Eifersuchtswahnes.' *Zentralbl. f. Psychoanal.,* **2.**

PAYNE, C. R. (1914-15). 'Some Freudian Contributions to the Paranoia Problem.' *Psychoanal. Rev.,* **1-2.**

PFEIFFER, S. (1920). 'Paranoia-ähnliche Mechanismen während einer Hysterieanalyse.' (Unpublished.)

PICHON-RIVIERE, ENRIQUE (1947). 'Psicoanálisis de la Esquizofrenia.' *Rev. de Psychoanal.,* **5.**

PIOUS, W. L. (1949). 'The Pathogenic Process in Schizophrenia.' *Bull. Menninger Clin.,* **13.**

*RÁDO, S. (1926). 'The Psychic Effects of Intoxication: Attempts at a Psycho-Analytic Theory of Drug Addiction.' *Int. J. Psycho-Anal,* **7.**

*(1933). 'The Psychoanalysis of Pharmocothymia.' *Psychoanal. Quart.,* **2.**

*(1953). 'Hedonic Control, Action Self and the Depressive Spell.' In: *Depression* ed. Hoch and Zubin. (New York: Grune & Stratton.)

*(1958). 'Narcotic Bondage.' In: *Problems of Addiction and Habituation* ed. Hoch and Zubin. (New York: Grune & Stratton.)

REICH, A. (1936). 'Klinischer Beitrag zum Verständnis der paranoiden Persönlichkeit.' *Int. Z. Psychoanal.,* **22.**

—— (1954). 'Early Identifications as Archaic Elements in the Superego.' *J. Amer. Psychoanal. Assoc.,* **2.**

REIK, T. (1927). 'Psychologie und Depersonalisation.' In: *Wie man Psychologe wird* (Vienna: Int. Psychoanal. Vlg.)

*RICKMAN, J. (1925). 'Alcoholism and Psycho-Analysis.' *Brit. J. Inebriety,* **23.**

*RIGGALL, ROBERT (1923). 'Homosexuality and Alcoholism.' *Psychoanal. Rev.,* **10.**

*RIVIERE, J. (1936). 'A Contribution to the Analysis of the Negative Therapeutic Reaction.' *Int. J. Psycho-Anal.,* **17.**

—— (1948). 'Remarks on Paranoid Attitudes seen in Analysis and Everyday Life.' (Unpublished.)

*ROBBINS, BERNARD (1935). 'A Note on the Significance of Infantile Nutritional Disturbances in the Development of Alcoholism.' *Psychoanal. Rev.,* **22.**

*ROCHLIN, G. (1953). 'The Disorder of Depression and Elation.' *J. Amer. Psychoanal. Assoc.,* **1.**

RÓHEIM, G. (1922). 'Völkerpsychologisches in Freud's *Massenpsychologie und Ich-Analyse.' *Int. Z. Psychoanal.,* **8.**

*(1923). 'Nach dem Tode des Urvaters.' *Imago*, **9**.

ROSEN, J. (1946). 'The Method of Resolving Acute Catatonic Excitement.' *Psychiat. Quart.*, **20**.

(1947). 'The Treatment of Schizophrenic Psychoses by Direct Analytic Therapy.' *Psychiat. Quart.*, **21**.

(1950). 'The Survival Function of Schizophrenia.' *Bull. Menninger Clin.*, **14**.

ROSENFELD, H. (1958). 'Some Observations on the Psychopathology of Hypochondriacal States.' *Int. J. Psycho-Anal.*, **39**.

SAUL, L. J. (1947). 'Some Observations on a Form of Projection.' *Psychoanal. Quart.*, **16**.

*SAVITT, ROBERT A. (1954). 'Extramural Psychoanalytic Treatment of a Case of Narcotic Addiction.' *J. Amer. Psychoanal. Assoc.*, **2**.

*(1963). 'Psychoanalytic Studies on Addiction: Ego Structure in Narcotic Addiction.' *Psychoanal. Quart.*, **32**.

SCHILDER, P. (1922). 'Zur Pathologie des Ichideals.' *Int. Z. Psychoanal.*, **8**.

(1925). *Introduction to a Psychoanalytic Psychiatry.* (New York: Nerv. ment. Dis. Co., 1928; Int. Univ. Press, 1951.)

(1930). 'The Neurasthenic Hypochondriac Character.' *Med. Rev. of Reviews*, **36**.

(1935). *The Image and Appearance of the Human Body.* (London: Kegan Paul.)

SCHILDER, P. and SUGAR, N. (1926). 'Zur Lehre von den schizophrenen Sprachstörungen.' *Z. f. Neurol. u. Psychiat.*, **104**.

*SCHMIDEBERG, M. (1930). 'The Role of Psychotic Mechanisms in Cultural Development.' *Int. J. Psycho-Anal.*, **11**.

(1931). 'A Contribution to the Psychology of Persecutory Ideas and Delusions.' *Int. J. Psycho-Anal.*, **12**.

SCHOCKLEY, F. M. (1914). 'The Role of Homosexuality in the Genesis of Paranoid Conditions.' *Psychoanal. Rev.*, **1**.

SEGAL, H. (1950). 'Some Aspects of the Analysis of a Schizophrenic.' *Int. J. Psycho-Anal.*, **31**.

SHORVON, H. I. (1946). 'The Depersonalization Syndrome.' *Proc. Roy. Soc. Med.*, **39**.

*SIMMEL, E. (1928). 'Psycho-Analytic Treatment in a Sanatorium.' *Int. J. Psycho-Anal.*, **10**.

*(1930). 'Zum Problem von Zwang und Sucht.' (Bericht über den V. Allgemeinen ärztlichen Kongress für Psychotherapie in Baden-Baden.)

*(1949). 'Alcoholism and Addiction.' *Yearbook of Psychoanal.* ed. Lorand. Vol. 5. (New York: Int. Univ. Press.)

SPITZ, R. (1958). 'On the Genesis of the Superego Components.' *Psychoanal. Study Child*, **13**.

STÄRCKE, A. (1914). 'Rechts und Links in der Wahnidee.' *Int. Z. Psychoanal.*, **2**.

(1919). 'The Reversal of the Libido-Sign in Delusions of Persecution.' *Int. J. Psycho-Anal.*, **1**.

(1935). 'Die Rolle der analen und oralen Quantitäten im Verfolgungswahn und in ähnlichen Systemgedanken.' *Int. Z. Psychoanal.*, **21**.

STONE, L. (1954). 'The Widening Scope of Indications for Psycho-analysis.' *J. Amer. Psychoanal. Assoc.*, **2**.

SULLIVAN, H. S. (1931). 'The Modified Psychoanalytic Treatment of Schizophrenia.' *Amer. J. Psychiat.*, **11**.

SZASZ, T. S. (1957). *Pain and Pleasure: A Study of Bodily Feelings.* (New York: Basic Books.)

*TAUSK, V. (1915). 'Zur Psychologie des Alkolischen Beschäftigungs-delirs.' *Int. Z. Psychoanal.*, **3**.

(1919). 'On the Origin of the Influencing Machine in Schizophrenia.' *Psychoanal. Quart.*, **2**.

THORNER, H. (1955). 'Hypochondria.' In: *New Directions in Psycho-Analysis* ed. M. Klein *et al.* (London: Tavistock.)

WAELDER, R. (1924). 'The Psychoses: Their Mechanisms and Accessibility to Influence.' *Int. J. Psycho-Anal.*, **6**.

*WEIJL, S. (1928). 'On the Psychology of Alcoholism.' *Psychoanal. Rev.*, **15**.

*(1944). 'Theoretical and Practical Aspects of the Psychoanalytic Therapy of Problem Drinkers. *Quart. J. Stud. Alcohol,* **5**.

*WEISS, E. (1926). 'Der Vergiftungswahn im Lichte der Introjektions-und Projektionsvorgänge.' *Int. J. Psychoanal.*, **12**.

(1947). 'Projection, Extrajection and Objectivation.' *Psychoanal. Quart.*, **16**.

WEISSMAN, P. (1954). 'Ego and Superego in Obsessional Character and Neuroses.' *Psychoanal. Quart.*, **23**.

WEXLER, M. (1951). 'The Structural Problem in Schizophrenia: Therapeutic Implications.' *Int. J. Psycho-Anal.*, **32**.

*WIKLER, ABRAHAM (1952). 'Mechanisms of Action of Drugs that Modify Personality Function.' *Amer. J. Psychiat.*, **108**.

WINNICOTT, D. W. (1945). 'Primitive Emotional Development.' In: *Collected Papers.* (London: Tavistock, 1958.)

WULFF, M. (1911). 'Die Lüge in der Psychoanalyse.' *Zentralbl. f. Psycho-anal.*, **2**.

*(1932). 'Über einer interessanten oralen Symptomenkomplex und seine Beziehungen zur Sucht.' *Int. Z. Psychoanal.*, **18**.

YOUNG, D. A. (1943). 'An Anal Substitute for Genital Masturbation in a Case of Paranoid Schizophrenia.' *Psychoanal. Quart.*, **12**.

# INDEX

Abraham, Karl, 35, 41, 96, 104, 131, 170, 219, 224, 235
Ackermann, N. W., 34
Acting out
  analyst tempted to collude in, 159, 205, 206, 207
  case material, 207–8, 210–14
  'characters', 208
  as a defence against a confusional state, 214
  to deny dependence, 178
  diminished by analysis of paranoid anxieties, 205, 206
  in drug addiction, 128–31, 140, 236, 239
  in everyday life, 208
  an inevitable part of all analyses, 200
  and impairment of ego function, 208
  by lateness, 19, 27
  in mania, 204
  by missed sessions, 24
  'partial' differentiated from 'excessive', 201
  and paranoid-schizoid fixation, 204, 209, 215
  by regressive behaviour, 205–8
  as rejection of primal objects, 202–6
  by termination of analysis, 39, 43
  in treatment of schizophrenia, 208–14
Addiction, see 'Drugs' and 'Alcoholism'
  to food, 142, 232 ff.
Alcoholism
  critical review of literature, Chapter 13
  delusions in, 218, 230
  homosexuality and, 219
  infantile masturbation and, 217, 219, 226
  depression and, 220
  mania and, 218, 221, 227, 237
  manic-depressive psychosis and, 226, 236

  oral fixation in, 219, 221, 226, 235
  role of parents in aetiology of, 231
  symbolic value of alcohol in, 237
  treatment of, 231
  See also 'Drugs–addiction to'
Alexander, F., 41, 67, 131
Anal (see also 'Faeces')
  fantasies, 29, 39, 40
  sadistic impulses
    towards breast, 60
    towards analyst, 111
    masked by genitality, 40
Analyst
  containing projected bad parts of patient's self, 81, 164, 176
  containing projected good parts of patient's self, 48, 89, 166
  envy of his sanity by patient, 163, 164, 194
  pressure on, to act out with analysand, 159, 206
  representing analysand's primary object, 205
  in role of functioning integrating ego, 166
  in role of superego, 85, 87, 152, 206
Animism, 37
Anxiety, see separately under 'Depressive' and 'Paranoid'
Ambivalence, 21, 28
Auto-erotism, 104, 115, 116, 221

Balint, M., 170
Barkas, M. R., 105
Bender, L., 41
Benedek, T., 42, 232, 233
Beres, D., 145
Bergler, E., 17, 36, 235
Bibring, G., 26
Bion, W. R., 158, 168, 169, 208
Bleuler, E., 180
'Bluff', 87, 101, 102
Boredom, 195
Breast, see 'Mother's breast'